The Fate of Law

The Amherst Series in Law, Jurisprudence, and Social Thought

Each work included in The Amherst Series in Law, Jurisprudence, and Social Thought explores a theme crucial to an understanding of law as it confronts the changing social and intellectual currents of the late twentieth century.

The Fate of Law, edited by Austin Sarat and Thomas R. Kearns

Law's Violence, edited by Austin Sarat and
    Thomas R. Kearns

Law in Everyday Life, edited by Austin Sarat and
    Thomas R. Kearns

The Fate of Law

Edited by Austin Sarat and Thomas R. Kearns

Ann Arbor

THE UNIVERSITY OF MICHIGAN PRESS

First paperback edition 1993
Copyright © by the University of Michigan 1991
All rights reserved
Published in the United States of America by
The University of Michigan Press
Printed and bound by CPI Group (UK) Ltd, Croydon, CR0 4YY

1994   1993   4   3   2

Library of Congress Cataloging-in-Publication Data

The Fate of law / edited by Austin Sarat and Thomas R. Kearns.
     p.   cm. — (The Amherst series in law, jurisprudence, and
social thought)
     Includes bibliographical references.
     ISBN 978-0-472-10244-0 (alk. paper) - ISBN 978-0-472-08239-1
     (pbk. : alk. paper)

     1. Law—Philosophy.   2. Feminism—Philosophy.   3. Structuralism.
I. Sarat, Austin.   II. Kearns, Thomas R.   III. Series.
K235.F375   1991
340'.1—dc20   91-14408
                                                          CIP

British Library Cataloguing in Publication Data
The fate of law. — (The Amherst Series in Law,
   Jurisprudence, and Social Thought).
   1. Law. Theories
   I. Sarat, Austin   II. Kearns, Thomas R.   III. Series
   340.1

ISBN13 978-0-472-10244-0 (cloth)
ISBN13 978-0-472-08239-1 (paperback)
ISBN13 978-0-472-02369-1 (electronic)

Acknowledgments

The concerns of *The Fate of Law* were the subject of a course we taught together for three successive years beginning in 1988. We gratefully acknowledge the invigorating interest and intellectual companionship of our students in that course. We would also like to express our appreciation for the stimulation provided by Lawrence Douglas and Victoria Saker, our colleagues in the Amherst College Program in Law, Jurisprudence, and Social Thought, and by Nathaniel Berman and Kristin Bumiller, participants in Law and the Social Order, an earlier stage of the present program. Finally, we are grateful to the Mellon Foundation and to Amherst's President Peter Pouncey, without whose interest and support this project would not have been possible.

Contents

Editorial Introduction
Austin Sarat and Thomas R. Kearns 1

Partial Justice: Law and Minorities
Martha Minow 15

The Postmodern Transition: Law and Politics
Boaventura de Sousa Santos 79

Disciplines, Subjectivity, and Law
Robin West 119

The Law Wishes to Have a Formal Existence
Stanley Fish 159

A Journey Through Forgetting: Toward a
Jurisprudence of Violence
Austin Sarat and Thomas R. Kearns 209

Contributors 275

Index 277

Editorial Introduction

Austin Sarat and Thomas R. Kearns

Legal scholarship, and law itself, is undergoing one of those occasional periods of rupture in which traditional assumptions no longer seem adequate or satisfactory. Law is said to be "turning outward" in search of new grounding;[1] legal scholarship seems to be undergoing a rapid "rotation"[2] in which attempts are made to accommodate the contradictory and conflicting challenges of deontological liberalism, natural law, pragmatism, interpretive social science, economics, and several varieties of critical social theory.[3] Some of those challenges are regarded as potent enough to "distort the purposes of law and threaten its very existence."[4] Others promise a way of thinking that will provide new rationality and coherence for legal decisions.[5]

---

1. Martha Minow, "Law Turning Outward," *Telos* 73 (1979): 79.

2. David Kennedy, "Rotations in Legal Scholarship" (Harvard University, photocopy).

3. Such accommodations are, however, always unstable. Because fashions in the legal academy change rather rapidly, it is often difficult to map the influence of any particular body of thought on legal scholarship. To take one example, namely economics, cf. Bruce Ackerman, *Reconstructing American Law* (Cambridge, Mass.: Harvard University Press, 1984), and Robert Ellickson, "Bringing Culture and Human Frailty to Rational Actors: A Critique of Classical Law and Economics," *Chicago-Kent Law Review* 65 (1989): 23.

4. See Owen Fiss, "The Death of Law," *Cornell Law Review* 72 (1986): 1. See also Paul Carrington, "Of Law and the River," *Journal of Legal Education* 34 (1984): 222. For responses to Carrington see "Of Law and the River" and "Nihilism and Academic Freedom," *Journal of Legal Education* 35 (1985): 1. Some scholars believe that the essential nature of law remains unchanged by the many intellectual challenges mounted by legal scholars. See Thomas Haskell, "The Curious Persistence of Rights Talk in the Age of Interpretation," *Journal of American History* 74 (1987): 984; and Stanley Fish, "Dennis Martinez and the Uses of Theory," *Yale Law Journal* 96 (1987): 1773.

5. See Richard Posner, *The Economics of Justice* (Cambridge, Mass.: Harvard University Press, 1981).

And even if one resists such apocalyptic or utopian visions, it seems safe to say that not since the emergence of legal realism, more than sixty years ago,[6] has there been both so much doubt and uncertainty and so much excitement and widespread interest in what is happening in the legal world.

While contemporary critiques of law are as diverse as they are numerous, no one would deny that feminist and poststructuralist writings are among the most wide-ranging and provocative. In this book, we ask about the fate of law in light of these two genres of contemporary critical thought. Because both feminism and poststructuralism had their genesis outside of legal scholarship, each asks us to think about the fate of law in light of cultural ferment, the reach of which goes far beyond law itself. It is from these large perspectives that the five original essays presented in this book hope to glimpse law's fate.[7]

But even with this wide angle of vision, our interest in this volume is not to achieve systematic statements of feminist or poststructuralist thought about law. Programmatic statements presenting the variety of feminist and poststructuralist criticisms of law can be found elsewhere.[8] We invite contemplation about how, if at all, law and legal scholarship have responded, or should respond, to feminist and poststructuralist challenges to claims about law's neutrality, objectivity, and capacity to limit and channel the exercise of power in American life.[9] Here we seek to assess just how seriously the challenges

---

6. See Laura Kalman, *Legal Realism at Yale, 1927–1960* (Chapel Hill: University of North Carolina Press, 1986). See also Joseph William Singer, "Legal Realism Now," *California Law Review* 76 (1988): 467.

7. All of the essays, except the essay by Sarat and Kearns, were presented as lectures at Amherst College. The essays by Minow, West, Fish, and Santos were also presented to the Amherst Seminar on Legal Ideology and Legal Process. We are grateful for the many contributions of the seminar.

8. See Catharine MacKinnon, *Feminism Unmodified* (Cambridge, Mass.: Harvard University Press, 1987); Ann Scales, "The Emergence of Feminist Jurisprudence: An Essay," *Yale Law Journal* 95 (1986): 1373; and Katharine Bartlett, "Feminist Legal Methods," *Harvard Law Review* 103 (1990): 829. See also Roberto Unger, "The Critical Legal Studies Movement," *Harvard Law Review* 96 (1983): 561; and J. M. Balkin, "Deconstructive Practice and Legal Theory," *Yale Law Journal* 96 (1987): 743.

9. See note 8 above. See also David Kairys, ed., *The Politics of Law* (New York: Pantheon, 1932); and Allan Hutchinson, ed., *Critical Legal Studies* (Totowa, N.J.: Rowman and Littlefield, 1989).

posed in each of these critical approaches should be taken and to draw out the lessons of such critical positions for law itself.

A unifying feature of the essays collected in this volume is that they all reject, or at least seriously question, claims of neutrality or objectivity in law and legal theory. They each manifest a belief that feminism and/or poststructuralist criticism of law has moved law and legal scholarship beyond an unproblematic and confident embrace of reason and rationality. They differ, however, in their assessment of the significance of that movement and in their understandings of how law has, and ought to, moved in response. Some see feminism and poststructuralism as having a disruptive and transformative influence on law, opening up new possibilities; others see greater resistance and resilience in current legal arrangements.

The bulk of mainstream legal scholarship has tended to view contemporary critiques of law, like those included in *The Fate of Law*, through the same lens through which it once surveyed the "revolution" of legal realism. There are, no doubt, some important resemblances. First, like the legal realists, many of today's critics are quite skeptical about the power and efficacy of legal rules, especially as devices to "tie down the world," to determine cases "in advance," and to eliminate discretionary judgment and politics from law. And again, like yesterday's legal realists, today's critics display the exuberance of those who see themselves as participating in an intellectual revolution.

Traditionalists in law and legal theory respond to these affinities with legal realism in a variety of ways. Some apparently believe, or perhaps they just hope, that there is nothing more in the new criticism than a warmed-over realism that will, in time, run its course. But others find reason, echoing the response of an earlier generation, to denounce contemporary challenges to law as reckless or nihilistic.[10]

References to realism provide an instructive frame for a reading of the essays in *The Fate of Law*. Those essays suggest, in fact, that similarities between today's critique of law and legal realism are both greater and less than many traditionalist responses suppose. Thus, it is important to see that today's critics are often vastly more thor-

---

10. Cf. Alan Altman, *Critical Legal Studies* (Princeton, N.J.: Princeton University Press, 1990); and Owen Fiss, "The Death of Law," *Cornell Law Review* 72 (1986): 1.

oughgoing than were most of the realists in disavowing Enlightenment assumptions about the capacity of reason and science to guide social progress. Most pointedly, today's critics almost universally reject the optimism of many realist thinkers regarding the power of the social sciences to provide law with neutral and objective groundings.[11] Contemporary thinkers are inclined to extend their doubts about law to the social sciences themselves and have noted, among other things, the ways in which law already constitutes much of the world that those disciplines attempt to study.[12] They conclude that this entanglement makes social science problematic as a grounding for law and legal decisions. While several of the contributors to *The Fate of Law* exemplify this skepticism, they offer no uniform replacement for the realist embrace of social science. Their challenge to social science is only a symptom of a more pervasive epistemological doubt that, when extended to law, reveals a conviction that law lacks any compelling formal grounding.

On the other hand, the contributions to this book would appear to refute any claim that today's critics are inescapably unconstructive or nihilistic. Asked to contemplate the fate of law in a world in which Enlightenment faith in reason and science has eroded, the authors whose work is presented in *The Fate of Law* have offered accounts and imaginings of law and law's fate that are distinctly, though diversely, engaged with reconstruction as well as criticism. Theirs is neither a message of despair nor a rejection of law *tout court*. On the contrary, some explore alternative ways of grounding law by reconceiving law itself; others identify external standards for law grounded in local practices and particular social narratives.

It appears, then, that the abandonment of Enlightenment ideals and realist optimism about social science need not end in dire predictions about the death of law. Nowhere in these essays is there any suggestion that the relentless skepticism of the past decade foreshadows the end of law; instead, while law's fate and the fate of legal scholarship appear unsettled—that is, not fated—and moving in a variety of directions, this is taken as a positive sign and an opportu-

---

11. See Mark Kelman, "Trashing," *Stanford Law Review* 34 (1984): 293.

12. See David Trubek, "Where the Action Is: Critical Legal Studies and Empiricism," *Stanford Law Review* 34 (1984): 575; and David Trubek and John Esser, "'Critical Empiricism' in American Legal Studies: Paradox, Program, or Pandora's Box?" *Law and Social Inquiry* 14 (1989): 3.

nity for reconsideration of law and law's relation to the social world. While each of the essays contributes to the critique of law, each seems fully accepting of law (in some form) and hopeful, if not confident, that law can and should be reimagined, reconfigured, and rescued.

Yet the constructive visions displayed in the essays do not display the homogeneity of, say, the realists' program. Rather, they exhibit a familiar feature of contemporary critical debate about law, namely, even in its most constructive mood, it tends to be characterized by diversity, by a pluralism of voices and viewpoints, and by differing, even warring, perspectives. Such diversity, pluralism, and difference contributes greatly to the excitement stirred by contemporary legal scholarship, but prevents us from putting together an anthology that is at once representative and reasonably brief. Thus, *The Fate of Law* is not a catalog or a comprehensive account of previously worked-out positions; the essays contained in this book do not present the full range of views an encyclopedic treatment would require.

Each of these essays speaks in its own voice; each confronts important contemporary developments in law and legal scholarship and locates them in relation to feminism and/or poststructuralism. However, the tone and style of the essays is by no means uniform; they display the unique intensities and passions of their authors. They range from broad and abstract historical and philosophical analyses to close readings of legal cases. Readers may find this tonal and stylistic pluralism jarring, but we think that one of the strongest themes of both feminist and poststructuralist writing is its openness, diversity, and impatience with uniformity. Thus, as editors, we have not tried to discipline the essays' style or homogenize their tone; each speaks for itself and explores the fate of law in its own way.

We begin with Martha Minow's "Partial Justice: Law and Minorities." Minow asks why, at this moment, we are worrying about the fate of law and responds by providing a comprehensive overview of what she argues are "sea changes" in the basic, taken-for-granted assumptions that provide coherence in our culture. Minow notes that such changes are reflected, first, in shifts in the alignments and coalitions among groups fighting over "issues of the day" and, second, in broad philosophical contests over the meaning and status of reason itself. She illustrates the first by discussing feminist debates about pregnancy and maternity leave benefits, as well as comparable worth. Here, Minow describes deep divisions within the feminist community that, in her view, reflect differences over "what law is or could be." She also sees those divisions at work in debates and "arguments within jurisprudence about basic concepts in theories of law," such as rights and the rule of law.

However, Minow does not seek to reconstruct jurisprudence; instead she advocates "storytelling" as a way of making sense of the changes, divisions, and debates that she has cataloged. One such story is a broad, sweeping narrative of the evolution of theories of knowledge, a story that Minow variously labels a "challenge to authority" and the "insiders' story." A second story, labeled the "outsiders' story," focuses on the experiences of women, children, members of racial and religious minorities, and disabled persons. Minow argues that developments within the "insiders' story" barely reach the "outsiders," or, when they do, they further marginalize outsiders or complicate their efforts at resistance and reconstruction. Poststructuralism, Minow argues, is the latest variety of the "insiders' story," and it, too, poses difficulties for the efforts of outsiders to gain a voice within law by calling into question their efforts to develop coherent selves and coherent identities. She sees many points of tension between poststructuralism and feminism and believes that they push law in different directions.

Poststructuralism focuses on the indeterminacy of legal language and the critique of rights, while the "outsiders' story," as illustrated by feminist and minority scholars, pays attention to the disadvantages that law imposes on particular groups in particular contexts. Minow identifies herself with the "outsiders' story" because of its insistence "upon the partiality of all stories." It is this emphasis on partiality and the embrace of the skepticism and openness it invites that Minow thinks is the appropriate response of legal scholars to the various stories she tells. She urges us to recognize law as a "set of practices and institutions situated within more than one narrative of human history," to embrace a theory of law that is "pluralist, heterogeneous, and localist," and to think about the fate of law by examining "actual problems, as defined and experienced by the people living through them."

In the next essay, Boaventura de Sousa Santos argues that the kind of pluralism, heterogeneity, and localism that Minow advocates is, in fact, on the horizon as law goes through what he calls the "postmodern transition." Santos attends to the material and structural conditions that make possible the transformation of law during this period of transition. He sees and describes a logical progression in capitalist political economy that provides, in his view, the backdrop for developments in critical social thought about law. The progression of capitalist development and the emergence of critical social thought about law provide the impetus for the kind of reconstruction of legality that both he and Minow envision.

Santos argues that we are witnessing the exhaustion of what he calls the "paradigm of modernity," an exhaustion brought about both by the successful completion of some of the projects of modernity and the recognition that "modernity is no longer capable of fulfilling some of its other projects." Modernity, as Santos sees it, is a historical period whose point of origin Santos places in the sixteenth century; the emergence of the modern is seen in the development of new forms of regulation (in particular, the state) and new resources for emancipation (Santos identifies rationality and rationalism as central to the emancipatory processes of modernity). He describes how the regulatory and emancipatory impulses of modernity take shape through three periods of capitalist development and argues that the exhaustion of modernity results from both its ambitions and its internal contradictions.

For Santos, it is the exhaustion of modernity that makes possible the transformation of law. He identifies this transformation with a process of decentering and pluralizing power, which in turn makes possible the "reinvention" of what he calls "minirationalities" freed from any totalizing discourse. Santos locates this decentering and pluralization in the history of ideas and associates it with the critique of "foundationalist epistemologies" and a revived interest in rhetoric and pragmatism. He argues, in addition, that the decentering and pluralization of power arise, in part, from the inability of the modern legal form to address "some of the serious problems of our age, from Chernobyl to AIDS."

The response to the exhaustion of modernity, in his view, is not to be found in the formulation of another philosophy but in the effort to identify "emancipatory everyday practices." Santos describes the exhaustion of modernity as the social condition necessary to allow for the proliferation of political and legal interpretive communities of the kind that Minow advocates. This development will, in his view, result in a "controlled dispersal" of law, the trivialization of state law, and the growth of what he calls a new "legal minimalism." In this new world of postmodern legality, the limits of social transformation through law will become more apparent, and other forms of "emancipatory practice" will emerge.

While Santos is hopeful about the liberation and liberalization of law, Robin West, in "Disciplines, Subjectivities, and Law," is much less optimistic. Feminism and poststructuralism go a long way toward undermining faith in the Enlightenment version of reason and rationality, yet she asks "whether and how we can criticize law, if not by reference to reason, by which is meant *either* categorical moral truths divined by pure reason or, alternatively, a theory of the good in turn grounded in universal but concrete truths about human nature, derived through rational methods of empirical inquiry." Her essay discusses three responses to this question.

The first is what she calls "legal authoritarianism." For the vast majority of mainstream legal scholars, the question West poses, the question posed by a serious engagement with feminism and postmodernism, is "oddly *irrelevant*." For them, reason has never been the standard against which particular laws should be judged. For most legal scholars, West contends, "it is *law itself*" that provides the standard. Any particular law is evaluated against law's own internal critical and normative apparatus. If feminism and poststructuralism have any relevance to mainstream legal scholars, it is to reinforce legal authoritarianism by providing a "sophisticated skepticism that philosophical studies and empirical science have nothing normative to offer." The critique of reason thus paradoxically reinforces the conservatism and self-referential quality of mainstream legal discourse. At the same time, West identifies a neopragmatist response within the mainstream legal academy (exemplified by the work of Stanley Fish whose essay follows West's) that takes the poststructuralist critique of reason seriously and concludes, in light of that critique, that there is no choice but to judge one act of power in light of another.

Next, West considers the response of two interdisciplinary movements in legal scholarship—law and economics, and law and humanities. Both represent efforts, which West thinks have largely failed, to find normative standards external to law itself. West tells a story of parallel development in what are generally thought of as two dissimilar intellectual movements, development in which an initial critical impulse is domesticated as scholars confront the limits of reason. For law and economics, the inability to know subjective preferences and tastes leads to the substitution of expressed consumer preferences and wealth maximization as the standard of judgment that is offered to law. West contends that this substitution means that what law and economics offers is itself already constituted by the prevailing patterns of power in society; thus, law and economics, like mainstream legal scholarship, ends up judging one set of power relations, law, by another.

For the law and humanities scholar, the inability rationally to apprehend communal well-being or happiness functions analogously to the economist's inability to know subjective preferences. Because of this alleged defect or inadequacy of reason, the humanist substitutes participation in interpretive communities or in the explication of canonical texts as the measure of value that law should advance. West argues that, for the humanist, the test of law is its capacity to create values that accord with those represented in the literary canon or that create the conditions necessary for interpretive community. Yet it is circular, West argues, to criticize law by reference to the values of great texts, since the greatness of a text is a product of similar operations of social power to those that produce law itself. As a result, the law and humanities movement ends up, because of its disillusionment with reason itself, criticizing one effect of power in light of another.

To end the circularity that West sees in these responses to the question of how to evaluate or criticize law from an external point of view, we must reexamine the possibility of knowing subjective states and community well-being by questioning rationality as a standard of knowledge. West claims that "arational knowledge," in particular what she calls sympathy, can provide a standard for judging law. For her, the response to feminist and poststructuralist critiques of reason is to liberate us from reason itself and to discover a new source of inspiration for law and legal decisions. These critiques do not diminish law or render it more plural and partial; they open up the possibility of a transformation that is widespread and all encompassing.

In contrast to West's suggestion that law can and should be transformed from the outside by being made responsive to the "politics and struggles of the heart," Stanley Fish argues that law, in order to be law, must be insulated and unresponsive. In his judgment,

feminism and poststructuralism help us see the partiality and indeterminacy, the inconsistencies and contradictions in legal discourse;
such critical specification of what law is reveals elements seemingly
external to law that are already incorporated within legal discourse.
For Fish, the rhetorical practices of law are self-generating and self-
perpetuating; law like any other practice is, in his view, largely impervious to theory and external criticism. Thus it succeeds in having
a formal existence.

Both feminism and poststructuralism are incorrect in assuming
that law has been or could be some other way. As Fish sees it, the law
wishes to have a formal existence and is rhetorically resilient in maintaining its formalism. Law assimilates extralegal concerns into its
own categories and, as a result, is able to fashion an autonomy out
of the very material it then rhetorically pushes away in the name of
that autonomy. Law's fate is to continue to maintain itself through
ever more ingenious rhetorical ploys. It has not been derailed, nor
does he believe it will be derailed, by critical exegesis.

Fish argues that there are two major threats to law's autonomy,
to its ability to maintain its formalism. The first is morality; the second is interpretation. While Fish treats these threats separately, he
believes that they pose essentially the same threat, that is, to reduce
law to merely an effect of something outside itself. Fish examines two
doctrines in contract law—the parol evidence rule and consideration—the first to reveal how law both repels and incorporates interpretation; the second to provide a similar analysis of the relationship
of law and morality. The law incorporates interpretation and morality, and at the same time, denies that it is doing so. As Fish argues,
to be efficacious, law's formalism must be the product of, and responsive to, the very forces that its formalism is meant to hold in check.
Law, he says, creates itself out of the very materials that it is obliged
to push away. This inconsistency is hardly the critical flaw assumed
in many contemporary critiques; it is, in Fish's view, a mark of law's
"amazing . . . success."

For Fish, law's formality and its autonomy are largely rhetorical.
Law's rhetoric works to tell two stories at once, to tell two stories as
if they were one. Inconsistency and irrationality in doctrine are what
enable law to do its work. Law, Fish proclaims, is thoroughly rhetorical and always engaged in effacing its rhetoric. He urges his readers
to pay attention to the conditions under which law's rhetorical dual-

ity, its capacity to be what it denies and incorporate what it seeks to expel, succeeds.

As Fish contends, it may be necessary to focus on law's rhetorical powers if we are to understand its resistance to critical attack and its remarkable capacity to employ linguistic and interpretive devices to absorb and deflect external challenges. In "A Journey Through Forgetting: Toward a Jurisprudence of Violence," Sarat and Kearns do not deny law's rhetorical virtuosity when they contend that contemporary mainstream and critical jurisprudence appear to be on the verge of forgetting that law is not merely a matter of words, but is centrally involved in the social organization of violence. Law does not merely curtail violence; it also inflicts pain and death. Far from denying law's rhetorical powers, this essay might be read as providing disturbing proof of those powers. It explores how law and legal theory have managed to focus attention on the necessity of law's violence as a response to the violence outside law and, miraculously, have also managed to expunge law's own violence from the pages of legal texts and the minds of legal scholars. It is difficult to imagine a more thoroughgoing display of rhetorical power than this concealment of law's violence.

According to its own story, law appears to be immersed in the bloody business of violence, yet the day-to-day texts of law are quite "bloodless," unstained by, and seemingly oblivious to, the sordid business at hand. Sarat and Kearns retrace what they call law's "official story" as it unfolds in the canon—in Hobbes, Austin, Hart, and Dworkin—as well as in contemporary critiques, in an effort to illuminate the steps by which law's violence has become nearly invisible in legal scholarship. They uncover a persistent and pervasive concern with law's alleged affinities with reason and rationality that, especially in the canon, displaces and distances law's violent nature. This preoccupation is plainly challenged in contemporary critiques that deftly disclose the violence of legal interpretation and encourage a clear-headed appreciation of laws' rhetorical and interpretive resourcefulness. But these critiques, too, leave the story of the way rhetoric and interpretation become pain and death largely untold.

Thus, Sarat and Kearns suggest that a further step is required, namely a retelling of law's story that resists, or at least holds off, our desire to believe that law's violence is somehow different from ordinary, numbing force. Such a story would resist, too, the congenial notion that law's violence can be tamed by reason. Whether it is possible to tell a story that bridges the gap in law's pretensions—between its appeals to reason and its reliance on force—and also links interpretive violence with pain and death would appear to be the central issue facing a jurisprudence of violence.

It is impossible to discern whether the response to feminist and poststructuralist criticism of law will be a reconstructed legality or a legal order ever more resilient in its capacity to resist radical transformation. Moreover, attempting to discern the pattern of law's response is somewhat odd, especially when it is tied to the question of the fate of law. Such a title seems to suggest the calm measure of detached Enlightenment reason, of teleology, of scientific rationalism, even of prediction, from which each of the essays in this book seeks to distance itself.

But perhaps we can read our own title differently, and advance by retreating to an earlier view in which fate had more mystical associations and in which to talk of fate was to engage in a telling of the past rather than a prediction of the future, to try to unravel promises already made, decisions already arrived at, or a destiny already sealed. Perhaps the fate of law is not to play the hero in a melodrama written by Thrasymachus or Hobbes. Perhaps we will come to see that the feminist and poststructuralist critique of law is part of its reconstruction and continuous revitalization; perhaps it is the ironic fate of law to be reconstructed or revitalized by those very ideas, for example, compassion, engagement, even politics, that law has for so long tried to exclude. To talk about the fate of law in this way is not to bemoan the tragedy of the modern condition, the iron cage of a depleted Weberian rationalism;[13] it is to witness the rescue of the modern condition from itself.

Or perhaps law's fate is neither so well settled nor so precarious as we might imagine from time to time. Each of the essays in this book claims or implies that law's fate it substantially undetermined. They explore contingent possibilities rather than describe fixed routes of resistance or change. This suggests that law's fate may be no more fixed than a Sisyphean reconstruction and revitalization in reaction to changes in the practices and beliefs on which law depends. But

---

13. David Trubek, "Max Weber's Tragic Modernism and The Study of Law in Society," *Law and Society Review* 20 (1986): 573.

one thing seems clear: law's fate is neither so well settled nor so precarious as to make further discussion of that fate either unnecessary or impossible.

Partial Justice:
Law and Minorities

Martha Minow

I was surprised and delighted to be asked to speak on the topic "The Fate of Law."[1] I was surprised, because this strikes me as a tall person's topic, a topic for someone who can survey the entire world of law and comment on its overall development. To discuss "The Fate of Law" is an invitation to make statements that cast shadows. My work tends to look at the margins and corners, especially at people such as women, children, and persons with disabilities. I am interested in people who have not been the central subjects of theories of law, people who have lived in law's shadows.

At the same time, I was delighted to be asked to speak on "The Fate of Law" because the invitation gave me permission to stop and ask, what do contemporary developments in jurisprudence mean for people who historically have been marginalized by law and legal theory? Do their experiences and perspectives register in contemporary theoretical debates? Do emerging lines of theory offer avenues for reordering law to include those who have been excluded or subordinated?

These questions interest me, and I will take this chance to address them. Still, I confess a worry that the topic, "The Fate of Law," presents a trap. It implies that something has changed, something is

1. I thank Joe Singer, Mary Joe Frug, Mary Ann Glendon, Frank Michelman, Michael Ryan, Austin Sarat, Avi Soifer, Elizabeth Spelman, Cass Sunstein, Saul Touster, and members of the Amherst Seminar for their comments; my essay would be even more partial, but for the help of these good friends. I also thank the faculties of law at the University of Connecticut and at McGill and Queen's universities for vibrant discussions of the themes in this essay.

new, and some danger has appeared in the life of the law. It implies an imagined life cycle for law—a birth, youth, and maturity—and, perhaps, a decline toward death. "Law's Fate" conveys a greater sense of frailty, or speculated limits, than, say, "Law's Empire."[2] Moreover, "Law's Fate" as a topic sets up expectations that are themselves contestable. One expectation is that law matters in some important way, and that its fate—whether continuous or discontinuous—matters. Yet, one of the insights offered by many scholars of legal history is that law is generally much less important than we lawyers tend to think.[3] Law neither confines people's behavior nor works as an independent force in history.[4] Another expectation is that one—I—could assess the fate of a cluster of institutions, practices, and ideologies associated with if not all human history, then at least with the last several centuries of Western civilization. Advice from historians, sociologists, and anthropologists make me doubt any such assessments freed from my own situated perspective.

I am most intrigued by the possibility that to talk about the fate of law is to make explicit what, in another era, may have been so taken for granted that no one needed to speak of or speculate about it. Imagine, for example, someone posing as a topic for a lecture series in twelfth-century Rome, "The Fate of Religion." Or someone asking, on April 15th of this year, "The Fate of Taxes." As an initial topic, therefore, I ask, why would people, like yourselves, want to hear about "the fate of law" at this moment? What is going on, that could make this seem an interesting or even important subject? Why would intelligent people be wondering, at this moment, about "The Fate of Law"?

I cannot help but note that, at this moment, we have recently witnessed grand jury investigations of the Attorney General of the United States, televised Senate hearings on the constitutional beliefs

---

2. See Ronald M. Dworkin, *Law's Empire* (Cambridge, Mass.: Harvard University Press, 1986).

3. This was a major contribution of the school of legal history initiated by J. Willard Hurst.

4. That is not to say that there is not autonomy of legal discourse or a distinction between legal institutions and other institutions. The point instead is that the culture of law may provide some ideals and some practices that enable resistance to prevailing social and economic forces, even while legal practices and decisions generally support and enforce those prevailing forces. See, e.g., E. P. Thompson, *Whigs and Hunters: The Black Act* (London: Allen Lane, 1975).

of Supreme Court nominees, and a highly publicized criminal trial of a military official who defended his role in a foreign policy scandal as inspired by the president's law or a still higher law. My first conjecture is that, deeper than these current affairs topics, there are a series of legal and political debates that signal shifts in generally accepted assumptions about law and society. Along with the usual controversies over turf and policy, I hear some new arguments that realign old foes and old colleagues into new coalitions and new disagreements. A challenge to the pornography industry joins radical feminists and conservative religious leaders in common cause—or collaborations of convenience. Similarly, civil rights activists seeking sanctions for "hate speech" inspire opposition from some defenders of civil liberties, and thus divide long-standing coalitions. Fundamentalist religious groups who oppose secular humanism in public school textbooks find supporters among left-wing critics who challenge the suppression of subgroup identity and group conflict by government officials. Opponents of abortion and advocates for the rights of disabled persons join forces to oppose feminists and others on medical treatment issues for handicapped fetuses and infants. People in very different quarters argue that the law should not constrain them because they listen to a higher law or personal conscience. Interests in community unite people who criticize liberal individualism for the contrasting reasons that traditional authorities need reinforcement and that traditional authorities exclude many from full participating membership.

Why are comrades and opponents shifting alignments? I think that traditional assumptions, usually so deep as to seem natural or incontestable, are newly open for discussion. This has happened before. We have named such periods of history the Reformation and the Enlightenment to indicate these sea changes. What I see before us are new debates about rights, about the rule of law, about foundations for belief and the nature of truth, and about the relations between individuals and society. These are standard topics in studies of jurisprudence—studies by prudent and even not-so-prudent jurists. Yet, current debate among scholars, lawyers, and politicians digs deeper into cultural presuppositions than it often has. The debates about these standard topics these days include even what should count as a persuasive argument in the debates themselves. I will speculate first about the shape of recent debates and then pursue their reverberations in the standard topics of jurisprudence. Finally, I will offer contrasting histories that attend to people both at the margins and at the center of legal theorizing.

Sea Changes

How do people know when they are living through historic changes in the assumptions that undergird their culture? One clue is the shifts in alignment among groups over issues of the day. Another clue appears in the work of artists who provide some reflections on cultural practices. Claes Oldenberg's sculptural depiction of law, in the atrium of the Loyola Law School in Los Angeles, perhaps provides such a clue to some tumult in law. His sculpture is a ladder, leaning precariously, with a can of paint perched on its top rung—the paint splurting out in a moment of frozen disaster. First-year students reportedly find much comfort in this sculptural depiction of their chosen field. But perhaps this image captures the sense of impending disaster experienced by people who turn to law rather than by the law itself.

The self-perception of legal scholars that historic shifts are occurring can be gleaned by the metaphor of a "fight" or "battle" that commonly appears in descriptions of developments in legal theory over the past decade. In an explicit dispute waged by self-identified contestants, legal scholars have competed over what should count as good work and what the enterprise of legal scholarship should address. Many law schools in the late 1980s either experienced such a fight or discussed the battle at other law schools with concern. Even selecting the terms to describe the fight is a contentious issue. One version of the dispute identifies, on one side, the defenders of rationality. They believe that it is possible and wise to conduct public affairs by identifying goals, devising alternative strategies to achieve those goals, evaluating the costs and benefits and other consequences of those alternatives, and selecting the one that maximizes the achievement of the goals. Theirs is an instrumental rationality, but many who hold this view also believe that ends, as well as means, can be selected through reason. And rational people, after due discussion, should be able to agree.

On the other side, according to this view, a disparate crew of challengers criticize the model of rationality for failing to describe the behavior of people under law and for failing to offer sufficient self-consciousness about the self-interests of legal actors. They emphasize the disagreements in society and the points of view typically silenced by the lawyer's conclusions about what is "sound public policy" or "reasonable standards of care." They note the disingenuity embedded in an idea like "rational consensus," for it either reduces rationality to what all would agree upon or reduces consensus to the position that some elite group has designated as rational. Attentive to dissent, some critics challenge the model of rationality for disguising the operations of power and the allocation of resources in society. They argue that power and resources fundamentally determine what can and cannot be articulated as a goal to be accomplished by the legal system. "Rationality" then becomes the label assigned to the views of those who have more power and more privilege. Proponents of this view urge the study of false consciousness and agenda manipulation. They want to unearth suppressed viewpoints and subjugated discourses. Some imply that, some day, we could produce a genuine version of the kind of inclusive discussion and rational process of persuasion imagined by the rationalists, but only after much else changes. Others maintain that we cannot now know how to imagine relationships between knowledge and power and between reason and politics to posit after such changes, and continuing efforts to do so are simply mistaken efforts to hang onto patterns from the past. Some critics recommend refining analytic techniques to puncture persistent claims to rationality in legal argument; others urge thick descriptions of the operations of power. Some look to the power of metaphor, imagery, and nonrational modes in the formation of desires and the conveyance of meaning; still others promote utopian visions and speculations.

Perhaps paradoxically (or parasitically), explorations of the self-delusions of rationality tend to adopt the standard forms of rational argument. The critics write law review articles, complete with footnotes and step-by-step arguments, and only infrequently depart from this form. Yet, they fit materials from poets, rock music, and European social theorists into footnotes; they import into law reviews dialogues, personal anecdotes, and reflections on the law review form. It is not sufficient to fold these innovations back within the traditional forms; the challengers have found numerous and inventive ways to disturb them from within.

Organizing the debates in terms of the defenders of reason and its critics is one, and one disputable, version of the fight. One of its serious defects is the tendency to obscure the variety of challenges offered to traditional legal argument and legal theory. Some among those I have called the challengers reject the very distinction between reason and emotion, or reason and power, as remnants of the categories they seek to combat. Others deny the psychological resonance and moral acceptability of a rationality modeled upon utilitarian cost-benefit analysis and its premise of autonomous individualism. In order to elaborate the beliefs shared by members of a particular community, some investigate the intellectual moves that count as rational within courtrooms and law schools. Some imply a faith in seeking the truth while criticizing what has counted as truth in the past. Some others assault the very goal of seeking the truth as insensitive to the epistemological and political diversity opened up by the challengers. Many emphasize that perceptions and preferences are unavoidably conditioned by local and contingent beliefs and practices, and, therefore, no general, universal framework of knowledge or persuasion—no science of law as defended by the rationalists—is possible.

Some scholars, lawyers, and political figures seem confused by the conflict. Some simply draw on the challengers' views while working within the rationalist model. Some try to assimilate the challengers to previous categories of thought and cabin their arguments as points of agreement or disagreement with particular legal positions. Others claim that the challengers simply revive old and familiar positions developed by the legal realists in the 1920s, or even by the ancient Sophists. Some practicing lawyers assume that the challengers are communists; some political figures try to superimpose national political divisions on the internal law school fights. President Reagan gave a speech celebrating the emergence of the "Federalist Society" as a response to "critical legal studies." But these efforts to order the law school debates according to other frameworks show widespread failures to engage with the debates themselves.

If taken seriously, I think that the contemporary debates in legal theory foretell a shift in paradigms, to use Thomas Kuhn's now-familiar term. The very familiarity of Kuhn's idea attests to the change. He wrote about how changes in the sciences, and by analogy, in other knowledge-seeking endeavors, are resisted by members of the expert community, who are wedded to the prevailing paradigm for seeking and testing knowledge. Yet, anomalies, instances that do not fit, may persist and resist the experts' readiness to explain them away. When many experts begin to notice repeated failures in the paradigm, they may grow more speculative, more theoretical, more willing to debate the ordinary ways of working and understanding so taken for granted when the paradigm seemed to work. Talk of paradigms, and paradigm shifts, echoes throughout universities, businesses, and even the popular press. New stories describe minority viewpoints as anomalies that test prevailing paradigms. A satiric comic sings the song, "Brother, can you paradigm?"

If taken seriously, the debates between rationalists and challengers in legal scholarship could shed light on developments in legal practice. In many ways, practicing lawyers have even more corrosive skepticism about rational consensus as a way to explain law then do legal scholars. It is lawyers, after all, who acknowledge that judges do not act according to universally shared reason, but according to their own political and personal preferences; lawyers use every available research technique to discover what has mattered to a particular judge in the past in order to produce a persuasive argument in the future. It is lawyers who presume the irrationality of juries, while believing in their own abilities to predict—or manipulate—jury behavior. The law firm representing MCI staged mock trials before juries who were selected to match, by demographic characteristics, the members of the actual jury in a suit against AT&T. By testing alternative theories and methods of presentation before the mock juries, the lawyers selected the arguments most likely to succeed for their clients, and thus fed the results of their studies back into the system.

Some lawyers are joined by scholars in looking at the ways that ostensible challenges to power in the name of rationality become ever more subtle extensions of it. Critics of alternative dispute resolution—mediation, arbitration, and the like—have explored this route, as have some observers of the medical profession. These critics document how the established profession tends to absorb the profession's pockets of resistance and thereby confirm the profession's monopoly rather than allow some competition. Thus, some hospitals include midwives in their medical team for childbirth; some adopt acupuncture as part of a medical management of pain. Courts and law firms have embraced mediation, and brought it under their roofs, rather than allowing it a separate path as an alternative to the formal system. Critics—including legal scholars, legal services attorneys, and other public interest lawyers—have expressed greater reservations about the new dispute resolution techniques and cautions about new packages for poor people's justice.

For me, the seriousness of changes in law—and the sense that the ocean is shifting even as we stand here—hit home in discussions during the past two years among women lawyers about pregnancy and maternity leave benefits. This issue sharply divided people who usually vigorously work together in law reform efforts. The problem emerged from a clash between federal and state laws. In two memorable federal cases, the Supreme Court rejected constitutional and statutory challenges to private employers' decisions to exclude pregnancy benefits from health care.[5] The Court reasoned that the employer did not draw a forbidden distinction on the basis of sex, only one on the basis of pregnancy. Since women could be both pregnant and nonpregnant, this was not an instance of sex discrimination. With this auspicious beginning, perhaps it is a good development that litigation on related issues proceeded on statutory rather than constitutional grounds. When the Court interprets statutes, its judgments can be more quickly overturned—by legislatures—than when the Court construes the Constitution, for then only the slow and complex process of constitutional amendment remains as an avenue for correction. Indeed, Congress responded to the Court's statutory ruling by enacting a statute—the Pregnancy Discrimination Act—that bans discrimination on the basis of pregnancy as well as any other impermissible sex discrimination.[6] But now, if differentiation on the basis of pregnancy is forbidden, does this mean that states may not require pregnancy or maternity leaves—a distinction, or discrimination, that helps women? Litigation over this issue culminated in a recent decision by the Supreme Court. The Court considered whether the Pregnancy Discrimination Act itself forbids even favorable treatment on the basis of pregnancy. Does the requirement of nondiscrimination mandate the same treatment, or does it permit special treatment?

---

5. Geduldig v. Aiello, 417 U.S. 484 (1974) (equal protection clause); General Electric Co. v. Gilbert, 429 U.S. 125 (1976) (Title VII). Countries with universal health care wisely avoid such problems.

6. 42 U.S.C. §2000e(k) (1982) (amending Title VII).

Advocates for women's rights argued about this with a kind of intensity and distress that helped me understand why brothers could fight brothers in the American Civil War. Writing briefs on opposing sides of the case, women's rights groups went public with the division. At a meeting in Washington, D.C., in the fall of 1987, opponents within the community of women's rights advocates met to discuss our differences. Some maintained that any distinction on the basis of pregnancy—any distinction on the basis of sex—would perpetuate negative stereotypes and the denigration and exclusion of women. Others argued that denying the facts of pregnancy and the needs of new mothers could only hurt women; treating women like men in the workplace violated the demands of equality. Can equality be secured through similar or through different treatment? Importantly, many advocates for women agreed that the workplace itself was the problem, because employers had the traditional male employee in mind as the model worker—with a full-time wife/mother at home. The very phrase *special treatment,* when used to describe pregnancy or maternity leave, treats men as the norm and women as different or deviant from that norm. None of the advocates for women's rights accepted this male-centered view. In this sense, we are divided merely over the tactic to be used to alter the relationship between work and family.

Well, not entirely. The division among advocates for women plunged deeper than mere tactics in at least two respects. First, we disagreed about what goal we actually sought: pregnancy and maternity leaves, more flexibility in work hours to accommodate demands of any dependents at home, or even more flexibility in work hours for whatever reason a worker wanted. Second, we differed over how much to accept and agree within prevailing frameworks of analysis versus how much to challenge those frameworks directly. Some who wanted this larger challenge acknowledged the risks of losing but stated that we should not seek only what we could win. There is more at stake in our strategy than winning, there is the matter of symbolic expression and resistance. In these respects, the disagreements begin to suggest the larger debates about law and the stakes of those debates, including assaults on the modes for seeking change designated by the legal system itself.

One of the most contentious disputes among us involved whether we should rest simply with the divisions expressed within the group of articulate, well-educated, and relatively powerful advocates for women's rights, or instead go and seek out perspectives of women in rural and distant communities who had even less access to courts, legislatures, and instruments of power. Were we engaging in exclusionary practices of the very sort we rallied to oppose? Was it really our domain to try to determine leave policy, or would a more democratic procedure, one that assures equality in the right to decide, design a process for more women—or all women in the country—to answer the issue? We did not answer this question, and we disagreed about its importance as well. Instead, we fought over what arguments, advocated in the room, we should endorse.

One inventive group argued for retaining the language of sameness as the predicate for equal treatment, while urging the Court to preserve pregnancy and maternity leaves by calling for comparable benefits for men. To the surprise of many of us, this is the approach that later convinced the Court. The majority opinion, written by Justice Thurgood Marshall, said that the correct question is not whether the ban against pregnancy discrimination also forbids special accommodation, but, instead, whether a workplace rule satisfies the ban against pregnancy discrimination if it allows both men and women to combine work and family.[7] It is a temporary resolution, however, for the decision was ambiguous about whether employers can, or must, provide comparable benefits for men, or for nonpregnant employees. Legislators and lobbyists are now similarly embattled on these issues. Many observers predict that employers will simply hire fewer women, or communicate that employees who actually elect to take the leaves will lose out on the job in the long run. According to others, the very process of trying to predict consequences is a waste because any reform will ultimately hurt women until women's power in society increases generally. Advocates for further change argue that pregnancy is a social issue, not a women's problem. Still others dispute the very idea that "women" represents a meaningful or coherent group with shared interests, and emphasize differences of race, class, and religion that make it difficult to talk of what is "good for women."

A similar conflict occupies discussions of comparable worth. Through lawsuits and other legal initiatives, reformers seek to rectify

7. California Fed. Sav. & Loan Ass'n v. Guerra, 107 S. Ct. 683, 694 (1987).

inequities in pay based on gender segregation in the workplace, and to revalue traditional "women's" work that the marketplace has devalued. They ask, why should secretaries receive lower pay than truck drivers; why should telephone operators receive lower compensation than telephone salespeople? Reason, claim the proponents of comparable worth, can be used to expose the prejudices that have both confined women to particular jobs and underpaid them. Reason can guide reevaluations of the social contribution made by different kinds of work. Advocates of comparable worth claim that it is possible to assess the relative value of a given job skill and line up the valuation of jobs on this basis. Its opponents object that comparable worth requires comparing apples and oranges—and departs from the one objective source of measurement, the marketplace. Thus far, we seem to have a contest over whether the marketplace is rational, and over whether other sources of reasoned evaluation can be as, or more, reliable.

The divisions of views quickly becomes more complicated. Some advocates for women support the idea behind comparable worth but object that any measure of the value of a given job skill will ultimately draw on the market value of that job, and thus revalidate the market's devaluation of traditional women's work while making the gender-based critique more elusive. Thus, these critics would argue, if comparable worth analysis uses the new industry of job evaluators, the new doctrine may simply cloak the persistent undervaluation of such skills as taking care of people, handling paperwork, and managing interpersonal dynamics in the guise of objective and positive social science. Moreover, they would claim, we have no benchmarks, accessible through reason, that are free from patterns of discrimination.

This position is likely to invite the rejoinder: on what foundation can you base your assertions of discrimination, if there is no rational corrective to the "undervaluation" of women's jobs? Perhaps it is this worry that leads others to urge a broadly based challenge to divisions of job responsibilities, such as the distinction between nurses and doctors. Nothing short of major social reconstruction, according to a blueprint not yet written, will do. Still other advocates for women stop far short of calling for revolution. Instead, they oppose comparable worth or other alternatives on the grounds that they would deter women from seeking more challenging and more rewarding roles offered in traditional "male" jobs. In this view, women should aspire to be doctors, not better-paid nurses. The most recent retort to this claim is that if many women become doctors, then the work of doctors, too, will become devalued. We cannot reason our way out of existing patterns of power relationships and images of gender. Our very efforts to reason about them may lead us, mistakenly, to exacerbate the problems.

Each of these examples suggests deep conflicts within groups seeking to change social and legal practices. Such conflicts may be the predictable side effects of reform activities. Torn even in small decisions over legal tactics by the old debate over reform versus revolution, and splintered by repeated political losses and the frustrating search for toeholds in the existing systems, reformers throughout history have often had more divisive debates among themselves than with their ostensible foes. Yet, I sense that the divisions that I have heard within reform camps expose profound conflicts over what law is or could be. Should we construct society according to categories that distinguish between what is natural and what is socially constructed and therefore subject to change? What counts as truth and what counts as illusion in legal argument? What relationships between individuals and society are possible or desirable? Any of the questions may divide those who believe that existing methods of rational argument afford methods to formulate goals and achieve them, and those who believe that our very tools of reason and proof encode the problems we seek to tackle. The latter group argues that we reproduce the problems, rather than disentangle ourselves from them, in the rationalist legal alternatives we debate.

The conflicts manifested by debates among reformers are matched, these days, by the tensions among traditionalists who confront a world more fluid and volatile than they would choose. Let me couple these glimpses of how reformers experience and express the shifting paradigms with an equally brief suggestion of what traditionalists may be feeling. I use as examples an evaluation of the practices of the former Solicitor General of the United States and current law school debates over law school curriculum planning.

A recent book by a journalist, Lincoln Caplan, criticizes the former Solicitor General of the United States, Charles Fried, for politicizing the office of the nation's lawyer before the Supreme Court. In *The Tenth Justice* (1987), Caplan details the manner in which many distinguished lawyers who have held the office of Solicitor General built up, through the decades, a reputation for integrity, neutrality, and excellence in legal analysis and judgment before the Supreme Court. The Solicitor General has served, in many ways, as a judge as well as an advocate, screening the cases that various agencies of the federal government had lost in lower courts and deciding which to take to the Supreme Court. In addition, the Solicitor General has played a powerful role as friend of the Court—amicus curiae—weighing in with views about the federal government's interests in cases involving private parties or the states. The Solicitor General's track record of success before the Court reflects and sustains the respect and deference earned by the lawyers in that office. Indeed, the lawyers built a reputation of independence from partisan concerns, excellence in professional craft, and self-restraint in the exercise of notable, but relatively unaccountable, power. Caplan charges Charles Fried, a professor at Harvard Law School and an appointee of President Reagan, with having betrayed the trust earned by his predecessors by badgering the Court with partisan, political viewpoints. In short, Caplan claims Fried violated professional standards by politicizing the office. Urging controversial applications of some precedents and the overturn of others, Fried and his staff also triggered unusual criticisms from members of the Court.

As a former clerk to a Justice of the Supreme Court, and as an inveterate Court watcher, I confess that I initially found Caplan's criticisms telling and troubling. I had grown to respect the office of the Solicitor General and the standards of excellence it represented. I, too, had noted the apparent decline of the office as it descended from near-judicial tones into the scrappy style of zealous adversariness. I reacted as someone accustomed to the genteel mores of a club that excluded most challengers of its members' understanding of the world. I also reacted as someone who lacks sympathy for most of the political program of the president whom the former Solicitor General aggressively sought to represent. Seeking reversals of the Court's positions on abortion, private discrimination, affirmative action, and governmental obligations, Fried's agenda was almost diametrically opposed to my own. Thus, it seemed especially delicious to me that I could join with people who disagree with my political purposes in apparently neutral criticisms of Fried's methods.

Yet, there is something misleading about criticism based on professional standards rather than open disagreement with the goals pursued by the office. On reflection, I realized that the traditions of professional craft and independence celebrated by the Solicitor General's office in the past helped to produce and monitor a narrow compass of debate, excluding discussions of ideology. Were I to consider the range of precedents I would like overturned, and the aggressive posture a systematic law reform effort would require, I too would want the office of the Solicitor General available to change the law more often and more dramatically than it has in the past. It seems odd for me to defend Charles Fried, whose views on nearly every legal subject depart significantly from my own, but this is the kind of strange alignment that I find symptomatic of our sea change. The claim to neutrality in the name of professional standards should not be allowed to obscure the significant political fight between conservatives and progressives. If we now find conservatives and progressives united against what has been a middle-of-the-road approach, we are witnessing a growing view that political changes should be debated and not curtailed by assumptions that we all fundamentally agree.

What, then, does this mean for the notion of "professional standards"? Professional standards imply the guidelines to which all upstanding professionals adhere. Yet, professional standards may call upon the Solicitor General to screen out many cases that would rock the apparent rational consensus of the Court's jurisprudence. The alleged virtues of neutrality and rational consensus in the name of professionalism become the attributes of reigning authorities. Once challenged as simply the decorum that accompanies the ideology in power, these virtues become ready casualties of challenges from ideologies either more conservative or more radical. The earmarks of a "sound" or "well-crafted" legal argument may themselves be open to attack in an era filled with challenges to the underlying assumptions of the political agenda behind particular legal rules.[8] If professional standards mean Burkean incrementalism, they should be subject to challenge, along with any other political choice.

At the same time, means as ends deserve debate and evaluation. I think that regardless of its announced or implicit ideology, legal

---

8. See Peter H. Irons, *The New Deal Lawyers* (Princeton: Princeton University Press, 1982); Robert Cover, *Justice Accused: Antislavery and the Judicial Process* (New Haven: Yale University Press, 1975) (describing periods of challenge to and transformation of the fundamental assumptions behind the constitutional scheme).

advocacy should be judged in terms of its candor about what is being debated and about how a proposed interpretation would change prior interpretations. Caplan charged Fried's office with citing rules for propositions for which they did not stand, for claiming that proposed interpretations are not new but are already settled by existing law.[9] Dishonest means used in search of passionately sought ends should themselves be debated; it is a particular ideology that demands complete honesty in argument about means as well as ends. I myself would urge this ideology within legal argument today as part of a commitment to expand participation in and challenges to the exercise of power under law,[10] and I think the demand for honesty in legal argument would not unduly constrain efforts to change the law by either progressive or conservative reformers. The essential point is that law itself is unavoidably political. Society makes choices through law about what to value, what to permit, what to punish, and what to prohibit. These choices include rules about what kinds of changes can be contemplated and how those changes are to be debated and evaluated. That he "politicized" the office is not a good basis for criticizing Charles Fried, even for those of us who disagree with his goals; that he may have concealed some of what he was seeking raises an issue of a different sort.

Another present-day dispute occurs in law school curriculum discussions. Based on developments in legal practice as well as legal scholarship, many law faculties have recently decided to instruct students in a field called law and economics. Students need to be proficient in a method of analyzing the costs and benefits of legal rules and practices. This is the method used in antitrust cases, tort cases, and, increasingly, in other fields as well. The practice of law itself has become a competitive business. Analysis of the costs and potential returns for a lawyer or firm handling any given matter is a critical component in law practice, as well as an increasingly important element of evaluating substantive legal policies. The availability of dam-

---

9. This is not the time or place to pursue this challenge to Fried's office, although I register it because I myself have encountered misleading citations in briefs written by the office during Fried's tenure, and because I believe that it is worth distinguishing between honest arguments for change and dishonest arguments for results couched as though they involved no change.

10. See "The Rule of Law" section below.

ages for a tortious injury depends largely on the lawyer's assessment that the case is worth taking through the system.

How should the school teach the methods of analysis used in law and economics? If it is merely an elective, its advocates say, it comes too late and remains too marginal. Yet, if it becomes part of the required curriculum, many traditional instructors feel both incompetent and undermined. The insistent search for costs and benefits is not what they know how to teach. Economic analysis also seems to degrade reasoning through the application of legal doctrine, reasoning by analogy, and cultural transmission of respect for precedents that the traditional teacher tends to emphasize. Others may reject the extreme form of consequentialism animating economic analysis of law; they defend a view of law's protection of rights beyond a utilitarian calculus.[11]

Despite these possible sources of resistance, a growing cadre of scholars trained formally or informally in economics now mount sophisticated courses in the economic analysis of law and produce elaborate scholarship in the same vein. Its very foreign qualities disable colleagues from evaluating the work by law-and-economics scholars. The rise of economic analysis of law introduces academic specialization of a sort that ends the law schools' claim to be the last refuge for generalists. Law and economics looks "hard" and its adherents can claim rationality is on their side; they explicitly articulate their assumptions and explicitly assess costs and benefits. Yet law and economics analysis poses a challenge to traditional legal analysis that traditionally celebrated case-by-case adjudication and accommodation of conflicting principles. Law and economics analysis introduces a different paradigm of rationality, and neither economic analysis nor traditional legal analysis can neutrally adjudicate the choice between them.

Some professors, including those identified with the left-wing intellectual project known as critical legal studies, object that law and economics relies on slippery concepts that do not disclose their assumptions and yet claim a power to resolve difficult disputes. One such concept is transaction costs. Critics charge that such concepts appear able to provide analytic power, yet they remain manipulable

---

11. It is possible to defend legal rights within a utilitarian calculus, but many legal academics would resist this approach as giving up the fight before it begins.

and subject to redefinition. Therefore, a concept like transaction costs seduces students with a seeming certainty when the purpose of law school should be to challenge comfortable certainties—or so critics allege. For the critics, law and economics seems to offer a scientific method for solving legal problems, but it actually disguises important choices and values about how to treat people. Some of these critics may choose to conduct their own classes as critiques of law and economics, or as elaborations of their own critical methodologies, informed by developments in European social thought, such as Marxism, critical theory, or deconstruction. Some of their colleagues, in turn, may doubt whether these courses belong in law schools. Taken together, the law and economics courses and the critical legal studies courses probe the underpinnings of law in ways that may intrude on the mainstream, traditional courses. Students instructed to ask about costs and benefits in one class and about power relationships in another start to question the traditional course that contains only discussions of legal rules and policies.

Thus, a traditional, open-minded academic who believes in academic freedom may grow troubled about current curricular and scholarly debates. Of course, anyone should be able to teach whatever seems true or useful—yet, a shift in some courses affects others. The standard, traditional class will change if students are learning approaches with entirely different assumptions and methodologies down the hall. The traditional teacher will now have to respond to questions about consequences, costs and benefits, and questions about why precedent or analogy matter. Strangely similar challenges may come from students intrigued by courses that deconstruct legal doctrines and demonstrate patterns of rhetoric and particular political agendas that accompany supposedly rational legal analysis. Never regarding the traditional materials as controversial, much less ideological, the traditional teacher now has to identify and defend assumptions. Some traditionalists might disdain any feelings of self-doubt.[12] They may view critical legal scholarship as an appalling in-

---

12. I think here of Allan Bloom, whose book, *The Closing of the American Mind: How Higher Education Has Failed Democracy and Impoverished the Souls of Today's Students* (New York: Simon and Schuster, 1987), became a runaway best-seller in the United States. From his vantage point, the introduction of alternative perspectives in the undergraduate program represents a decline in standards and a loss of the rigor represented by instruction in the classics. He objects particularly to African-American stud-

troduction of politics or of a watered-down academic study of philosophy and social theory by amateurs; they may object that students
no longer learn law, much less that law has right and wrong answers.[13] They may simply assert that standards are falling, and reas-
sert their own curriculum and teaching style as the standard.

As long as the debate proceeds from the queries, have standards
declined, or what happened to reason, the dice is loaded; these are
questions framed by the traditionalist camp. But where is there a
place to stand without joining one or another camp? If reason itself
is contested, how are we to think about the contest? These answers
arise in new arguments within jurisprudence about basic concepts in
theories of law. These debates, too, solicit odd bedfellows, and raise
from another direction the problem of where to stand in order to
know.

Old Rigging, New Knots

Alongside shifting currents in contemporary legal debates, I believe
there are new contests over classic questions in the study of justifications for law. Scholars and activists are engaged in debates over
rights, the rule of law, foundations for belief and the nature of truth,
and the relations between individuals and society. These are debates
that include what even counts as a persuasive argument in the debates themselves. Here is an admittedly rationalist account of these
debates.[14]

---

ies and feminist scholarship—as well as to rock and roll. The parallels to law school
curricular changes are incomplete, yet intriguing.

13. Some law school innovations may resist such a Bloomian charge by asserting
lineage to the rationalist tradition. Indeed, unlike the changes in the undergraduate
curriculum, the study of law and economics has been defended because it adds rigor
to legal studies. From at least some vantage points, the economic study of law increases
the "rationality" of law by heightening attention to objectives, alternatives, and consequences. Critical legal studies has also been defended for raising the intellectual quality, sophistication, and rigor of legal analysis and scholarship. In these respects, innovations in legal education may represent the gradual improvements that come from
borrowing work from the universities, admittedly with the usual lag time required for
ideas to cross the street to the law school.

14. Roberto Unger suggests how unavoidable—and unavoidably important—the
tools of rationalist discourse are, even in the critique. See Roberto Unger, *Knowledge
and Politics* (New York: Free Press, 1975).

Rights

In the popular press and political volleys, the rights debate is somewhat crude: some pundits assert rights whenever they mean wants;
others oppose any right that was not well established before they
were born. Legal and political scholarship actually is not so different.
Some scholars trace new rights from technological change or from
social movements. Others attack a "rights industry" that is run by
professional advocates, law professors, and publicists for manufac-
turing rights that undermine settled expectations and civil society.
The debate produces a sharp division over constitutional interpretation. Advocates of a notion of evolving standards of justice and fairness square off against those who demand evidence of the original
intent of the Constitution's framers to support any claims of constitutional protection. Oddly, though, some individuals seem to shift
methodological camps, depending upon which particular interest
seems at stake.

   These are long-standing disputes, with positions that have been
familiar in legal and political circles for generations. The supporters
of evolving rights, in this century, have been aligned with "progressive" political reforms, advancing the rights of groups like blacks,
women, native Americans, and other groups traditionally lacking full
political participation. Those who demand evidence of original intent
or long-standing pedigree for rights usually stand with established
property interests and traditionally privileged persons. There have
always been exceptions; some claim to find strong authority for
change in the original intent of the constitution.

   Yet more recent contests over rights point to some realignments.
The right to life movement, for example, rallies members of fundamentalist religions who usually oppose legal change; they argue, in
essence, for the recognition of rights for a new class composed of
fetuses. Here, right to life advocates rely on and strengthen the argument that rights come not only from official legal sources but also
from conscience; although they couch their argument as an attack
on the Supreme Court's activism in *Roe v. Wade*, they seek, at this
point, judicial activism not only to reverse that case but also perhaps
to protect Operation Rescue activists and to enlarge the state's regulation of pregnancy and medical treatment decisions about newborns.
Their opponents, for the most part, defend the right to privacy, no-

tions of autonomy, and boundaries of permissible governmental regulation. Yet these very rights arguments by the pro choice activists collide, in a different direction, with arguments introduced by critical legal scholars about all kinds of rights. The critical legal scholars are a diverse group of progressives and activists who landed in law schools and launched a critique of rights as incoherent, mystifying, and alienating. Despite an explicitly left-wing political agenda, the critical legal scholars echo conservative authors who castigate the proliferation of rights for undermining community. Critical legal scholars undoubtedly yearn for a different community—an egalitarian, and perhaps, socialist, one—while traditional conservatives invoke conventional communities anchored in established authority and hierarchy.[15] But they create a challenge to liberal ideals of individual autonomy and privacy alongside challenges prompted by conservatives, defending community values and traditions.

These are not simply flip-flops, with people switching allegiances in the battle over rights depending on particular instrumental purposes, but, instead, shifts that seem to mirror the debate over rationalism. The earlier divide between those who saw evolving rights and those who demanded documentation for rights represented a contest over what counts as authority. People may have disagreed about whether human reason could discern authority for rights in shifting social need or, instead, in interpretations of texts or assertions about nature. But they agreed that human reason was essential to articulating and enforcing rights. People involved in earlier contests implied that rights have something even more fundamental to do with rationality. They argued that people deserve rights because of their shared capacities for reason, and rights can be discerned and effectuated through processes of reasoned debate and judgment.

Today, some critical theorists contest the premises of individual autonomy, conscious subjectivity, and universal capacities for reason that underlie rights traditions. They also challenge the claim that reason guides legal argument and judgment. They focus instead on the impossibility of reason as an ideal removed from history and

---

15. See Richard Parker, "Issues of Community and Liberty," *Harvard Journal of Law and Public Policy* 8 (1985): 287 (comparing conservative republican community and populist republicanism).

politics. They stress class conflicts that suffuse and yet remain submerged by legal disputes. They maintain that legal texts lack determinate meanings because critical ambiguities within the tests can only be resolved through an endless recursiveness, referring to other texts, which refer to other texts. And they locate indeterminacy in key words or concepts, encoded with suppressed and contradictory meanings.[16] These are not simply charges that the particular rights that exist now are too limited, or too embedded in existing social and economic arrangements, although critics often make these charges as well. Instead, the critical legal studies critique of rights maintains that the very process of thinking about oneself in terms of rights produces alienation, a harmful sense of distance from personal experience and meaning, and profound interference with interpersonal understanding.[17]

In a different way, the right to life activists challenge the predicates of rationality behind a system of rights. They seek to secure rights for fetuses but fetuses lack rationality; and the activists rely on divine, rather than rational, authority. Moreover, conservatives have played upon the splits within the liberal coalition, and attacked abstract liberal notions of justice for producing governmental invasions in the home and the neighborhood.[18] The conservatives and fundamentalists do not themselves argue against governmental intrusions, however—and, indeed, advocate rights for severely disabled newborns against parents or medical personnel who would withhold treatment.

The dividing lines are new. Some liberal defenders of abortion rights try to revitalize rationalist models of individual choice as the premise for women's rights and positivist justifications for rights. This approach links rights to official acts of courts and legislatures rather than conscience, nature, or divine authority. Other defenders of abortion rights reject the framework of autonomy and individual-

---

16. Critiques of rights for indeterminacy are not restricted to the critical legal studies camp. See, e.g., Peter Westen, "The Rueful Rhetoric of 'Rights,'" *UCLA Law Review* 33 (1986): 977 (critiquing rights for masking ambiguity in reference to interests vs. entitlements and for carrying powerful rhetorical force nonetheless).

17. See Peter Gabel, "The Phenomenology of Rights-Consciousness and the Pact of the Withdrawn Selves," *Texas Law Review* 62 (1984): 1563.

18. See Allen Hunter, "The Role of Liberal Political Culture in the Construction of Middle America," *University of Miami Law Review* 42 (1987): 93.

ism and, instead, argue that women's systematic inequality requires this amount of freedom.

A backlash against feminism and against racial justice reforms often unites business and labor groups while requiring, paradoxically, both a revived defense of the traditional family as a communal enclave away from competitive individualism, and a revitalized individualism, attacking special governmental assistance through welfare and employment rights. Liberal defenders of civil rights build defenses against the two-fronted assault of conservatives who would withdraw enforcement of civil rights on the law books, and radical critical theorists who attack even the ideal of rights as misleading and alienating. In many ways, the contest over rights exposes another dispute—one over the ideal of the rule of law.

The Rule of Law

"The Rule of Law" represents a philosophy of government by law rather than by men[19] or sheer power. It has a particular history and particular proponents. Committed to governance through general rules, consistently and fairly applied, the rule of law postulates (1) rules, (2) officials who enforce them, and (3) norms about the pronouncement and enforcement of those rules. Some rules articulate rights and their corresponding duties or immunities; others simply command standards of obliged conduct, enforced by the police power of the state. The rule of law as an ideal imbuing all rules and their interpretations emerged with a particular historical struggle that toppled regimes of feudal and royal authority and their attendant methods of personal preference, favors, and loyalty.

Adherents to the rule of law embrace norms of impartiality, neutrality, objectivity, and universality. These norms are also currently under attack. One attack comes from litigators and scholars concerned with the situations of women, children, disabled people, and members of religious, racial, and linguistic minorities, gays and lesbians, and other groups.[20]

---

19. Usually, quite literally. See Hanna Fenschel Pitkin, *Fortune Is a Woman: Gender and Politics in the Thought of Niccolo Machiavelli* (Berkeley: University of California Press, 1984).

20. Other disfavored groups include incarcerated felons, prostitutes, drug addicts, alcoholics, persons with terminal illnesses, and persons with contagious diseases.

The critics claim that legal rules and legal institutions fail to achieve the aspirations of impartiality, neutrality, objectivity, and universality. They argue that supposedly impartial legal rules actually prefer some and disadvantage others. An equality principle that approves descriptively similar treatment for everyone neglects some; a law requiring public classroom instruction in English neglects the situation of students whose primary language is Chinese, Spanish, or French. Many rules impose a disparate and negative impact on members of minority groups or women. When the military or a private employer imposes a dress code that bans nonstandard headgear, there is a special, serious impact on a member of a religious minority that requires special head coverings that is different from the burden on the individual who simply wanted to wear a baseball cap. Despite claims of universality, neutrality, and objectivity, the law hypothesizes a "typical person" and then fails to accommodate—or even penalizes—those who do not fit the law's own preferred type.

Moreover, demands for neutrality can stymie remedial efforts to overcome the effects of past discrimination and exclusion. Neutrality, in its dominant version, would prevent affirmative action in employment and school admissions, despite ample evidence that decision makers excluded people in the past and hampered their progress on the illegitimate basis of minority group membership. So goes one kind of challenge to law's familiar goals of impartiality, neutrality, objectivity, and universality. This challenge suggests that these goals are still worthy, but unfulfilled. The rules of the game must be made still more general, and remnants of particular images of persons and their needs must be cleared away. Some would say that such reforms could salvage and reinvigorate the ideal of neutrality; others remains suspicious of any claims to avoid hidden assumptions about the archetypal person.

Yet, a contrasting challenge cuts more deeply into the aspirations of the rule of law. From this view, the very aspirations to generalize, to abstract from particular experience, to devise universal rules, and to see impartially are impossible and self-deluding. From this angle, we should revel in particularity, we should admit that abstraction is no better than concrete analysis, we should accept case-by-case or individualized justice as what law is and can at best be. Legal argument must engage never-ending permutations of the multiple and inconsistent values of this society. There are no certain meanings of authoritative texts, no question can ever be settled, and conflict should be embraced rather than resolved. Some would even argue that rules that set boundaries and close off some decisions for reconsideration must be made suspect, even if those decisions were hard won and overcame prior oppression. I may be grouping together views expressed by people who would never embrace one another, but I suspect they have more in common than they admit. Surely, they have more in common than those who defend the norms of universality and impartiality, and even more than those who criticize the failure of these norms but still seek their fulfillment.

Let me sort out the disagreements in terms of the norms and assumptions supporting the rule of law.[21] First, the assumption that law works through rules, pronounced and enforced by officials,[22] draws challenges from several quarters. Jürgen Habermas seeks to reconstruct a basis for legality, yet his work maintains that no authority, and no rule, is legitimate unless it could be articulated and agreed to in an "ideal speech situation" where there are no distorting power relations or social constraints and nothing remains undiscussed by anyone who would want to discuss it. Habermas similarly grounds rationality in the "life world" and thus hints at a way to locate authority in the structures of lived experience rather than in state officials. Michel Foucault has argued that rules no longer emerge solely from legal officials, but instead work through the disciplinary mechanisms of professionals who promulgate standards and norms in schools, workplaces, bureaucracies, families, and other social institutions.

Other scholars advocate hermeneutic and interpretive methods to reject any implication that rules or their meanings are fixed. The hermeneutic approaches, in contrast, follow Hans-Georg Gadamer and Ludwig Wittgenstein, and locate the meanings of rules in historically situated, communal practices. The interpretation of rules, in this sense, depends upon groups of people with shared social practices and forms of life that permit, and indeed produce, multiple and shift-

---

21. I am assisted in this discussion by Margaret Jane Radin, "Reconsidering the Rule of Law," *Boston University Law Review* 69 (1989): 781.

22. This is admittedly the positivist version of the rule of law. Is there a natural rights version? See, perhaps, Michael Moore, "A Natural Law Theory of Interpretation," *Southern California Law Review* 58 (1985): 277; Michael Moore, "Moral Reality," *Wisconsin Law Review* 1982, 1061 (elaborating a coherence view of moral reality).

ing pragmatic meanings.[23] For these people, law is an interpretive process engaging those who make rules and those who follow them—and those who resist them or give new meanings to them in their acts of partial compliance.[24] What, then, would be the fate of norms like impartiality, neutrality, objectivity, and universality? They are remade through commitments to view judges as engaged in, rather than separate from, the communities. Context is necessary for making meaning, and specificity and particularity are necessary for doing justice. Some hermeneutic approaches challenge the emphasis on a coherent state authority implicit in the rule of law, and search for cultural contexts to replace coherent state authority. The state cannot help but be hostile to competing sources of authority, even as these competing sources—such as religious traditions—may be central to people's abilities to make meanings in their lives. Robert Cover emphasizes the significance of contests among plural, normative communities for meaning.[25] For him, judges who are officials of the state must accept responsibility for the violence they do when their judgments conflict with the norms generated by a subcommunity, and must try to avoid suppressing those competing sources of normative obligation and meaning.

Once again, the new debate over rationalism is implicated.[26] For the rule of law depends on a particular view of reason: those who apply and those who follow rules share goals and practices of rationality, and the entire system of rule by law is defended through a

---

23. Robert Cover elaborates such a view in "Foreword: Nomos and Narrative," *Harvard Law Review* 97 (1983): 4; Joan Williams and Margaret Radin defend such a view in Williams, "Critical Legal Studies: The Death of Transcendence and the Rise of the New Langdells," *New York University Law Review* 62 (1987): 429, 491–95, and Radin, "Reconsidering the Rule of Law." Ronald Dworkin seems drawn to such a view and yet retains aspects of positivist thought. See Dworkin, *Law's Empire*.

24. See William Forbath, Hendrik Hartog, and Martha Minow, "Introduction: Legal Histories from Below," *Wisconsin Law Review* 1985, 759. See also Hendrik Hartog, "The Constitution of Aspiration and 'The Rights That Belong To Us All,'" *Journal of American History* 37 (1987): 1013.

25. See Cover, "Nomos and Narrative"; Carol Weisbrod, "Family, Church and State: An Essay on Constitutionalism and Religious Authority," *Journal of Family Law* 26 (1987–88): 741.

26. Paradoxically, a kind of reason is required in the very critique of the claims of reason. See p. 32, n. 14 (discussion of Unger). Within the critical hermeneutic practices, this kind of self-reflective critique of the method of the critique itself would be de rigeur.

rational defense that rules promote liberty and security. The hermeneutic challenge doubts an idea of reason abstracted from context and
generalizable across communities. In rejecting objectivity, the interpretive approach also rejects subjectivity, or mere self-conscious
awareness as the route to knowledge. All knowledge depends on a
culturally and historically situated shared world of meaning. Norms
cannot be separated from facts; justifications depend on the community in which those statements matter.

That community is not just a set of ideas, either: it represents
actual institutional practices, anchored in and produced by educational systems, advertising, religious traditions, and corporate practices. Interpretation occurs within a community and depends on a
circular process of seeking to understand a whole in terms of its
parts, and parts in their contribution to the whole.[27] And the whole
is not just a text, such as the text of the Constitution, but also the
institutional practices in which it was produced and within which its
current interpreters live and act. Interpretation depends on the situated perspective of particular people, and yet the very fact of their
situation means that they can never fully grasp actions or meanings
in a different context. All attempts to understand will be rooted in
and dependent on particular social and institutional contexts.[28] A
tendency within hermeneutics to talk only about cognition, argue
some of its exponents, must be checked by attention to the material
and institutional settings of interpretation itself.[29]

The hermeneutic challenge to the rule of law, in turn, tugs at
another, still deeper, source of current debate: what is truth and
what are the foundations of knowledge?

Truth's Foundations

Of course, the nature of truth and its demonstrations have occupied
philosophers, and lawyers, for centuries. But historians and philosophers have recently framed narratives about shifting conceptions of

---

27. See Hans-Georg Gadamer, *Truth and Method*, 2d ed. (London: Sheed and
Ward, 1979).

28. This view is actually shared by Kuhn, Rorty, Mead, Dewey, and maybe
Heidegger too, as well as hermeneutic scholars, such as Gadamer and Ryan.

29. This is, in part, a critique of Rorty, who tends to remove the question of
knowledge from power and material, institutional settings.

truth and its foundations—or lack of foundations. Western philosophers, at least since the Enlightenment and probably since Plato, have tried to ground truth and knowledge on a foundation beyond history.[30] Human reason can discern truth. Science, for example, is a method for constraining individual bias and testing hypotheses about the world against the raw data. There is a world to be discovered through human rationality.

Current scholars from many camps challenge the view that we can know the world and test our knowledge against it. Some perhaps controversial, and contentious, philosophers, psychologists, and linguists attack the notion that a world can be perceived free from the interests or situated perspective of the perceiver. Some historians of science identify the power of groups of scientists, socialized to share ideas about truth and paradigms of inquiry that ward off, rather than accept, challenge. The idea of scientific rationality is itself a historical artifact, subject to changing mores of specific scientific communities. Literary theorists and anthropologists emphasize the interaction between the observer and the observed and the reader and the text. In seemingly contradictory fashion, they tell us of the elusiveness of anyone else's subjectivity, and yet they also assert that knowledge claims fail if they do not attend to another's subjectivity. Indeed, in search of understandings of intersubjectivity, many contemporary scholars argue that no one can completely know his or her self. We each know about the self only by reference to the shared social dimension of language. Scholars in numerous fields emphasize how knowledge of any sort expresses and reflects particular relationships of power, specific cultural situations, and historical context. Even if there is a "there" there, our ways of claiming to know it are misleading. Our idea, for example, that mysticism is less "true" than science may be a sign of cultural ethnocentrism. Many responses to these charges emerge in recent scholarship, but they have not restored the notion of truth to a place beyond debate; currently, defenses of a reality that can be discovered vie with other approaches for faithful adherents.

Thus, contemporary scholarship has shaken the claims of scien-

---

30. See Richard J. Bernstein, *Beyond Objectivism and Relativism: Science, Hermeneutics, and Praxis* (Philadelphia: University of Pennsylvania Press, 1983); Alasdair C. MacIntrye, *After Virtue: A Study in Moral Theory* (Notre Dame, Ind.: University of Notre Dame Press, 1981); Richard Rorty, *Philosophy and the Mirror of Nature* (Princeton: Princeton University Press, 1979).

tific naturalism permeating law and legal claims to knowledge and validity. There are strong continuities here with work by turn of the century pragmatists and their fellow travelers, the legal realists, but it has taken more than half the century for these ideas to resurface as a serious theme in legal scholarship.[31] Theorists who make this point are often charged with nihilism, which implies that law has in the past represented some grounded or teleological beliefs. There is a certain irony here, which actually affords a clue to the shifting tides. For one target of attack by contemporary critics is the commitment to relativism embraced in the prevailing legal system. Granted, defenders of the system would not acknowledge relativism as an ideology but instead treat it as the sophisticated path between the absolutisms that have animated right- and left-wing politics. Some critical—and some noncritical—theorists charge that the liberal commitment to relativism actually undermines moral judgments that could gain leverage against the status quo.[32] Yet, in reply, these critics are charged with undermining any basis for values. Like legal realists earlier in the century, current critics inspire ad hominem attack because they challenge the idea that each individual has access to universal truth through reason that transcends history—and thereby destabilize law's role as a guardrail for liberal relativism.

Unwinding these paradoxes takes time, and needs context. Edward Purcell's book, *The Crisis of Democratic Theory*, provides a powerful narrative context that at least tries to account for these paradoxes. Purcell connects the prominence of science and the proliferation of social sciences with a crisis in legal and democratic theory in twentieth-century America. Philosophers had already located the basis for knowledge in the human mind and its tests of the world, rather than in a divine order. Then, both natural and social sciences emphasized "objective" methods to minimize the role of the observer and to test hypotheses through carefully collected data about concrete, observ-

---

31. See generally Edward A. Purcell, Jr., *The Crisis in Democratic Theory: Scientific Naturalism and the Problem of Value* (Lexington: University Press of Kentucky, 1973); James T. Kloppenberg, *Uncertain Victory: Social Democracy and Progressivism in European and American Thought, 1870–1920* (Oxford: Oxford University Press, 1988). The progressives themselves were divided, especially between those who emphasized a faith in the scientific method, and those who emphasized power and politics. Some, like Dewey, tried to unite these themes.

32. See Alex Aleinikoff, "Constitutional Law in an Age of Balancing," *Yale Law Journal* 96 (1987): 943.

able things. Yet, Einstein's theory of relativity and his demonstration of non-Euclidean geometry sent shock waves through the intellectual communities precisely on the question of truth and its foundations. Relativity rejected the premise that time and space are absolute, and explained, instead, that they are mutually dependent. Different people, situated in different places, would observe the timing of events differently. We each, however, need a theory to tell us what we see. Non-Euclidianism proved the viability of alternative systems of geometry, following contradictory postulates, and challenged the idea of one rational universe that could be grasped through deduction from a priori premises.[33]

Philosophers pursued the possibility of multiple logics, and social scientists devised theories of multiple explanations for human behavior. Anthropology in particular, exploring and celebrating the varieties of the human experience, flourished in the early part of this century. And legal theorists rejected abstract concepts as the basis for legal reasoning and called for empirical study rather than perpetuating a closed, deductive system.[34] Each of these initiatives seemed to tear apart the idea that knowledge rests on principles standing outside human history. Each of these initiatives expressed faith in human reason to discover the facts of human experience and to build knowledge from them.

Yet, the risk that these developments would undermine the basis for moral and legal judgments, leaving only relativism, became a crisis when the United States confronted war with Fascism. Relativism seemed to threaten the intellectual bases for rejecting totalitarianism. It was unacceptable to lack a moral basis for objecting to totalitarianism, yet no absolute basis for truth or morals could gain academic support. According to Purcell's account, there seemed no middle way out of totalitarianism on the one side and, on the other, nihilist emptiness lacking even a critique of totalitarianism. United States scholars in diverse fields resolved this tension in the 1930s by proclaiming the values of U.S. pluralism, tolerance, and cultural consensus, adding up to a theory in defense of relativism itself.[35] Theorists forged a belief in nonabsolutism and experimentalism—a belief

---

33. Purcell, *Crisis*, 47–72.
34. Legal realists such as John Dewey and Karl Llewellyn advocated this view.
35. At Yale, Lasswell and MacDougall led this reconstruction; at Harvard, it was Hart and Sacks.

that supported democracy, science, and social science and grounded knowledge in culture. It was a theory to challenge and reject ideologies, but it became an ideology itself, an ideology justifying the status quo by the very claim that it was nonideological.[36]

Current challengers to theories that assert foundations for legal knowledge often receive the *nihilist* label.[37] The current challengers essentially pick up the thread of the same intellectual developments that earlier legal theorists used to demolish a priori legal concepts. By probing the influence of the observer on the observed, some linguists, art theorists, literary critics, and anthropologists have emphasized the cultural context of knowledge and the necessarily partial quality of any interpretation. Some current legal theorists borrow from this work and claim that legal certainty can be found in the communities of interpreters whose conventions govern a given interpretive project.[38] Others seek to show the endless possibilities within any given text.[39] Still others explore the possibilities for practical or dialectical reason,[40] or for narratives explicitly constructing meanings rather than claiming to discover them.[41] If "narratives"—and rhetorical truths—are all there is in philosophy and history, then philosophers and historians can claim no greater truths than writers in other fields.[42] A far cry from earlier views of truth as grounded in facts and

36. Purcell, *Crisis*, 272.

37. See Joseph William Singer, "The Player and the Cards: Nihilism and Legal Theory," *Yale Law Journal* 94 (1984): 1; John Stick, "Can Nihilism Be Pragmatic?" *Harvard Law Review* 100 (1986): 332.

38. See Owen Fiss, "Objectivity and Interpretation," *Stanford Law Review* 34 (1982): 739; Stanley Fish, *Is There a Text in this Class?* (Cambridge, Mass.: Harvard University Press, 1980); Michael Walzer, *Interpretation and Social Criticism* (Cambridge, Mass.: Harvard University Press, 1987).

39. See Jacques Derrida, "Structure, Sign, and Play in the Discourse of the Human Sciences," in *The Structuralist Controversy: The Languages of Criticism and the Sciences of Man*, ed. Richard Macksey and Eugenio Donato (Baltimore: Johns Hopkins University Press, 1972), 247. David Kennedy, Clare Dalton, and Gerald Frug have most notably deployed this approach in legal scholarship.

40. See Theodor W. Adorno, *Negative Dialectics*, ed. E. B. Ashton (New York: Seabury Press, 1973); Clifford Geertz, *Local Knowledge: Further Essays in Interpretive Anthropology* (New York: Basic Books, 1983). In law, Drucilla Cornell and Frank Michelman are proponents of this view.

41. See Jerome Bruner, *Actual Minds, Possible Worlds* (Cambridge, Mass.: Harvard University Press, 1986).

42. Some (Ricoeur, Rorty, Geertz) emphasize that narrative is all there is, but that is our way of making meaning. Others (Derrida, Hayden, White) stress that

discovered by human reason, the current debaters join those who seek foundations for truth in human conventions and those who challenge the very idea of such foundations.[43] Some advance, and others dispute, an alternative to foundations in the social situation of the individual: the individual's identity and understandings depend on a language and form of life shared with others. This dependence provides some closure; it tests for what counts as a claim or a persuasive story. The interpretive turn in talk of truth engages old and new debates about the relationships between individuals and communities.

Individuals and Communities

People have long debated the proper relationships between individuals and society—and between individuals and the state. Forged in the nineteenth century, a version of this debate that still prevails in many places divides those who emphasize individual liberty and restrict community and state to vehicles for protecting that liberty, from those who promote collective forms of government and economic organization to meet human needs. Proponents of liberty—associated with laissez-faire—warn against governmental power, and point to totalitarianism, including governmental economic planning, as the real danger. The collectivists charge the laissez-faire view with indifference and even exploitation of workers and the poor amid increasing industrial development. It is a familiar debate with at least a century-long duration; its rhetoric reverberates even in recent presidential campaigns.

Yet, if these battle lines ever mapped onto actual policy choices, they do not do so now.[44] The government is inextricably bound up in economic and other regulation; and the commitment to protect individual liberty remains strong and yet is largely rhetorical, as tech-

---

philosophical arguments cannot be disassociated from language and its forms of representation; at the same time, language itself cannot be fully controlled by human reason because words bring something beyond transparent reference to our understanding of the world.

43. A current debate divides "essentialists," who attribute, for example, sex differences to biology, and social constructionists, who maintain that differences are all socially constructed. Feminists and antifeminists crosscut this divide.

44. See Aviam Soifer,"The Paradox of Paternalism and Laissez-Faire Constitutionalism: U.S. Supreme Court, 1888–1921," *Law and History Review* 5 (1987): 249.

nological and bureaucratic forms connect each of us to others in complex and unavoidable ways. Virtually everyone recognizes that "libertarian law" is no less a function of political choice and no less dependent on state enforcement than socialist law. These days, fewer people engage in arguments about which side, after all, won the contest between laissez-faire and collectivism.

Theorists and politicians who dig beneath standard rhetoric actually realign the standard views. Communitarianism—as opposed to collectivism—is a new rallying cry; its legal form is typically called "republicanism," to emphasize the importance of participatory self-governance through which each individual exercises regard for the interests of others. The new communitarianism, or republicanism, draws supporters from traditional liberal and conservative camps—leaving liberal advocates of privacy and libertarians who favor deregulation of the economy on the other side of the line, staring at one another.

Some of the new republicans worry about the traditional baggage of hierarchy and exclusion that accompanied republican ideology in the past. Others worry more about the enduring power of self-interest that could defeat the virtues of other-regarding deliberation. What they share, however, is a strong critique of the notion that individuals are, or ever should be, merely autonomous and self-interested. Even if the notion of individual autonomy were only a political choice, rather than a metaphysical claim, new republicans worry that this choice undermines the development of mutual regard and a politics of virtue in favor of a politics of self-interest. As a metaphysical or empirical question about human nature, the new republicans find support in the work of linguists, psychologists, sociologists, and philosophers who stress that the self is unavoidably embedded in society and in personal relationships. Our most private thoughts depend on participation in a shared, public language. The boundaries of the individual's ego depend on successful, continuous relationships with others. The very idea of autonomous individualism is a social construct, produced for the enjoyment and well-being of members of a particular class and community. The meanings of meaning and the nature of knowing depend upon communal activity. Literary theorists get into the game, by stressing the author's dependence on readers for the construction of meaning in the text. The new commu-

nitarians split, however.[45] Some talk of the community as a normative idea, others reject the very idea of normative ideals and instead
emphasize processes, located in time, of particular communal deliberations. Individuals cannot know or command themselves except
in relationship with others, because no self is bounded; each self
mutually defines others.[46]

Mirroring the split within the communitarians is a division
among their opponents between those who defend the sovereign,
independent self as a defense against community power, and those
who doubt not only the existence of bounded, sovereign selves, but
also the existence of coherent, meaningful communities. Thus, there
are thinkers who warn that new cozy communitarianism is a guise
for imposing the views of some on the many. Some urge a new
understanding of the individual subject as simply the effect of cultural codes; dissolving separate identities could level hierarchies and
promote equality. Others worry about talk of an other-regarding, or
even decentered self and see dangers in dissolving the individual into
an all-enveloping community. Similarly, some oppose the very claim
that one can know another as well as oneself, because this denies an
irreducible difference between people, if only marked by separate
skins. Claims to know the other may mask the paternalism, racism,
and chauvinism that historically has hidden in the language of abstract universalism.[47] Some anticommunitarians reject any claims to
knowledge and normative reason that could treat "community" co-
herently as illusory. Neighbors, fellow workers, and readers of the
same magazines might all be contestants for the reference group
signaled by "community," but most such groups lack ongoing,
shared interactions. Privacy, personality, and identity are fictions—
but so is the idea of a community joining mutually implicated
selves.[48]

---

45. I leave for another time the question of whether this split itself refutes their
theories.

46. See Drucilla Cornell, "The Poststructuralist Challenge to the Ideal of Community," *Cardozo Law Review* 8 (1987): 989.

47. See Elizabeth V. Spelman, *Inessential Woman: Problems of Exclusion in Feminist
Thought* (Boston: Beacon Press, 1988) (exploring the risk of false essentialism within
works by Plato and Aristotle and works by Simone de Beauvoir and Nancy Chodorow).

48. See Peter Sloterdijk, *The Critique of Cynical Reason,* trans. Michael Eldred (Minneapolis: University of Minnesota Press, 1987), 59–61.

Thus, although a communitarian/individualist division persists, newcomers join and regroup around this division and form a new crosscutting split. Cutting across those with communal instincts and those who deny them is a challenge to the sovereignty of the self.[49] It is a challenge that shakes the intellectual predicates for basic liberal rights: the premises of rationality, universality, and generalizability in the rule of law, notions about a correspondence between perceptions and the truth, and notions of the sovereign subject who has capabilities for rational action.

Reflections

Current debates make standard subjects within jurisprudence interesting and lively. Just as the legal disputes over proposed regulations of pornography have introduced new themes to constitutional law courses, these philosophic disputes about rights, rule of law, truth, and the self and community enliven discussions in law school classes with arguments from new angles. It might seem that now is the time to articulate a new jurisprudence, building up from a new, improved theory of the self as unbounded or fundamentally social[50] to devise new conceptions of rights as features of relationships;[51] new approaches to the rule of law as a hermeneutic process;[52] and new views of truth and meaning as foundationally communal.[53] Many provoca-

---

49. Sloterdijk calls it "the critique of the illusion of privacy" or the idea that we are each Somebody—when instead "Our true self-experience in original Nobodiness remains in this world buried under taboo and panic. . . . The living Nobody, in spite of the horror of socialization, remembers the energetic paradises beneath the personalities" (*The Critique of Cynical Reason*, 73). Interestingly, a song in the long-running musical, *A Chorus Line*, pursues the same theme when a member of the cast recalls an acting class in which she was urged to dig deep into herself, but she found nothing there.

50. Or interdependent; see Joseph William Singer, "The Reliance Interest in Property," *Stanford Law Review* 40 (1987): 611. Or a theory of the individual as biologically connected to others; see Robin West, "Jurisprudence and Gender," *University of Chicago Law Review* 56 (1988): 1 (suggesting how women's capacity for pregnancy provides a starting point for a theory of the self).

51. This has been a project of mine at times. See Martha Minow, "Interpreting Rights: An Essay for Robert Cover," *Yale Law Journal* 96 (1987): 1860.

52. See Cover, "Nomos and Narrative"; Radin, "Reconsidering the Rule of Law."

53. Many legal scholars approach the problem of truth with an interest in narrative and hermeneutic interpretations. See James Boyd White, *When Words Lose Their Meaning* (Chicago: University of Chicago Press, 1984); Gerald Lopez, "Lay Lawyer-

tive and innovative scholars are engaged in just such projects, and it is a moment of interdisciplinary fervor in legal scholarship, enacting in this very eclecticism a challenge to old boundaries.

But I will not proceed here along these lines for several reasons. First, to do so is to leave in place the definition of the project of jurisprudence that existed before any of the current challenges. Rebuilding the pieces without reconsidering the whole misses different sets of questions altogether. Assimilating new challenges to prior paradigms is more likely to resist than explore the questions they pose. This idea has been explored eloquently by others who have addressed incommensurate worldviews. For example, a mathematician considered how two-dimensional creatures would assimilate a sphere to their perceptions of a circle or a series of bigger and then smaller circle sphere's movement through the plane. The perceptions from two-dimensions could not conceive of the possibility of a body in three dimensions.[54] Perhaps John Dewey was right when he wrote that "intellectual progress usually occurs through sheer abandonment of questions together with both of the alternatives they assume—an abandonment that results from their decreasing vitality and a change of urgent interest. We do not solve them: we get over them."[55] Whether or not Dewey was right, the stalemate reached by many theoretical debates is often a sign that the problem cannot be solved, or cannot be solved at the level of analysis at which it has been posed. It is a sign that we need to cut the cards in a new place to see what else is in the deck.

Second, only by asking different questions can we consider what has been left out or suppressed by legal theory in the past. Reconstructing jurisprudence with new answers to traditional questions about the self, the rule of law, truth's foundations, and relations between individual and community might help shore up law's foundations by infusing legal theory with contemporary intellectual devel-

---

ing," *UCLA Law Review* 32 (1984): 2; Fiss, "Objectivity and Interpretation"; Sanford Levinson, "On Dworkin, Kennedy, and Ely: Decoding the Legal Past," *Partisan Review* 51 (1984): 248.

54. See Edwin Abbott, *Flatland: A Romance of Many Dimensions* (New York: Barnes and Noble, 1983).

55. John Dewey, "The Influence of Darwinism on Philosophy," in *The Middle Works, 1899–1924,* ed. Jo An Boydston, (Carbondale, Ill.: Southern Illinois University Press, 1977), 4:14.

opments—but this enterprise would neither offer glimpses into the motivations for those new intellectual developments nor inquire into how legal theory historically has screened out some perspectives while reinforcing others. We might even consider how philosophies about law are not a pastime or a game, but instead part of the cultural belief systems that make some questions seem hard and some seem easy.

Finally, although this may restate my previous points, the challenge to rationality, like the challenges to objectivity, impartiality, neutrality, and universality in law, expresses a very modern sensitivity to the relationships between knowledge and power. We cannot know without standing somewhere, and because we are situated somewhere, we cannot see everything. Once we have considered this challenge, it is hard, if not impossible, to resume a faith in a reason that would transcend the situation of the reasoner. And yet once we recognize this, it seems possible to reconstruct reason to take its—our—own limits into account. Discussions about rights, the rule of law, truth, and relations between individual and community enact this conversation but do not move beyond it.

At this moment, just like at other scary times, I think we often turn to stories. We tell stories to make meanings out of what we do not understand. And perhaps, through our stories, we come to think we understand. The stories I would like to tell raise the question of vantage point. How would shifts in assumptions and practices in contemporary legal theory appear to people who are privileged—and how to people who are less so? And, if we can tell more than one story about how we got to where we are, does that enrich our knowledge or cut us loose from our moorings—or both?

Partial Histories

What historical story can make sense of these shifting lines of debate in political and legal theory? If I take seriously the possibility that where one stands limits what one can see and know, I suspect that there are several stories, each varying based on the point of view and topics selected for emphasis. As I offer two stories, then, they should be read as an invitation to contemplate still a third, and a fourth. My stories are deliberately and perhaps provocatively sweeping and ambitious. They are "tall persons" stories; even though, as I think will be obvious, they each are no more that partial accounts.

The first goes back to Copernicus, and to the Reformation, to trace a narrative of intellectual challenges to the conception of unified authority. Copernicus challenged a divine conception that placed the earth at the center and, paradoxically, advanced a scientific theory that supplanted divine explanations with man-made ones. The Reformation assaulted the theory that each individual needed a church official to intervene with God and advanced the view that each individual had direct access to the divine. These challenges, in different ways, began to place "man" at the center of the understanding of the universe and of human experience. Replacing ideas of a divinely ordered, hierarchical universe that obliged individuals to accept their social station and the norms declared by religious officials, the challengers focused attention on human reason as an avenue for truth seeking and human affairs as the center of concern.[56] Renaissance humanism built foundations for the Enlightenment. Later historians could tell of an "Age of Reason." The Enlightenment was also concerned with the limits of reason, yet, within those limits, it shored up the faith that, through reason, people could unmask illusions and mistakes and find order in the universe. Human authority, justified through right reason, could prompt demands for restrictions on the sovereign powers of the government. This ultimately helped to fuel demands for democratic self-government. Human authority replaced divine authority; the authority of the divine sovereign is supplanted by the human sovereign and by the sovereignty of reason.

But new developments unsettled this new order. Creative thinkers in many fields challenged faith in human authority and reason during the nineteenth and twentieth centuries. Marx argued that material structures had greater influence than ideas on the nature of society and on human consciousness, and introduced the idea that people could be deluded about their own wants and interests. Freud gave new impetus to the insights of literature about human passions, drives, and unconscious motives contending with reason and control. Nietzsche criticized the illusions of morality and argued that religion and other belief systems disguised a more fundamental will to power. Einstein and Heisenberg emphasized the influence of the observer on the observed and challenged faiths in direct human perceptions

---

56. In a sense, these developments revived earlier concerns of the Greeks and the Gnostics and even in some ways the early Hebrews.

as reliable bases for reasoned understanding. Wittgenstein introduced new doubts about how we mean and know. Shattering the
faith in human reason in different ways, these modernist critiques
nonetheless reinstalled a faith in the critical processes of discovering
and exposing illusion. After all, if one could now comprehend the
insights of Freud or Marx or any of the others, a greater understanding, and a greater grasp of "reality," could follow. The authority of
reason is unmasked as illusion, yet this very phrasing undergirds a
strengthened faith in the use of human intelligence to approach understanding and control of the world.

Perhaps it was Nazism and the Holocaust that shook even this
belief and presaged a third phase of challenges to authority. Linguists
and philosophers have argued that it is not reason, not sense perceptions, but the structure of language itself that explains our meanings.
And the structure of language—the relationship between particular
symbols and their references in the world—is arbitrary and assumes
meaning only through familiarity with particular cultural practices.[57]
History creates stories about the past in terms of familiar and comforting narrative schemes.[58] Philosophers and literary theorists dub
themselves postmodern and attack the "consoling myths" of human
mastery through reason.[59] There can be no knowledge without a
standpoint. Marx and Freud simply and wrongly projected their own
nineteenth-century European experiences as universal. Knowledge
conditioned by a particular human standpoint cannot be generalized
enough to afford a total scheme of explanation. Knowledge can only
be contingent and affected by the perspective of the knower. There
are no possible grounds for calling a particular view distorted, because the idea of distortion summons up a baseline against which the
distortion could be measured. Not only is there no God's-eye point
of view, there is no possibility of a humanly made facsimile; detach-
ment is impossible, and there is no universal grounding for knowledge or experience.[60] Even the concept of the self, the individual, as

---

57. Critical figures here are Saussure, Frege, Quine, and Wittgenstein.

58. See Hayden White, *Metahistory: The Historical Imagination in Nineteenth-Century Europe* (Baltimore: Johns Hopkins University Press, 1973).

59. See, e.g., Jean-Francois Lyotard, *The Post-Modern Condition: A Report on Knowledge*, trans. Geoff Bennington and Brian Massumi (Minneapolis: University of Minnesota Press, 1984).

60. See Hilary Putnam, *The Many Faces of Realism* (LaSalle, Ill.: Open Court, 1978); Thomas Nagel, *The View from Nowhere* (New York: Oxford University Press, 1986).

a coherent integration of body and mind is an artifact of a particular cultural narrative rather than the truth. Human subjectivity reflects the structures of thought and social practice through which a particular human individual develops, rather than a sovereign being, with intrinsic traits, preferences, and desires. Features of identity, grasped by a person, are constructed by society and accepted or resisted by the individual; in either form of engagement, the individual's identity depends on social patterns of thought rather than emanations from the self. There is no bounded personality having its own experiences and consciousness. There are also no determinate structures outside individuals—Marxism, structuralism, and all such schemes of total explanation are partial human constructions, mistaken in their very claim to have grasped the truth. After this wave of "postmodernism," what is left?

At this point, theorists diverge. Habermas seeks to salvage the rationalist project by searching for conditions under which communication could be dislodged from patterns of power and suppression; his critics fault him for reviving sovereign rationality and suppressing unconscious and marginal perspectives. Some who would ally partly against Habermas maintain that the perpetual criticism of rationalism in any guise points toward a political practice of displacing power, diffusing domination, and enlarging egalitarianism.[61] Yet others imply that even this revives a totalizing pattern of thought that must be undone.[62] This view animates at least some of the work known as critical legal studies.

Some see a similar division in contemporary fiction: there are those who seek a better, less-deluded version of reality and others who concede there is no reality to be discovered—only invented worlds. Novels, they claim, should draw discomfiting attention to their very inventive strategies rather than pretending to capture an external reality. Not only novels and philosophic tracts, but also cultural mores, customs, and legal practices can be understood as texts,

---

61. Michael Ryan, *Marxism and Deconstruction: A Critical Articulation* (Baltimore: Johns Hopkins University Press, 1982); Michael Ryan, "Deconstructive Philosophy and Social Theory," in *Displacement: Derrida and After*, ed. Mark Krupnick (Bloomington, Ind.: Indiana University Press, 1983).

62. Important here are Nietzsche and Paul de Man. Derrida tries to have it both ways, and indeed claims so must we all, because we can only work within figures and narratives, and differences that constitute all identities elude us.

subject to the interpretive process of reading their invention, rather than finding some reality in them. Texts, themselves, have no authority and depend on their readers to make meaning; readers have no basis for their reading other than their engagement with the process and their attention to the risks of pretending to discover a priori truths. Theorists advocating another version of this point claim that texts and contexts intermesh so much that we cannot even talk about their separation meaningfully; texts depend on outside references and, indeed, the relations to outside references make up the text.[63] Language endlessly defers its reference; even the self is lost in a play of language and stream of differences. Critics turn toward irony and a heightened sense of the comic or absurd; intellect cannot resolve choices.[64] Criticism should be conceived as an infinite progression that refuses to identify a center because it is always decentered and self-contradictory.[65] Power is everywhere. End, for now, of the first story. It could be called the story of the "legitimation crisis," or the "challenge to authority." Instead, let me call it the "insiders' story," so that I may call the next the "outsiders' story."

This is a story of exclusion and resistance. It is about the theories and experiences of people made marginal by the first story—women, children, members of racial and religious minorities, and disabled persons. The intellectual and political revolutions that altered a medieval world of divinely inspired and justified relationships of hierarchy and mutual obligation did not do very much to change the stations of these individuals. Largely excluded from consideration in political theory and assigned to subordinate roles by law, these people had little chance to assert themselves, to partake of the society of sovereign individualism, even though Enlightenment ideas held the latent promise of extending liberty and equality for all. Theories of social contract, and even, for the most part, the ideas of the Reformation, imagined independent Christian, white men who were heads of households. These theories did nothing to prevent industrialism from subordinating women in a private sphere; nor did these theories

---

63. See Patricia A. Parker, *Literary Fat Ladies: Rhetoric, Gender, Property* (New York: Methuen, 1987).

64. See Ihab Habib Hassan, *The Postmodern Turn: Essays in Postmodern Theory and Culture* (Columbus: Ohio State University Press, 1987), 167–87.

65. Jonathan D. Culler, *On Deconstruction: Theory and Criticism after Structuralism* (Ithaca, N.Y.: Cornell University Press, 1982).

constrain European or American settlers from enslaving Africans and killing and defrauding native Americans. Children remained thought of as both savage and innocent and subject to the orders of their fathers and mothers; disabled persons were occasionally considered bedeviled, and often sent to institutions or vaguely tolerated within a community; members of religious minorities lacked political and commercial freedoms.

In the insiders' story, what counts as the next phase of dethroning authority barely reached the outsiders, and in some ways, reiterated their marginal status. Marx and Engels urged reconstruction of the hierarchical family, but only by celebrating "productive" work, with little challenge to the historic devaluation of reproduction and women's traditional contributions. Freud notoriously conceived of women as inferior to men in both their psychic dependence and their untrustworthiness as reporters of their own experience. He did offer a basis for understanding mentally ill persons as more like than unlike everyone else. But the waves of psychological services and new methods for education and social management influenced by psychology helped to justify a massive surge of diagnostic labeling, hospitalization, and differentiation of people on the basis of mental disabilities.[66]

Other early twentieth-century intellectual developments challenging prior conceptions of a determinate universe reached the marginal groups only to reiterate their marginality. Instead, the fields of eugenics and medicine attained peak authority as professionals and opinion leaders used them to assign labels of inferiority and defectiveness based on race, ethnicity, gender, and alleged measures of intelligence. Protest and reform efforts by and on the behalf of marginal people started a cycle of energetic organizing, accomplishment, and decline in the middle of the nineteenth century with abolition and the "Woman" movement. A new cycle started with the Progressives who sought to clean up city morals and politics, expand political participation, and implement protective legislation on behalf of working people. Whatever the motivations, much of the Progressive-era reforms seem, in retrospect, to be devices by middle-class activists

---

66. Some pragmatists, especially Dewey, promoted a conception of children's natural capabilities and argued for education centered on children's needs rather than adults' demands. This view received considerable attention, but did not gain wide acceptance.

to control the behavior of new immigrants, women, and mentally disabled persons. Another phase of reform appeared in emergency actions adopted nationally during the early New Deal, followed by the establishment of major structural reforms of labor relations and securities and banking practices. In the margins of these reforms, some African-Americans and some white women found new work opportunities, but little of the structural renovation of the government reached problems of racism and sexism.

Excluded groups and their supporters began resistance efforts in the nineteenth century, renewed them with growing success at the turn of this century, and again in the 1950s, 1960s, and 1970s. The rhetoric of rights and the idea of the rule of law were central to many of these resistance and reform activities. Organizers and spirited speakers interested in marginal groups found analogies and even plain textual support in basic legal documents for the demands of inclusion. Movements for abolition, temperance, women's suffrage, and child labor laws rested on assumptions that morality and law should converge, and that the inclusive language of the Declaration of Independence and the Bill of Rights should be taken seriously rather than treated as code words for free, white men.

Deliberate efforts to use the legal system to bring about changes in the status of blacks, women, disabled persons, and children engaged members of these groups and their supporters. In the early part of this century, white, middle-class women devoted themselves to social work and developed, in inchoate form, ideas of a caring and responsive community.[67] In the 1960s and 1970s, recipients of such "help" challenged the social control devices of the welfare state and public regulations, devised self-help groups and political organizations for welfare recipients, former mental patients, alcoholics, and others previously defined as dependent and in need of care. White women, minorities, disabled persons, and others who were previously disempowered—and their sympathizers—began to have access to established educational institutions. They challenged traditional curricula and scholarship for excluding or suppressing their experiences and perspectives. Feminist and African-American perspectives

---

67. William Simon, "The Invention and Reinvention of Welfare Rights," *Maryland Law Review* 44 (1985): 1. See also Martha Minow, " 'Forming Underneath Everything That Grows': Toward a History of Family Law," *Wisconsin Law Review* 1 (1985): 819.

on history, literature, philosophy, social science, and science challenged the canons of traditional knowledge and opened the way for
more pluralist study.[68] Of course, educational institutions reacted.
Sometimes their administrators and faculties shored up "standards"
to recreate exclusions, and sometimes they ghettoized the alternatives into marginal parts of the universities.

Somewhere around this time, postmodernism enters. Some of
the themes of postmodernism are surprisingly congenial challengers
from the margin who, like postmodern theorists, dispute assertions
of universalist reason that claim to be objective but instead express a
particular perspective and pattern of power. The postmodern emphasis on multiple realities, plural possibilities, and no privileged position for any particular method or perspective is consonant with the
egalitarian impulses of feminism and other movements from the margins. Indeed, the very preoccupation of many postmodernists with
"difference" seems a ready point of connection for those whose identities have largely been forged by reference to the "norm."

But, on the question of identity, postmodernism poses difficulties for resisters from the margins. Maintaining that the self and
identity are not integral but constructed can assist a challenge to the
traditional privilege given to some identities. However, this same
assault on the meaning of identity can undermine new sources of
pride and strength for those who reclaim and reconstruct identities
of difference once foisted upon them. The postmodern challenges to
a coherent self that processes and makes sense of experience undermines the claims to know "the black experience" or "women's point
of view." Many within marginal groups object to this result; others
argue that further "deconstruction" of identity is necessary if the
knowledge claims are ever to work against exclusion. Undermining
assertions of "the minority experience" may promote greater attention to the varieties of minority experiences and thereby boost the
project of resistance. Yet to the extent that this undermining pulls the
rug out from under any effort to critique the white, male experience,
resistance can be obstructed anew. Similarly, the postmodern objection to any claims of objectivity or God's-eye view can strengthen
challenges to the claims of truth or value that have degraded the

---

68. It is early yet to report, but there are emerging works, in various academic fields,
from Asian-American, native American, gay and lesbian, and disability perspectives.

58	THE FATE OF LAW

experiences of women, minorities, and all persons of "difference."
Yet the same objection could disable critiques of power and powerlessness. The very assertion of past degradation may be treated now
as simply one among many points of view.

Many postmodernists also seem, to activists from the margin,
politically disengaged and quiescent. From the vantage point of marginal groups, the emphasis on indeterminacy can be complicity or a
sophisticated guise for favoring the status quo. Postmodernism
seems to remove the very levers against power at the moment they
have been seized by those who have lacked them. If power is everywhere and nowhere, and there are simply plural points of view with
no ground for commensurate experience, who is to say what oppression is or what should change? Those from the margin, like postmodernists, seek out difference, emphasize the fictional and constructed
qualities of human experience, and celebrate the crack-up of authoritative structures of knowledge and power. But many from marginal
groups reject work that implies passivity and indifference, that
doubts the validity or grounding of experiences of domination, and
that hides the handles on the status quo just when its critics reach to
grasp them. From the margin, truths are not merely relative to language. Language is relative to power.[69]

The insider and outsider stories especially clash when it comes
to law. The insider story of the successive challenges to authority tells
of disagreement between those who pursue the indeterminacy of
legal language—and hope to enlarge the possibilities for human freedom and choice by urging perpetual criticism—and those who seek
conditions free from domination, where true discourse can take
place. The outsider story mirrors that debate but puts it in a different
form. The outsiders challenge the pretended inclusion and neutrality
of law, but emphasize and seek to reform the exclusion and disadvantage law imposes on particular groups, in particular contexts. In legal
scholarship, this contrast is most vivid in the debate over rights. The

---

69. Some postmodernists may respond that the focus on discourse enables, rather
than disables, attention to power by demonstrating how everything is held together
by force, not reality. Some theorists from marginal groups inventively work to remake
strategies from postmodernism to explore material, rather than figurative, differences
and suppressions. See Barbara Johnson, *A World of Difference* (Baltimore: Johns Hopkins
University Press, 1987); Elizabeth A. Meese, *Crossing the Double-Cross: The Practice of
Feminist Criticism* (Chapel Hill: University of North Carolina Press, 1986). There are
undoubtedly more permutations of debate and dialogue.

fight between critical legal scholars and their erstwhile feminist and minority colleagues exemplifies the contest between insider and outsider views. In this more fine-grained examination, the fight is among those who share the paradigm shift represented by the critique of reason.

Scholars associated with the critical legal studies movement have assaulted rights discourse as formal, incoherent, indeterminate, and empty. The language of rights can be used to justify opposite results. The logical, self-sealed system is itself radically incomplete. Moreover, legal language can guarantee ideals like equality and impartiality in the abstract but not in practice, because the social and economic worlds remain patterned with inequality and partiality. Simply imposing rules of formal equality and neutrality on top of a world that is not that way reproduces the distributions of power already in the world.

Feminists have also criticized rights. Feminists claim that rights have embodied a male point of view, disguised as neutral and universal. Feminists challenge, in particular, the worldview that takes men's desires and experiences as the norm and seeks privacy, security, and liberty with little ability to acknowledge or protect women's experiences. Feminists have struggled to introduce women's points of view in the legal treatment of rape, pregnancy, and abortion. These examples show an ambivalent relationship to the language of rights. Feminists have been able to invoke conceptions of autonomy behind rights discourse as a way to challenge the traditional male point of view embedded in legal rules about rape, pregnancy, and abortion. Thus, feminists have asserted that it is not "reasonable" for a man to assume that a woman who says "no" and does not put up a physical struggle has consented to rape; it is discrimination on the basis of sex to have an apparently "neutral" rule that excludes pregnancy benefits from an employer's health-care package; and it is an invasion of a woman's privacy and autonomy to force her to bear a child she does not want. These arguments depend on the language of rights and the conception of an autonomous individual implicated in it.

Feminists also criticize these arguments for constraining and limiting challenges to existing practices. Thus, some dispute the very emphasis in criminal law on the state of mind of the rape defendant rather than victim's (or survivor's) refusal to consent. Some feminists

argue that, in a male-dominated society, all acts of heterosexual sex—
not just those where a woman says no—should be understood as
rape. Similarly, some criticize as insufficient the law reforms that
accommodate a woman's pregnancy, but fail to remake the
workplace and child-care responsibilities so that pregnancy is a problem and responsibility for men and women. Further, the privacy
rationale for women's abortion rights fails to address the economic
questions of access to medical care. Moreover, the privacy doctrine's
conception of autonomy cannot capture the situation of a pregnant
woman with a fetus growing inside her, and leaves open the question
of the fetus's rights, as recent litigation about forced caesarean sections and fetal surgery suggests.

In these and other contexts, many feminists worry about using
rights language because it may shore up the illusion of abstract
universalism that disguises a male point of view. The language of
rights thus could strengthen, rather than challenge, assumptions and
practices that hold together the exclusion or domination of women.
Some feminists analyze the hidden messages about women in law
and in legal teaching materials. They seek to explain judicial decisions through the power of cultural images rather than through an
abstract theory of rights that risks recreating the attitudes feminists
seek to resist.[70] But feminists also worry about a critique of rights
that reduces the availability of rights in securing minimal safety and
respect in a legal system that makes rights the coin of the realm.
Contemporary feminists believe that legal rights could provide answers or even assure safety from basic physical danger. Feminists use
rights, like all language constructed without women in mind, to
translate claims so those with more power can hear and may be
compelled, by their own investment in their world, to respond.

Similarly, minority scholars have engaged in a "critique of the
critique of rights."[71] Some argue that the idea of autonomy has been
so much denied to minorities that the recent critical challenge repre-

---

70. Mary Joe Frug, "Re-Reading Contracts: A Feminist Analysis of a Contracts
Casebook," *American University Law Review* 34 (1985): 1065; Clare Dalton, "An Essay in
the Deconstruction of Contract Law," *Yale Law Journal* 94 (1985): 997.

71. Minority scholars include women of color; here is a dramatic instance of the
awkwardness of categories that have prevailed for those who have been excluded,
because the very effort to name the excluded so often appears as "women and minorities" and apparently, excludes those who are both. See Judy Scales-Trent, "Black

sents a new invasion.[72] Other minority critics charge critical legal scholars with the self-absorption of elite isolation.[73] Many minority scholars maintain that when critical legal scholars demonstrate the indeterminacy of rights, they produce doubts about moral grounding—yet the experiences of minority groups in slavery, in internment camps, and in continuing social practices of discrimination provide a basis for knowing that change, and change in a particular direction, is justified. Minority scholars defend the grounding of normative intuitions in experiences of exclusion and oppression, but it is a sophisticated understanding that includes great familiarity with the indeterminacy and emptiness of rights rhetoric as practiced. Mari Matsuda puts it this way:

> How could anyone believe both of the following statements? 1) I have a right to participate equally in society with any other person. 2) Rights are whatever people in power say they are. One of the primary lessons [critical legal scholars] can learn from the experience of the bottom is that one can believe in both of those statements simultaneously, and that it may well be necessary to do so.[74]

For feminist and minority scholars, the risk of creating a newly self-deluding theory by asserting normative intuitions based on experience is slight. A lesson often drawn from the experiences of exclusion is sensitivity to who else or what else may also be excluded by any reform. To speak of women's experience may occlude the varieties of women's experiences, or may posit one experience—probably that of Western, middle-class, heterosexual, secular women—as the norm while suppressing others. Yet, knowing about how earlier claims of the universal human experience excluded them, the women

---

Women and the Constitution: Finding Our Place, Asserting Our Rights," in *Harvard Civil Rights–Civil Liberties Law Review* 24 (1989): 9; Kimberle Crenshaw, "Demarginalizing the Intersection of Race and Sex: A Black Feminist Critique of Antidiscrimination Doctrine, Feminist Theory and Antiracist Politics," *University of Chicago Legal Forum* 1989, 139.

72. Patricia Williams, "Alchemical Notes: Reconstructing Ideals from Deconstructed Rights," *Harvard Civil Rights–Civil Liberties Law Review* 22 (1987): 401.

73. Harlon Dalton, "Minority Critique of CLS: The Clouded Prism," *Harvard Civil Rights–Civil Liberties Law Review* 22 (1987): 438.

74. Mari Matsuda, "Looking to the Bottom: Critical Legal Studies and Reparations," *Harvard Civil Rights–Civil Liberties Law Review* 22 (1987): 338.

asserting knowledge of "women's experience" can hear and accept the challenge that their own view is partial. There is no one reality, no one version of the truth: the task is to search out the many truths.

Another lesson is that challenges from the margin remake the understanding at the center; "each time we let in a new excluded group, . . . each time we listen to a new way of knowing, we learn more about the limits of our current way of seeing."[75] Like many postmodernists, the scholars from the margin emphasize the provisional and incomplete quality of any moment of knowledge and insight. All knowledge is partial. No person can know everything, and, indeed, no person can know more than what his or her cultural, material, and physical situation would permit. And everyone's knowledge is, in some sense, favorable to themselves, their perspective, their experience. Knowledge claims are constructed through the perspective of particular people, in particular social and historical situations. The task is to make the process of knowing attentive to its inevitable partiality.[76] This means paying attention to the standpoint of historically denigrated groups to glimpse truths obscured by the dominant view. But it also means challenging the underlying scheme defining the dominant and the dominated, looking for the multiplicity within each point of view—because the very effort to remedy understanding will reinstate a new version of the prevailing order. And attention to inevitable partiality also means resisting the temptation to adopt the standpoint of the excluded as the new truth. It is a corrective lens, but leads to another partial view.

This exploration echoes exchanges among the postmodernists. They, too, oppose any new total explanation, any point of view that claims to be the truth, any new canon of the authoritative texts. But unlike the postmodernists, whose politics often remain hidden or diffuse, the scholars from the margin feel the urgency of political action and the need for aspiration, direction, and change. Outsiders treat law, as other cultural tools, as a method to interrogate our practices rather than reconfirm them.

As might be obvious by now, I identify and sympathize with the

---

75. Carrie Menkel-Meadow, "Excluded Voices: New Voices in the Legal Profession Making New Voices in the Law," *University of Miami Law Review* 42 (1987): 52.

76. If this sounds like a universal, it also reimagines universality by making it self-reflexive.

feminist and minority scholars. It is not that the outsider story is the "true" one. I am too convinced of the various challenges to unitary authority and totalizing theories to accept that. But I incline toward the outsider story because of its insistence upon the partiality of all stories, and its simultaneous commitment to normative commitment and skeptical critique. Yet postmodernists may respond, with some force, that I have fallen into the old trap of consoling myths of reason, and the particular mistake of treating identities and experiences as essential and grounded rather than shifting and containing their opposites.[77] I agree that no identity or experience is grounded "all the way down."[78] Instead, language, culture, and history shape who we are and what we think we are. There are differences that matter for now, because they have mattered; the powerful may need the powerless, but that does not make the two interchangeable or undermine a critique of the distribution of power. Any theory that seems to produce quiescence and a sense of helplessness is not good enough. I especially worry about theories that sand away the toeholds recently secured by those who have historically faced exclusion just as they begin to challenge these historic patterns.

But I also worry that there is a trap in thinking about the stories as if one were right and one were wrong. This neglects the likely emergence of a third, and even a fourth story. And supposing that one must choose a "right" story recreates the problem each of the stories, in its own way, documents: any claim to know the unmitigated truth faces both the probable prospect of future dethroning and the probable charge of excluding or suppressing the viewpoint or experiences of those with less power to tell the story. Instead, the stories, I think, provide an occasion for a strategy discussion. Here is one that I can imagine, because it reflects discussions taking place among academics and activists in the late twentieth century.

Six women, gathered at a meeting to discuss past and future directions for a public policy that addresses women, consider how much their discussions are occupied with assertions of identity and

---

77. See Kelman and Kennedy, as discussed in Marie Linda Park, "Radical Women and Radical Men: Tensions between Feminist Legal Theory and Critical Legal Studies" (senior thesis, Harvard College, 1988).

78. This is a reference to the story about the person who believed that the universe rests on the back of a turtle which, in turn, rests on the back of many more turtles—it is turtles all the way down.

standpoint. Some talk about the importance of racial identities and class-based experiences in assessing past and future reforms that ostensibly address women and condemn contemporary analyses for neglecting these themes. Others charge that themes of sexual orientation, disability, ethnicity, and religion remain unspoken, even in this meeting. Still others emphasize how every comment reflects the social and economic situation of the speaker: how the academics speak to preserve their expertise while justifying its relevance to broader politics, and the activists speak to challenge the scholars as irrelevant. Here is a bit of the conversation, with the speakers identified by the categories that are, themselves, under debate.

A white, heterosexual, female academic. "I think that as long as we act out identity politics we are stuck; if you talk about the black feminist and activist perspective, and I talk about the viewpoint of the white feminist historian, we will reinvigorate the very categories of difference we were trying to undermine. And we will strengthen the assumptions about knowledge, power, and identity that we've tried to challenge in all feminist work."

A black, heterosexual, female activist. "I just don't agree with you. We still haven't taken seriously the exclusion of women of color in the planning of political strategies, and you're asking me to stop talking about it? What is there to talk about if we don't talk about our identities?"

A Chicana, heterosexual activist (speaking to the white academic). "I think you're scared, I think if we talk about the exclusion of women of color, you have to lose some privilege."

A white, lesbian activist and academic. "I don't think it's about fear; I think it's a desire to avoid making differences seem essential, or inherent, because that denies how much we choose who we are and forces us into the frameworks we did not create."

The Chicana activist. "I see what you mean. But it's just not going to work. We are just beginning to articulate the ways in which the policies devised by white feminists leave us out; it seems like silencing us to say, 'Don't talk about the Chicana perspective.'"

A second white, heterosexual academic. "I think the thing to do is not to resist talk of difference, but to immerse in it. Then we'll see in fact that talking about the black or Chicana or lesbian perspectives themselves are too rigid and general and likely to submerge more differences. Just as when a group of all women come together to discuss our shared interests, we begin to discuss our differences, when people assert the interests or viewpoint of women of color, people will also begin to talk about differences among that group, and then still further differences."

A second Chicana activist. "That's funny, because I was just thinking about how we're all the same underneath, say, in our physical vulnerability and yet capacity to be powerful."

The first white woman. "You know when we first arrived we thought our differences were professional, but then we realized we are all the same, in our desires for political change and our efforts to work for it with whatever tools we have. When we've focused on the differences of race and ethnicity neglected by the last wave of white feminists, something important has happened. We've stopped talking about inclusion—including those who are different in our already existing project—and we've started talking about partnership, with agendas we mutually shape."

The black woman. "What has been especially powerful to me, though, has been to be with enough women of color that I can validate my own perspective. But I see the danger of refueling lines of differences we've been oppressed by all our lives. The only way out is through; we can't escape this stage of talking differences. We can't skip over our claims to be heard until we're heard and don't need to demand it."

And the conversation continues. My inability to do justice to the conversation without identifying the women by the categories they themselves debate may capture the particular, peculiar historical moment in which I write. Identity politics, claims of rights, assertions of knowledge based on perspective and experience, all risk entrenching the patterns of social and legal structures that produced exclusion by race, gender, class, and other lines of difference. By claiming to talk as outsiders, we risk reentrenching rather than challenging the lines of power and meanings that make us outsiders. We risk denying continuing differences among people labeled as the same, and denying similarities among people labeled as different. We run the danger of paying homage to another false god, now called identity, rather than sovereignty of the state, or sovereignty of reason; we risk the distraction of intense fights among people who agree about so much, but still remain shut out as relative outsiders.

Is it possible, then, to embrace a perspective or a story while remembering it is contingent? Together, postmodernists and outsiders criticize not only the supposed certainties of human reason. The critics also challenge the uses of knowledge to shore up rather than to resist power. Those who want to resist and remake prevailing patterns of power and authority understandably join the critique of apparent certainties in human reason, for those certainties have often disguised and legitimated the exclusion and denigration of many people. Uncertainty—heightened awareness of the limits of any claim to knowledge—can provide a new basis for self-reflective knowledge and a new basis for respecting others. The challenge from the outsider, though, is not nondirectional. It is not merely a call for inclusion within structures that otherwise remain unchanged. Nor is it an invitation for chaos, within which critiques of oppression are asserted to cover everyone equally. Everyone is not oppressed equally, even if everyone has hurts.

In the contexts of our lives, we do, and we must, make choices about what to accept and what to resist. Theories of law, I think, should work to connect the theories to contexts, and invite others to challenge the partiality of the effort. Introducing the outsider story demonstrates the partiality of the insider story. An intriguing task, for those concerned with law, would be to imagine and construct a jurisprudence from the outside. But to embark on this seriously would mean soliciting ever more additions and challenges; there is not just one perspective from "the outside." Moreover, as relative outsiders become relative insiders, white women and members of minority groups help to make the margin the center and then need others to remind us what we have failed to see.

After postmodernism and after the outsider critique of postmodernism, I think that we need a new way to think about law. If knowledge and values express the partiality of the human perspectives from which we know and judge, then law cannot be justified as the absolute, universal, summative organizing frame for political and social life. We need to understand the partiality of perspective embedded in law but treated as natural or given, as when we assume that "affirmative action" alters the givenness of things, or when we assume that a "maternity leave" is a special treatment, departing from the normal benefits for workers. We also need to understand law as itself partial, in several senses. Law is only one of many sources of normative authority in people's lives; religious groups, cultural traditions, customs, economic analysis, and certainly other forms of meaning influence what we choose and what compels us. Law itself is not monolithic. What the statute books and Supreme Court announce have, at best, a tangential relationship to what local trial courts do; very few trial decisions are ever reviewed, and the local culture of local courts is more authoritative than the sources of law we teach in law school. And even those cases going to court or prompting people to lobby their legislators or other officials are very few in comparison to the enormous number of daily actions and decisions we all take that implement or resist legal order. In a pluralism of legal worlds, legal authority depends, at least in part, upon our own participation and our own choices about what to accept and what to resist.

If we stand back, then, and ask about the "Fate of Law," it is possible to be both overwhelmed and underwhelmed. How can we describe, much less evaluate, the multiplicity and variety of legal methods and human engagement with law? In light of the partiality of any version of law or its history, I suggest we resist the monolithic language of "The" "Fate" of "Law." None of these items is singular, and talking that way obscures the multiple sources and meanings of laws. I do think we can and should theorize, try to talk about the meanings of this partiality and uncertainty for a reason: The reason is to exercise humility and to enable more people to define the terms of their own inclusion in society.

Many new questions crop up in light of these stories. How can law provide a lever for challenging exclusion if law defines the terms of exclusion? How can law embrace partiality without declining into moral relativism and incoherence or indeterminacy? Both the insider and the outsider stories criticize the traditional earmarks of the rule of law—generality, universality, impartiality, and neutrality. Yet without them, how can law provide measures for criticizing the persistence of oppression?

Again, I do not think we can, or should, answer questions posed at this level of abstraction. I will not propose an approach to law that takes the categories and questions of established philosophies of law as the point of departure. To do so would enshrine their assumptions even in disputing their particulars. Thus, I will not offer an outsider view of rights, or of the rule of law, or foundations for truth, or relations between individuals and communities. These are categories thrown into high relief by legal theories that have largely neglected their own situation or relationship to power. Instead, I will sketch a stance for approaching questions that become legal problems, while maintaining an awareness of both the insider and outsider stories about where we are.

Partial Justice

I would like to pursue the insights of either the insider and outsider narratives—and both of them together. This means recognizing that law is a set of practices and institutions situated within more than one narrative of human history and more than one social experience. Law itself should not be misunderstood to be a shared language. That would revive a myth of rational consensus that the competing narratives belie. Rather than using a legal language or a language of theory that speaks on a universal plane, my own conclusion is that I should work on legal theory by working on problems in specific contexts. According to old criteria, this would not be recognized as legal doctrine, or as jurisprudence. The challenge, then, includes resisting the temptation to seek approval according to established mores and prestige values. My theoretical understandings would be deepened by sustained looks at concrete social problems, while attending to the larger questions they open. This means pursuing a theory in practice and a theory that is at once pluralist, heterogeneous, and localist.

What do I mean by pluralist, heterogeneous, and localist? By pluralist, I mean acting on the insight that perspectives are partial by seeking out alternative views, and by conditioning assertions of any one view with deliberate efforts to see its limits from a perspective beyond itself. For example, consider legal disputes between religious individuals and secular institutions that seem to interfere with their religious practices. Recent highly visible cases of this sort include a challenge to a military dress code requirement that forbade the wearing of even religious headgear, such as a yarmulke;[79] a suit attacking public school texts for imposing secular humanism and undermining parents' efforts to nurture their children's religious be-

---

79. Goldman v. Weinberger, 106 S. Ct. 1310 (1986) (ruling that the free exercise clause did not compel a religious exemption for the Air Force dress regulations). Congress later adopted legislation changing the dress regulations to permit the wearing of religious garments.

liefs;[80] and a claim against a state unemployment benefits scheme for denying benefits to an individual who was dismissed from her job after converting to a religion that forbade her from working on Saturday.[81] Long before anyone should reach a conclusion about what to do with such claims, there is the task of understanding them. Failure to grasp the partiality of secular understandings—and the partiality of the perspectives of secular judges who administer law—condemns such claims to perpetual misunderstanding before they are even calculated.

As two professors noted recently,

> When the law must deal with religion, it must use a language and a process steeped in objectivity, rationality, and empiricism to describe and evaluate experiences which are subjective, irrational, and unobservable. A religious language of faith, belief, and divine judgment seems out of place in the legal system. . . . To the religious person, it is more accurate and far more meaningful to describe religion as "spiritual" rather than "subjective" or "irrational." It is inevitable then that law will systematically devalue the religious experience. Legal language and process currently are incapable of capturing and conveying the essential meaning and significance of religion.[82]

The incommensurability of premises is especially pronounced when the secularist presumes to know what would and would not undermine or interfere with another's religious beliefs.[83]

---

80. See Mozert v. Hawkins County Pub. Schools, 657 F. Supp. 1194 (1986), rev'd No. 86–144 (6th Cir. 1987). The court of appeals rejected the claims by the religious parents.

81. Hobbie v. Unemployment Appeals Commission, 107 S. Ct. 1046 (1987). The Supreme Court demanded accommodation by the state, even though the complainant converted after accepting the job and, therefore, produced the conflict between the job and her religious beliefs.

82. Frederick Mark Gedicks and Roger Hendrix, "Democracy, Autonomy, and Values: Some Thoughts on Religion and Law in Modern America," *Southern California Law Review* 60 (1987): 1579.

83. See, e.g., Wilson v. Block, 708 F.2d (D.C. Cir. 1982), *cert. denied*, 464 U.S. 1056 (1983). There, Hopi and Navajo tribes opposed a federal decision to permit expansion of a ski resort on federally owned, nontribal land because the tribes used the land for performance of religious ceremonies and the collection of religious objects, and because the development would desecrate symbols of their faith. The court observed that only

A similar problem arises when a government implements a majority religious practice and minority-group members challenge this as an unconstitutional establishment of religion or interference with free exercise. Here, the members of the dominant culture—even if they are not observant practitioners of a mainstream religion—fail to grasp that their perspective disables them from understanding the intrusion experienced by members of minority faiths. Recent examples of this problem include the Supreme Court's rejection of a challenge to a public display of a Christmas crèche. The justices reasoned that the display served a secular purpose and that the symbols of Christmas are really national symbols.[84]

By seeking pluralist understandings in these settings, I hope a judge would do more than nod blankly with the statement that my own viewpoint is partial. Instead, the judge should seek out an understanding of contrasting viewpoints, at least until glimpsing how incomprehensible her own view must be to some others. Knowing the partiality of her own knowledge, information, and normative scheme may not change the outcome in some cases, but it should make the process of decision problematic. Further, by understanding the partiality of her own view, the judge may reach different conclusions some of the time.

By heterogeneity, I mean facing up to the multiplicity of discourses and frameworks for analysis that occupy legal spaces currently. In the instances of religious and secular conflict I have described, we need to work to become fluent in each without pretend-

---

a small portion of the land would be developed and even that would remain accessible to the tribes, and therefore found little impact on the tribes' religious practices; the court did not even address the argument about religious symbols. The judges were caught by their own organizing assumptions and did not realize how much they did not realize. See also Lyng v. Northwest Indian Cemetary Protective Ass'n, 108 S. Ct. 1319 (1988).

84. Lynch v. Donnelly, 465 U.S. 668 (1984). For a different set of arguments, see County of Allegheny v. American Civil Liberties Union, Greater Pittsburgh Chapter, 109 S. Ct. 3086 (1989). Another example arose when the Court rejected a state statute that directed the teaching of aspects of creation when the public schools give instruction on evolution as part of a balanced approach to what many fundamentalist Christians in the state perceived to be a curriculum otherwise invasive into their religious beliefs. Edwards v. Aguillard, 107 S. Ct. 2573 (1987). Here, the Court perceived instruction in creation as impermissible religion, and instruction in evolution as perfectly permissible science, even though the defenders of the statute argued that creation could be taught as a science, and that evolution was a religious belief.

ing to make each one mutually translatable. We each can learn to craft an analysis based on deontological rights theories, another couched in the economic vocabulary of utility maximization and cost-benefit analysis, and still another that looks to symbolic meanings, textual understandings, and communal stories. Arguments that persuade a given judge may well draw on all three strands. Importantly, each framework is not reducible to the others. Breathing vitality into multiple frameworks matters because the experiences and dilemmas we articulate in legal settings are too complex and multiple to be captured in any single framework. We are moved and we move others by articulating claims and theories that resonate with prior commitments or hopes, and the discourse of law should not predetermine the range of commitments and hopes to which we can appeal. Yet, to borrow an idea from economics, I think that anyone using one framework should internalize its costs—its undervaluing of what is valued by other frameworks—rather than imposing these costs as the externalities of its use. The damage to symbolic human dignity from cost-benefit analysis, for example, should be addressed within the context of cost-benefit analysis, not left as an attack by outsiders.

But if I only explore pluralist and heterogeneous approaches to concrete social problems, there will be something unacceptably lacking from the legal theories I propose. I am reminded of an essay, written by a college student, that I read recently. He described his experience with a new friend while studying together in England. The new friend was from Austria, and proved exceedingly generous and affable. The friend initially indicated some chauvinism about his own church, and asked the author about his religious affiliation. When the author said, "I'm Jewish," the friend replied, "Oh, no, they're everywhere." This was not, as it turned out, a random comment; the friend was indeed anti-Semitic and believed that Jews run an international banking conspiracy; he also believed that blacks are inferior to whites. The author of the essay wrote of his growing horror at his friend's attitudes, and his own self-doubt about how he could continue to maintain their friendship.

The Austrian seemed to epitomize Hannah Arendt's description of the banality of evil. This generous, kind person would undoubtedly be a loving father and good citizen—but could also have participated in the Third Reich. Obviously straining to understand, the author concluded that both he and his friend were products of their childhoods and their cultures. Since he, but for chance, might have been raised in Austria in the friend's family, the author found a basis for understanding and accepting his friend.

I remain troubled by this conclusion. That we are all products of our culture, our language, and our peers does not make the friend's attitudes acceptable. An understanding of the partiality of all perspectives does not make them all equally plausible or equally acceptable. Moral relativism of this sort is a mistake, not an answer.

Some say moral relativism results if we solicit and celebrate the view of those who have been excluded, degraded, or oppressed. Surely, this celebration of multiplicity topples the hierarchy that canonized one set of experiences as the norm. Yet the demand for that kind of pluralism does not and should not suspend the critique of power relationships that motivate it. When those from the margin seek tolerance and pluralism, we do not treat beliefs with indifference. We instead demand respect for difference. This is not the simple liberal commitment to tolerance either, for that approach leaves those with privilege too complacent about the comfortable place from which they are asked to tolerate or put up with those who are different. Instead, the struggle waged by the outsiders is for a process of continually dealing with difference in ways that enlarge people's understanding of the partiality of their own perspective. And while this struggle may seem a new assertion of a universal truth, I do not mean it to be so, for even this commitment to understanding the perspectives of others must remain contingent, partial, subject to challenge, and subject to change.

Given the Holocaust, Pol Pot, and other instances of genocide in recent memory, it should be hard to forget that, in ripe social circumstances, a "true belief" can mobilize people to do anything in the name of that belief. Yet we must remain equally vigilant against a kind of mutual acceptance and indifference that places oppression on an equal footing with any other human activity.[85] For law, the problem comes in several layers. Treating a theory of legal authority as well grounded and demanding obedience may mean losing sight of the partiality of those perspectives that capture legal authority.

---

85. Geoffrey Hartman, "Religious Literacy," *Conservative Judaism* 40, no. 4 (1988): 26 (discussing Yeats's view that "The best lack conviction, while the worst / Are full of passionate intensity").

Yet, encouraging skepticism and resistance toward legal authority may undermine a tool for redressing historical inequalities and restraints—and confuse the sense of some stopping points, some authoritative judgments, about issues of interpersonal, social, and political disagreement.

Thus, in addition to the several frameworks already visible in legal scholarship and judicial and legislative acts, I think we need to elaborate and refine what is as yet only an inchoate framework—a language we could use to describe and criticize power relations between people and between groups and also to examine the influence of social and economic structures in individual self-perception and choice.[86]

Lawyers and judges, and anyone using legal notions, should be better equipped to articulate and evaluate the material, institutional settings that make some people marginal and some people more comfortable with society's rules and benefits. We need more, not fewer, words and ideas about these things, and we need to make legal inquiries that can challenge rather than obscure how legal notions themselves contributed to this process of dividing the marginal and the comfortable.

Finally, when I urge a legal theory that is contextual, I am arguing for concrete sites for theory. Rather than starting with abstract concepts and looking for examples or illustrations, legal theory should start with actual problems, as defined and experienced by the people living through them. My talk may seem abstract, but I confess I have basically described the world and the people I know. These are the actual problems within legal scholarship and legal communities. Similarly, I have tried to pursue heterogeneity by acknowledging and even using contrasting modes of argument here, and I have tried to admit and explore the partiality of my own perspectives.

A commitment to local, concrete inquiries would switch the focus from, for example, questions about the fate of law if individual judgments cannot be reconciled, or if abstract concepts, like rights, no longer seem coherent or bounded. Those concerns are too stylized

---

86. Some people have been arguing for a discourse of needs; I fear that this is both too essentialist, positing something intrinsic to people rather than part of their social experience, and too individualized, lacking sensitivity to social structures. But the concerns about needs, I think, can be incorporated in a discourse of power relations.

to convey how they implicate and construct human experience. Centralized, governmental authority may govern people whose own normative commitments rest on incommensurate premises; people may comply, people may resist, people may live quietly with conflicts, and people may bring their conflicts into spheres of public attention and debate. We must not pretend that the law provides one comprehensive scheme that orchestrates all the legal relationships among subgroups and between the central government and each group; instead, law provides multiple languages and institutions within which to play out struggles.

In the Broadway musical *Pippin*, Pippin is a son of Charlemagne and spends the entire play preoccupied with his own fate. He hopes to be someone extraordinary, and he tries art, warfare, and sensual pleasure in this pursuit. Worn out, he is taken in by a widow and earns his keep doing chores around her farm. But finally a great opportunity to fulfill his dream of being extraordinary appears: he is invited to perform a dramatic and memorable feat of self-immolation—lighting himself up as a torch, as it were. Tempted, and torn, he finally refuses, and accepts instead an ordinary life of work and love amid daily commitments. At this point, the playwright arranges for Pippin to be stripped of most of his costume; one by one, pieces of the stage set and magical illusions of the theater are removed; even the lights are altered, so finally Pippin stands with his widow friend and her son, against the brick back wall of an otherwise bare stage. No more illusions, just daily life.

I think that is where we are. And I have no dramatic finale. I certainly do not choose self-immolation. I do choose a daily life of struggle for a better world. My own work tries to articulate specific alternatives, growing from concrete settings that we often miss when we talk at the level of abstraction usually represented by legal and rights language.

One example came to me when I worked on a dispute over the rights of a handicapped student in a public school. Similar disputes have worked their way through school systems and courts around the country. Federal legislation authorizes education for handicapped children and obliges school systems receiving federal funds to provide the "least restrictive" placement, but the legislation also requires schools to provide the "appropriate" educational program for each child diagnosed as handicapped.

Should a deaf student be mainstreamed in the classroom with all hearing students or assigned to a school for the deaf that can afford complete instruction in sign language and total communication? Or does the federal legislation require the participating school system to provide, within the mainstream classroom, a sign-language interpreter for the hearing-impaired student? This problem can be analyzed in terms of rights, in terms of economic costs and benefits, and even in terms of symbolism. I have suggested a different approach. This is not a solution to be adopted as federal legislation or as a federal judicial interpretation, nor do I mean it even as a solution for every school system. But, what if the school instructed the student's classmates in sign language, and treated the problem as theirs as well as hers? The legal framework, I think, should help members of the school community treat the "problem" of the education for the handicapped child as their own problem, not as her problem. Their choice then is not about whether to solve it, but how. They would have to devise the solutions, or temporary resolutions, quite locally. The law should provide a language through which people could gain attention from communities that otherwise proceed without them in mind. The legal rule can shift some preexisting assumptions, like the assumption that schools that failed to keep disabled persons in mind in their design are natural, and anyone who does not fit in must adapt or go elsewhere. A legal norm can demand a new approach: the school community must learn how to include the disabled person and not recreate the exclusionary experiences of disability. To do this will require inventive, local solutions.

What I suggest here is a way to treat law as our folding tents and tools for making temporary shelters before we break-up camp and move on to the next problem. Alternatively, for those who find that metaphor too free of conflict, we should view legal institutions and legal language as terrains for struggle over situated problems. It might be more comforting to think of law as a set of right answers, or a set of trump cards to play to resolve otherwise perpetual games. But recognition of partiality, I think, demands more of us. The problems I worry about are physical abuse, mistreatment of minorities by majorities, government officials who lack watchdogs, and disputes among people who share no commitments to resolve their problems peaceably. These are each problems where I yearn for a right answer and yet doubt the epistemology and political assumptions of a world of right answers. Examples of these problems I will now puzzle through, and invite you to join me. I wish I had an idea like sign-language-for-everyone for each problem, but I do not, as yet. Precisely because it is the search for different ways to connect across differences, I cannot do it alone. The enterprise can be put this way: can we make law a tool for helping us remake a world of distinctions so that people do not oppress one another? The inquiry can be generalized in this question: if we pursue partial justice, how can we make the instruments of a centralized legal system respect the settings where people make meaning without abandoning people to the power relations in which they find themselves? These are the kinds of questions I hope to explore in the future.

I hover close to paradox here, as I reach for a place to rest before turning to hear what you have to say. A commitment to partiality, to exploring the partiality of my own views from the vantage points of others, leads me to note the partiality of other views—even those that claim for partiality a kind of universality, albeit one situated in history, contingent on the material and intellectual context in which I find myself.

I do not think we will find answers to the problems I have sketched, or secret paths through the paradoxes. I cannot and will not propose a new principle or even a new procedure for addressing these themes. I do argue for a stance, a stance skeptical of claims to have found reliable moorings, but also a stance skeptical of skepticism. I also argue for a stance of engagement with the experiences of outsiders, the perspectives that seem hard to assimilate. This means rejecting the drift toward complacency often engendered by doubts about what is right. It also means elaborating narratives about insiders and outsiders, about power relations and structures, along with constant reminders that such narratives themselves are debatable and contingent.

I am not done. And neither are you. Wherever you find yourself in the debates I have described, you are implicated in them. If you hang onto steady certainties, you have closed off challenges that may not persuade you—but that mean a great deal to those who think you do not see their perspective. If you concede that there are multiple, irreconcilable perspectives, you may feed a complacency that further entrenches the particular perspectives that currently prevail. If you pursue the tensions between these positions, however, and engage

with the possibilities that you may not be right, you still may persuasively find some answers quite wrong. By engaging with what sur-
prises you, by encountering the bend of your own thought, you may
move someone else to let loose of a rigid belief; you may supply the
room for another to make room for you. You may help the partiality
of justice become its virtue rather than its hypocrisy.

The Postmodern Transition: Law and Politics

Boaventura de Sousa Santos

Historians will probably describe the twentieth century as an un-happy century. Reared by its androgynous parent, the nineteenth century, to become a wonder child, it soon revealed itself as a fragile and sickly child. When it was fourteen years old, it fell seriously ill with a disease that, like the tuberculosis or the syphilis of the period, took a long time to be treated and, indeed, was never completely cured. So much so that when it was thirty-nine years of age, it re-lapsed into an even more serious illness that was to prevent it from enjoying life with the full energy that usually comes with middle age. Though considered clinically cured six years later, it has since then always been in poor health and many fear a third serious re-lapse, which this time will most probably be fatal.

Much more patiently than Saint-Simon, who thought (in 1819) that it was getting too late for the nineteenth century to throw away its eighteenth-century heritage and assume its own character,[1] we have been waiting for the meaning of the twentieth century. In a book titled *The Meaning of the Twentieth Century*, Kenneth Boulding was content to characterize our century rather vaguely as the middle period of the second great transition in the history of humankind.[2]

I want to thank the colleagues of the Amherst Seminar for their invitation, for their stimulating response, and above all for having shared with me the atmosphere of their scientific community. I would also like to thank Maria Irene Ramalho, Simon Roberts, Nicos Mouzelis, Tim Murphy, David Trubek, Ronald Chilcote, and Stewart Macaulay for their comments on earlier drafts of this paper.

1. Henri Saint-Simon, *Oeuvres*, vol. 2 (Geneva: Slatkina Reprints, 1977), 212.

2. Kenneth Boulding, *The Meaning of the Twentieth Century* (London: Allen and Unwin, 1964), 1.

More recently, Ernest Gellner has regretted that the twentieth century version of history "has not yet been properly formulated philosophically."[3] And I myself wrote that the twentieth century ran the
risk of not beginning at all, that is, of not beginning before ending.[4]
Similar concerns have been hovering over the various conferences
on the appraisal of the century organized everywhere in recent years.
The result has been that many such appraisals have, in fact, been
appraisals of the nineteenth century and not of the twentieth century,
as they have purported to be.

However, in more recent years, there have been signs that this
biography of the century may be incomplete and, accordingly, that
the assessments and obituaries have been premature. It seems, indeed, that our century is now prepared to enjoy a full active life in its
senior year. But what is the real meaning of such signs? Do they
indicate realistic purposes and a sensible assessing of the strengths
and weaknesses needed to accomplish them in such a short time, or
are they an outburst of senile infantilism? Do they express a timely
sense of urgency or the self-defeating feeling of "belatedness" that,
according to Harold Bloom, plagues our culture and, particularly,
contemporary poetry?[5] Finally, even assuming that its projects and
purposes are realistic and worth pursuing, will our century have time
to pursue and fulfill them? Or, to ask a more honest and straightforward question: will we have time to become the children of the twentieth century?

Though one of the most ambiguous feats of our century is to
have transformed the sense of time into the sense of a lack of time, I
am inclined to give an affirmative answer and predict that the years
ahead will fully confirm my positive interpretation of our current
predicament. That is what I will try to demonstrate, with a certain
dose of tragic optimism taken from Heidegger.

This essay will consist of three main sections: in the first I will
present an interpretative analysis of the historical trajectory (or trajectories) of the paradigm of modernity and show the conditions that

3. Ernest Gellner, *Relativism and the Social Sciences* (Cambridge: Cambridge University Press, 1986), 93.

4. Boaventura de Sousa Santos, *Um Discurso sobre as Ciências* (Porto: Afronta-
mento, 1987), 6.

5. Harold Bloom, *The Anxiety of Influence* (New York: Oxford University Press,
1973) and *Poetics of Influence* (New Haven, Conn.: Henry R. Schwab, 1988).

have both contributed to its exhaustion and pointed to the emergence of a new paradigm. In the second section, I will present the profile of the emergent paradigm in broad lines by contrasting modern and postmodern critical theory. Finally, I will suggest some specific applications of the new paradigm in the field of law and politics. Each section begins with the enunciation of a main thesis followed by a justification.

The Rise and Decline of the Paradigm of Modernity in Advanced Capitalist Societies

The main thesis of this section is: The sociocultural paradigm of modernity emerged before the capitalist mode of production became dominant and will disappear before the latter ceases to be dominant. This disappearance is complex because it is, in part, a process of supersession and, in part, a process of obsolescence. It is supersession to the extent that modernity has fulfilled some of its promises, in some cases even in excess. It is obsolescence to the extent that modernity is no longer capable of fulfilling some of its other promises. Both the excess and the deficit in the fulfillment of historical promises account for our present predicament, which appears, on the surface, as a period of crisis but which, at a deeper level, is a period of paradigmatic transition. Since all transitions are both half invisible and half blind, it is impossible to name our current situation accurately. This is probably why the inadequate designation *postmodern* has become so popular. But for the same reason this name is authentic in its inadequacy.

The paradigm of modernity is very rich and complex, as capable of immense variability as it is prone to contradictory developments. It is based on two pillars, regulation and emancipation, each one constituted of three principles or logics. The pillar of regulation is constituted by the principle of the State, formulated most prominently by Hobbes, the principle of the market, developed by Locke and Adam Smith in particular, and the principle of the community, which presides over Rousseau's social and political theory. The pillar of emancipation is constituted by the logics of rationality as identified by Weber: the aesthetic-expressive rationality of the arts and literature, the cognitive-instrumental rationality of science and technology, and the moral-practical rationality of ethics and the rule of law.

The paradigm of modernity is an ambitious and revolutionary

project, but it is also internally contradictory. On the one hand, the breadth of its claims opens up a wide horizon for social and cultural innovation; on the other, the complexity of its constituent elements make the overfulfillment of some promises and the underfulfillment of some others hardly avoidable. Such excesses and deficits are both inscribed in the matrix of the paradigm. The paradigm of modernity aims at an harmonious and reciprocal development of both the pillar of regulation and the pillar of emancipation, as well as at the undistorted translation of such development into the full rationalization of collective and personal everyday life. This double binding—of one pillar to the other and of both to social praxis—will ensure the harmonization of potentially incompatible social values, of justice and autonomy, of solidarity and identity, of equality and freedom.

With the privilege of hindsight, it is easy to predict that the hubris of such an overreaching aim carries in itself the seeds of frustration: unfulfilled promises and irredeemable deficits. Each pillar, based as it is on abstract principles, tends to maximize its potentials, be it the maximization of regulation or the maximization of emancipation, thereby making problematic the success of any strategy of pragmatic compromises between them. Moreover, each pillar consists of independent and functionally differentiated principles, each of which tends also to develop a maximalist vocation, be it, on the side of regulation, the maximization of the state, the maximization of the market, or the maximization of the community; and, on the side of emancipation, aestheticization, scientificization or juridification of social praxis.

The paradigm of modernity emerged as a sociocultural project between the sixteenth and the end of the eighteenth century. Only at the end of the eighteenth century does the test of its implementation truly begin, and that moment coincides with the emergence of capitalism as the dominant mode of production in today's advanced societies. From then on, the paradigm of modernity is tied to the development of capitalism. Following the German tradition originating with Hilferding, developed by Offe and others, and now also accepted by English social scientists,[6] I distinguish three periods in

---

6. Rudolf Hilferding, *Finance Capital: A Study of the Latest Phase of Capitalist Development* (London: Routledge and Kegan Paul, 1981); Claus Offe, *Disorganized Capitalism*

this development.[7] The first period, the period of liberal capitalism, covers the whole nineteenth century, though the last three decades have a transitional character; the second period, the period of organized capitalism, begins at the end of the century and reaches full development in the interwar period and in the two decades after the war; finally, the third period, the period of disorganized capitalism, begins at the end of the 1960s and is still with us.

It is not my purpose here to give a full description of each period, but rather to mention those characteristics that will enable me to trace the trajectory of the paradigm of modernity throughout the three periods. My argument is that the first period already showed that the sociocultural project of modernity was too ambitious and internally contradictory. The second period fulfilled some of the promises of modernity (sometimes even in excess), but failed to fulfill others, while trying, by a politics of hegemony, to minimize the extent of its failures and to make them socially and symbolically invisible. The third period represents the consciousness of a threefold predicament: first, whatever modernity has accomplished is not irreversible and, to the extent that it is not excessive, it must be defended, but it can only be successfully defended in postmodern terms; second, the as yet unfulfilled promises will remain unfulfilled as long as the paradigm of modernity dominates; and finally, this deficit, besides being irreversible, is much greater than the second period was ready to admit.

I will, thus, try to show that, as we move from the first to the second and third period, the paradigm of modernity, as if animated by a laser-beam effect, narrows down the scope of its accomplishments at the same time that it intensifies them. Such a process of concentration/exclusion is adequately symbolized in the historical and semantic sequence of three concepts, all of them rooted in the modern: modernity, modernism, and modernization.[8]

(Oxford: Polity Press, 1985); H. A. Winckler, ed., *Organizierter Kapitalismus: Voraussetzungen und Anfänge* (Göttingen: Vandenhoeck and Ruprecht, 1974); Scott Lash and John Urry, *The End of Organized Capitalism* (Oxford: Polity Press, 1987).

7. For the characterization of the three periods, I follow Lash and Urry, *End of Organized Capitalism*, very closely.

8. There are striking parallels between this sequence and reason, rationalism, and rationalization.

The First Period

What is fascinating about the nineteenth century is that it features
the violent explosion of the internal contradictions of the project of
modernity. By that I mean the contradictions between solidarity and
identity, between justice and autonomy, and between equality and
freedom. Since these contradictions explode without mediation, both
the tendencies toward the narrowing of the project's scope and the
underlying aspiration of globality—that is to say, the ambition to
transform social reality radically—are clearly to be seen in each one
of the principles or logics of both regulation and emancipation. As
to the pillar of regulation, the idea of a balanced and combined development of the principles of the state, of the market, and of the community—which, contrary to commonly held views, was central to the
political philosophy of the eighteenth century of Adam Smith and the
Scottish Enlightenment[9]—breaks down, and in the ideological vac-
uum thereby produced three phenomena occur. First is the unprece-
dented development of the principle of the market as shown in the
first wave of industrialization, in the expansion of commercial cities,
and in the rise of new industrial cities. Second, there is an almost
total atrophy of the principle of the community. The community,
which for Rousseau was a concrete community of people inasmuch
as popular sovereignty belonged (in real terms) to the people, is
reduced to a dualist structure composed of two equally abstract elements: civil society, conceived as a competitive aggregation of particular interests, and the individual, conceived as a formally equal
and free citizen. The third phenomenon is the ambiguous development of the principle of the state under the impact of the first two
phenomena, as well as in the face of the contradictory claims of
laissez-faire, which, as Dicey noted, involved both the idea of the
minimal state and the idea of the maximal state.[10]
        The pillar of emancipation mirrors, with even greater clarity, the
convulsive tensions boiling inside the paradigm of modernity. The

        9. Jacob Viner, "Adam Smith and Laissez-Faire," *Journal of Political Economy* 35
(1927): 198; L. Billet, "Political Order and Economic Development: Reflections on Adam
Smith's *Wealth of Nations*," *Political Studies* 23 (1975): 430; and Boaventura de Sousa
Santos, "On Modes of Production of Law and Social Power," *International Journal of
Sociology of Law* 13 (1985): 302.
        10. A. V. Dicey, *Law and Public Opinion in England* (London: Macmillan, 1948), 306.

narrowing tendency, that is, the tendency toward exclusion and concentration, occurs in emancipation through the process of functional differentiation so well analyzed by Weber. As this process unfolds, the articulation among the three logics becomes more complex and their interpenetration in the *Lebenswelt* less probable. This may be observed, at the level of aesthetic-expressive rationality, in the increasing elitism of the romantic movement; at the level of cognitive-instrumental rationality, in the spectacular progress of the sciences and in their gradual conversion into a force of production; and, finally, at the level of moral-practical rationality, in liberal microethics (that is, moral responsibility referred exclusively to the individual), of the legal formalism of the German pandect, boosted by the codification movement, whose landmark was the Napoleonic Code of 1804.

But in my view, during this period, the pillar of emancipation is the organizational matrix of social and cultural phenomena, which, in marginal or deviant forms, bring to life the aspiration of a global and radical transformation of the social praxis inscribed in the paradigm of modernity. I select three such phenomena, one from the realm of moral-practical rationality and two from the realm of aesthetic-expressive rationality. The first one consists of the intellectual and social construction of the radical socialist projects and movements, both the so-called utopian socialism and the so-called scientific socialism. All these projects and movements point toward a full and harmonic realization in this world (even if this world is the phalanstery) of the ideals of equality and freedom, of solidarity and subjectivity that constitute modernity. The other two phenomena are romantic idealism and the great realist novel. I am not interested here in contrasting, as Gouldner does, classical and romantic thought, but simply in showing that, though in an elitist and sometimes consciously regressive form, romantic idealism represents the utopian vision of the full achievement of subjectivity.[11] In longing for the totality, for the origins, and for the vernacular, against the atomism, the alienation, and instrumentalism of modern life, and by placing aesthetics and poetry at the center of social integration, romantic idealism epitomizes the denunciation of and the resistance to the

---

11. Alvin Gouldner, *The Coming Crisis of Western Sociology* (New York: Avon, 1970), 115.

tendency toward exclusion and concentration in the social implementation of the paradigm of modernity.[12] On the other hand, the great
realist novel bears witness to a class—the bourgeoisie—that fails to
seize the historical opportunity of becoming a universal class and
bringing about a radical social transformation,[13] the same opportunity that Hegel had envisaged for the bureaucracy and Marx for the
working class.

In sum, the period of liberal capitalism sets in motion the social
process of exclusion and concentration but, as the contradictions of
the paradigm explode without mediation, it is still possible in this
period to formulate and activate, even if in a deviant or marginal
form, the radical and globalizing vocation of the paradigm, thereby
refusing to accept the irreversibility of the deficit in the fulfillment of
its promises.

The Second Period

The period of organized capitalism is truly a positive age, in the
Comtean sense. As a reasonable and mature adult should do (according to Comte), it starts by distinguishing in the paradigm of modernity between those promises that can be fulfilled in a dynamic capitalist society and those that cannot. It then concentrates on the former
and tries, through the hegemonic means of socialization and cultural
inculcation, to eliminate the latter from the symbolic universe of social and cultural praxis. In other words, this period begins by acknowledging the idea that the deficit of unfulfilled promises is both
inevitable and irreversible and then goes on to eliminate the idea of
deficit itself. This ideological transformation is translated in the transition from the broad concept of modernity to the narrower concept
of modernism.

---

12. See Hauke Brunkhorst, for whom "romantic modernism edges bewilderingly
close to the conservative or reactionary fundamental opposition to modern culture and
its utopian rationalism" ("Romanticism and Cultural Criticism," *Praxis International* 6
[1987]: 409). Similarly, according to Gouldner, "the revolutionary potential of Romanticism derived, in part, from the fact that although basically a critique of industrialism,
it *could* as well be used as a critique of capitalism and its culture" (*Coming Crisis of
Western Sociology*, 115).

13. According to Georg Lukács, "the central category and criterion of realist
literature is the type, a peculiar synthesis which originally binds together the general
and the particular both in characters and structures" (*Studies in European Realism* [Lon-
don: Merlin Press, 1972], 5). Hence, his definition of realism: "a correct dialectical

The process of exclusion and concentration can be traced both in the pillar of regulation and in the pillar of emancipation. As to regulation, the principle of the market continues the spectacular expansion initiated in the first period, taking on new economic and institutional forms: the concentration and centralization of industrial, banking, and commercial capital; the increasing regulation of markets; the proliferation of cartels; and the separation of legal ownership from economic control. As to the principle of community, the capitalist development and the expansion of the working class it entails, coupled with the extension of suffrage, produces a certain rematerialization of the community exemplified in the emergence of class practices and their translation into class politics. Trade unions and working-class parties enter a political space that, until then, was exclusively occupied by oligarchic parties and bourgeois organizations. The principle of the state suffers the impact of these changes and at the same time becomes an autonomous and active factor in their intensification and orientation. The state increases its ties both with the market, through ever growing interpenetration between the state bureaucracies and the large monopolies, and with the community, through the political incorporation of large sectors of the working class, increasing state intervention in the forms of collective consumption, in health and education, and in space management and social legislation; in other words, through the development of the welfare state.

These transformations amount to a profound redefinition of the paradigm of modernity whereby the degrees or types of solidarity, justice, and equality are chosen in view of their compatibility with the degrees and types of autonomy, identity, and freedom that are deemed necessary in a capitalist society (and vice versa). The reformulations lead to the emergence of two "realistic" promises that will be fulfilled to a great extent during this period: the promise of a fairer distribution of material resources and the promise of a greater democratization of the political system. The fulfillment of the first promise is made compatible with the continuation of a class society, while the fulfillment of the second promise is made compatible with the con-

conception of the relationship between being and consciousness" (119). See also Erich Auerbach, *Mimesis: The Representation of Reality in Western Literature* (Princeton: Princeton University Press, 1968), 454ff.; and Alan Swingewood, *The Novel and Revolution* (London: Macmillan, 1975), chap. 3.

tinuation of a bourgeois class-politics. Through a politics of hegemony it is then possible to convert this particular form of compatibility, which is, in fact, one among many others, into the only legitimate one, even, perhaps, the only imaginable one. Such conversion surfaces both in the gradual but steady marginalization of the communist parties and in the social-democratic transformation of the socialist parties.

In this second period, the pillar of emancipation undergoes transformations that are as profound as those described for the pillar of regulation and, indeed, convergent with them. These transformation are reflected in the transition from the culture of modernity to cultural modernism. By cultural modernism, I mean a new aesthetic-expressive rationality that extends, in this period, to both the moral-practical rationality and the cognitive-instrumental rationality. Modernism represents the climax of the process of concentration and exclusion that, in the realm of aesthetic-expressive rationality, takes the form of the radical autonomy of art (art for art's sake), the antagonistic opposition between high culture and popular culture, and the militant suppression of the social context, as symbolized by the architecture of the megapolis. Modernism is, thus, the social and cultural construction of "a great divide," in Andreas Huyssen's terms, and he is right in considering the "anxiety of contamination" as the most revealing characteristic of modernism, the anxiety of contamination by politics, morality, and popular and mass culture.[14] In my view, the same anxiety of contamination can be traced in the transformations occurring in the other two logics of rationality. As far as the moral-practical rationality goes, such anxiety of contamination is present in the theories of political representation which, by favoring vertical arrangements over horizontal arrangements, lead to the emasculation of the people.[15] The same anxiety of contamination is also present in the development of a formalist legal science opposed to any form of nonprofessional legal knowledge, which finds its extreme and most sophisticated expression in Kelsen's pure theory of

14. Andreas Huyssen, *After the Great Divide* (Bloomington: Indiana University Press, 1986), chap. 7.

15. These were the theories Hannah Arendt once considered as underlying the U.S. Constitution and responsible for its "fateful failure" to promote the politics of participation. See George Kateb, "Death and Politics: Hannah Arendt's Reflections on the American Constitution," *Social Research* 54 (1987): 605; and Fred Dallmayr, "Public or Private Freedom: Response to Kateb," *Social Research* 54 (1987): 617.

law.[16] In the realm of cognitive-instrumental rationality, the anxiety of contamination is present in the emergence of different positivist epistemologies, in the Mertonian paradigm of the scientific ethos, and, above all, in the Bachelardian epistemological rupture between scientific knowledge and common sense.[17]

The intensity of such transformations and accomplishments are the other side of the deficit of totality in which they are based and which they successfully manage to forget or suppress through their dynamism and hubris. The triumphant, shiny representation of the knowable and of the rational goes hand in hand with the dictatorship of the demarcations, the ruthless policing of the borders, and the expeditious liquidation of transgressors and transgressions. In this process, the pillar of emancipation becomes more and more like the pillar of regulation; indeed, the pillar of emancipation becomes the mental side of the pillar of regulation, a complex process that is rendered most eloquently in Gramsci's concept of hegemony.

My argument in the second section of this essay will, perhaps, be better understood if I remind us at this point that the process of concentration and exclusion that characterizes the trajectory of the paradigm of modernity in the period of organized capitalism had a very tumultuous start, rich in incidents that threatened its full development. The Russian revolution and the historical avant-garde of the 1920s are two cases in point. The Russian revolution was an attempt to give historical credibility to a new and radically different form of compatibility between degrees and types of solidarity, justice and equality on one side, and degrees and types of identity, autonomy, and freedom on the other. The attempt failed, both because of the failure of the revolutions in other capitalist countries (most notably the German revolution of 1918) and because of the Stalinist nightmare.

As to the avant-garde movements—futurism, surrealism, dadaism, Russian constructivism, proletcult, etc.—their most striking feature is that all of them attempt to reconcile art and life against the modernist canon in very different ways. It is well known how these

---

16. Hans Kelsen, *The Pure Theory of Law* (Los Angeles: University of California Press, 1967).

17. Robert Merton, *Social Theory and Social Structure* (New York: Free Press, 1968), 604; Gaston Bachelard, *Le Nouvel Esprit Scientific* (Paris: P.U.F., 1971); and *La Formation de l'Esprit Scientifique* (Paris: J. Vrin, 1972).

movements were either liquidated by fascism or Stalinism or were gradually absorbed in the modernist canon. But their cultural significance cannot be minimized, as Habermas does when he conceives surrealism as a mere moment of dissublimation of modern art and, as such, bound to fail.[18] Peter Bürger is, thus, right in emphasizing the cultural meaning of the avant-garde movements as the historical moment in which, for the first time, artists understand how the autonomy and the social status of art are engineered and function in capitalist societies.[19] In other words, their historical meaning lies in their early denunciation of the process of concentration and exclusion, the full consequences of which we are suffering now.

The Third Period

The period of disorganized capitalism is the most difficult to analyze, if for no other reason than because it is the period we are living in; the owl of Minerva is not privileged to fly at dusk, the only safe flight time for knowledge, according to Hegel.

Concerning the pillar of regulation, the most decisive transformations seem to be occurring in and through the principle of the market, and so much so that this principle seems to become truly hegemonic in the sense of being able to generate a surplus of meaning that spills over to the principle of the state and the principle of the community and seeks to colonize them. The dramatic growth of the world markets, coupled with the emergence of worldwide systems of production and economic agents (the multinational corporations), undermine the capacity of the state to regulate the market at the national level. The industrialization of the Third World, the expansion of international subcontracting and franchising, and the ruralization of industry have together contributed to destroy the spatial configuration of production and reproduction in the central countries: the traditional industrial regions are decharacterized and dein-

---

18. Jürgen Habermas, *Legitimationsprobleme im Spätkaitalismus* (Frankfurt: Suhrkamp Verlag, 1973), 118ff.

19. Peter Bürger, *Theory of the Avante-Garde* (Manchester: Manchester University Press, 1984). On the debate between Habermas and Bürger, see Jochen Schulte-Sasse, "Foreword: Theory of Modernism versus Theory of the Avante-Garde," in Bürger, *Theory of the Avante-Garde;* and Martin Jay, "Habermas and Modernism," in *Habermas and Modernity,* ed. R. Bernstein (Oxford: Polity Press, 1982), 125.

dustrialized and, in their place, reemerges, as a strategic productive factor, the locality, the local endogenous dynamics often based on complex mixes of agriculture and industry, of family production and industrial production. The extensive expansion of the market runs parallel to its intensive expansion, as witnessed in the growing differentiation of products and the consequent increase of choices and particularization of tastes and also in the ever-deeper commodification of the information from which virtually infinite opportunities for the expanded reproduction of capital result.

The impact of these changes on the principle of the community is wide ranging. As the wage relation becomes more flexible and precarious, the corporatist mechanisms developed in the second period (labor laws, industrial courts, collective bargaining) lose steam, and the trade unions, whose membership declines, lose bargaining power. The increased internal differentiation of the industrial working class and the dramatic expansion of the service class have contributed to decharacterize class practices and to prevent their easy translation into class politics. As a result, traditional working-class parties smooth out the ideological content of their programs and turn into catchall parties.

As both a cause and an effect of these transformations, the principle of the state is undergoing equally sweeping changes. In view of the transnationalization of the economy, the state sometimes seems to have become an almost obsolete unit of analysis and to have lost the capacity and the political will to regulate both social production and social reproduction. As it becomes externally weaker and internally less efficient, the state becomes paradoxically more authoritarian, acting through myriad ill-integrated bureaucracies, each one exerting its own microdespotism vis-à-vis increasingly powerless politically incompetent citizens.

The trajectory of the three logics of modern emancipation in the period of disorganized capitalism is best characterized by the social and cultural construct of both a sense of irreparable deficits and a sense of uncontrollable excesses that together lead to a syndrome of exhaustion and global blockage. This is most notably the case of the cognitive-instrumental rationality of science and technology. The involvement of science in the military-industrial complex, the ecological catastrophe, the nuclear threat, the destruction of the ozone layer, the emergence of biotechnology and genetic engineering—all these phenomena point to the idea that the promise of scientific progress inscribed in the paradigm of modernity has been fulfilled in excess and that this excessive fulfillment carries with it an unsettling deficit of meaning. As Rousseau predicted with maddening forethought, we have let ourselves be enslaved by the tools devised by Bacon and Descartes for our liberation.[20]

In the realm of aesthetic-expressive rationality, the deficit of meaning assumes the form of irrelevance and domestication. Modern art seems powerless to resist the commercialization of its uniqueness or the distraction with which it is contemplated. No matter how honorable Adorno's reasons to take modern art away from a leveling world into the high or into the deep,[21] the task seems quite implausible today, if not absurd: on the one hand, the elevation to the high is impossible in an age in which the infinites proliferate, even if they are bad infinites in the Hegelian sense, all of them standing on their tiptoes, forcing the artistic difference to make no difference; on the other hand, digging into the deep seems equally implausible, a Sisyphean task in the midst of profound superficialities endlessly juxtaposed, rhizomatic networks of meaning in Deleuze's sense. The extremely acute awareness of this impasse and the early denunciation of exhaustion and global blockage in this realm of emancipatory logic explain why the first face of the emergent paradigm of postmodernity has been an aesthetic-expressive one, as I will show.

Finally, in the realm of moral-practical rationality, the sense of exhaustion and global blockage is expressed in two major and interconnected ways.[22] In the first period, revolution and social reform occupied equally strong and rival positions in the symbolic universes of those groups interested in social transformation and emancipation. As the second period unfolded in the advanced capitalist societies, social reform gained a hegemonic position and the concept of revolution was swept under the carpet of social and political thought. Social reform meant basically peaceful and piecemeal social transformation by means of abstract and universal laws issued by the state. In the

---

20. Jean-Jacques Rousseau, *Oeuvres Complètes*, vol. 2 (Paris: Seuil, 1971), 52.

21. T. W. Adorno, *Ästhetische Theorie* (Frankfurt: Suhrkamp Verlag, 1981).

22. A powerful analysis of the sense of exhaustion and global blockage in the advanced capitalist societies can be found in Claus Offe, "The Utopia of the Zero-Option: Modernity and Modernization as Normative Political Criteria," *Praxis International* 7 (1987): 1.

third period, the merits of this solution are being questioned. The juridification or overlegalization of social reality has produced standardized social relations, that is to say, mass-produced, unidimensional social habitus, and the social empowerment of the popular classes it made possible was achieved by means of transforming autonomous citizens into clients (or even victims) of increasingly authoritarian state bureaucracies.[23]

Related to this there is a second sign of exhaustion and global blockage that presents itself as an ethical impasse. Both liberal ethics and legal reformism are based on microethics, on the attribution of moral responsibility to individuals and for individuals' actions. This paradigm may have worked more or less adequately in the first and in part of the second period, but today, in the face of the global danger of nuclear annihilation and ecological catastrophe, a situation is created for the first time in history in which, to quote Karl-Otto Apel, "in face of a common danger, men and women are called upon to assume a common moral responsibility."[24] The impasse lies in the fact that, while microethics is definitely inadequate to address this new situation, it has not yet been replaced by a macroethics capable "of organizing the responsibility of humankind for the consequences (and side effects) of their collective actions on a planetary scale."[25]

The exhaustion and global blockage of the logics of emancipation and the incapacity of any of the principles of regulation to secure a stable compatibility among contradictory claims and promises create a social and cultural context in which deregulation, contractualization, and conventionality within each sector of social life coexist, as Offe has recently emphasized, with a high degree of rigidity and inflexibility at the global level.[26] Everything seems possible in art and science, in religion and ethics, but, on the other hand, nothing new seems to be possible at the level of the society as a whole.[27] The

---

23. On this point, Sergei Moscovici makes a very strong statement: "at the beginning of the century we were certain that the masses would triumph, whereas towards the end of it we are all prisoners of leaders" (*The Age of the Crowd* [Cambridge: Cambridge University Press, 1985], 1).

24. Karl-Otto Apel, "The Situation of Humanity as an Ethical Problem," *Praxis International* 4 (1984): 250.

25. Ibid., 250.

26. Offe, "Utopia of the Zero-Option."

27. Cf. Offe's assessment of our contemporary condition: "on the one hand, nearly all factors of social, economic, and political life are contingent, elective, and

advanced capitalist societies seem condemned to suffer the excessive fulfillment of some of the promises of modernity and to forget or repress the deficit of unfulfilled promises.

As Max Weber showed better than anyone else the antinomies of the project of modernity in the first and second periods of capitalism so Habermas has shown the antinomies of the third period. As a matter of fact, we have to agree with him that the project of modernity is an incomplete project.[28] But while Habermas believes that this project can be completed in subparadigmatic terms, that is, by resorting to the cultural, social, and political tools developed by modernity, I submit that whatever is there to be completed can only be completed in terms and with the tools of a new, emergent paradigm.

Topoi for the Emergent Paradigm

The main thesis of this section is: The modern idea of a global rationality of social and personal life ended up disintegrating into a multitude of minirationalities at the service of a global, uncontrollable, and unaccounted for irrationality. It is possible to reinvent the minirationalities in such a way that they cease to be parts of a totality and become, instead, totalities present in many parts. This is the task for postmodern critical theory.

The interpretive description of the third period, the period of disorganized capitalism, is only part of the picture. As I have mentioned, in this period there have been accumulating the signs of the emergence of a new paradigm which, for the reasons I have indicated, can be designated as the paradigm of postmodernity. As to the logics of emancipation, since the late 1960s and mid-1970s, particularly in the United States, the aesthetic-expressive rationality of the arts and literature has undertaken a radical critique of the modernist canon, that is, the critique of modernization, standardization, and functionalism; a critique of the international style, of abstract expressionism, serial music, and classic literary modernism. Such a critique, as Huyssen rightly points out, is already present in the beat genera-

---

gripped by change, while, on the other hand, the institutional and structural premises over which that contingency runs are simultaneously removed from the horizon of political, indeed, of intellectual choice" ("Utopia of the Zero-Option," 8).

28. Jürgen Habermas, *Der Philosophische Diskurs der Moderne*, 2d ed. (Frankfurt: Suhrkamp Verlag, 1985).

tion of the mid-1950s.[29] The exhaustion of the modernist canon once perceived, the new beginning is sought, in architecture as well as in painting, theater, film, and music. The main feature of this new search is the desire to cross the borders between high culture and low culture, to mix the codes and reclaim the social context and the local vernacular, to value the *Gemeinschaft* over the *Gesellschaft*; in other words, to revive the adversarial, critical vocation of art, not by negating the world, as Adorno had maintained, but, on the contrary, by affirming the world and by diving deeply into reality.

In the field of the cognitive-instrumental rationality of the sciences and technology, the epistemological crisis of modern science dates back to the beginning of the century and has been deepening and widening ever since. The most important moments in this process are: Einstein's theory of relativity, the uncertainty principle of Heisenberg, the complementarity principle of Bohr, the noncompletion theorem of Gödel, the catastrophe theory of Thom, and, more recently, the theory of dissipative structures of Prigogine, the synergetics of Haken, the hypercycle of Eigen, the autopoiesis of Maturana and Varela, the implicate order of David Bohm, and the bootstrap philosophy underlying the S-matrix of Geoffrey Chew.[30] All these trends point to a new science. Its various names—Prigogine's new alliance, Fritjof Capra's new physics or Tao of physics, Jantsch's para-

29. Huyssen, *After the Great Divide*, 186.
30. H. Reichenbach, *From Copernicus to Einstein* (New York: Dover, 1970); W. Heisenberg, *Physics and Beyond* (London: Allen and Unwin, 1971); J. Ladrière, "Les Limites de la Formalization," in *Logique et Connaissance Scientifique*, ed. J. Piaget (Paris: Gallimard, 1967), 312; R. Jones, *Physics as Metaphor* (New York: New American Library, 1982), 158; J. Parain-Vial, *Philosophie des Sciences de la Nature: Tendences Nouvelles* (Paris: Klincksieck, 1983), 52; J. Briggs and F. D. Peat, *Looking Glass Universe: The Emerging Science of Wholeness* (London: Fontana, 1985), 22; René Thom, *Parábolas e Catástrofes* (Lisbon: D. Quixote, 1985); I. Prigogine and I. Stengers, *La Nouvelle Alliance: Metamorphose de la Science* (Paris: Gallimard, 1979); I. Prigogine, *From Being to Becoming* (San Francisco: Freeman, 1980) and "Time, Irreversibility, and Randomness," in *The Evolutionary Vision*, ed. E. Jantsch (Boulder, Colo.: Westview Press, 1981); H. Haken, *Synergetics: An Introduction* (Heidelberg: Springer-Verlag, 1977); and "Synergetics—An Interdisciplinary Approach to Phenomena of Self-Organization," *Geoforum* 16 (1985): 205; M. Eigen and P. Schuster, *The Hypercycle: A Principle of Natural Self-Organization* (Heidelberg: Springer-Verlag, 1979); H. R. Maturana and F. J. Varela, *De Maquinas y Seres Vivos* (Santiago de Chile: Editorial Universitária, 1973) and *Autopoietic Systems* (Urbana: University of Illinois Biological Computer Laboratory, 1975); David Bohm, *Wholeness and the Implicate Order* (London: Ark Paperbacks, 1984); Geoffrey Chew, "Bootstrap: A Scientific Idea?" *Science* 161 (1968): 762; Geoffrey Chew, "Hardon Bootstrap: Triumph or Frustration?" *Physics Today* 23 (1970): 23; F. Capra, "Quark Physics

digm of self-organization, Bateson's immanent mind, Bohm's implicate order—are the possible names of a postmodern science.[31]

Finally, concerning the moral-practical rationality of ethics and law, the limits of the liberal microethics and the legal form connected with it have been further exposed. This ethical and legal form is totally inadequate to address some of the serious problems of our age, from Chernobyl to AIDS. The point of the matter is that a new jus-naturalism is emerging, not as an abstract construct, but as the interstitial symbolic configuration of the new social struggles that I shall discuss.

At the level of the principles of regulation, the identification of postmodern signs is particularly difficult. What from a certain angle seems to be new and discontinuous with the past is, when seen from another angle, really an uninterrupted progress into the present. The principle of the market is the most ambiguous. On one side, the extensive and intensive expansion of the market makes it ever more difficult for any adversarial, alternative, socially useful and nonprofit oriented social or cultural initiative to succeed, so imminent is the danger of its being coopted, absorbed, domesticated, and converted into another sphere of capitalist production. On the other side, in the age of media and informational reality, the opportunities for a more democratic consumption and, even, production of knowledge are immense. The increased social and cultural competence that is to be expected may, indeed, materialize if the recent dramatic increases in productivity continue. The reduction of the working week, increasingly central in labor disputes, will expand leisure time and production will be displaced by consumption; in this case, the priority of production basic to the paradigm of modernity and present as much in social theory as in modernist architecture will collapse.[32]

---

without Quarks: A Review of Recent Developments in S-Matrix Theory," *American Journal of Physics* 47 (1979): 11.

31. Prigogine and Stengers, *La Nouvelle Alliance;* F. Capra, *The Tao of Physics* (New York: Bantam Books, 1976) and *The Turning Point* (New York: Bantam Books, 1983); E. Jantsch, *The Self-Organizing Universe: Scientific and Human Implications of the Emerging Paradigm of Evolution* (Oxford: Pergamon Press, 1980) and *The Evolutionary Vision;* Gregory Bateson, *Mind and Nature* (London: Fontana, 1985); Bohm, *Wholeness and the Implicate Order.*

32. C. Jencks, *Post-Modernism* (London: Academy Editions, 1987), 11ff.; Huyssen, *After the Great Divide,* 187.

As to the principle of the community, the relative weakening of class practices and of class politics has been compensated for by the emergence of new agonistic spaces that propose new social post-materialist and political agendas (peace, ecology, sexual and racial equality) to be acted out by new insurgent groups and social movements. In this respect, one might say that the twentieth century only begins in the third period of capitalist development. Indeed, the discovery that capitalism produces classes and that classes are the organizing matrix of social transformation was a nineteenth-century discovery. The twentieth century enters the historical scene only when it discovers that capitalism also produces racial and sexual differences and that these can also be nodal points for social struggles.

Finally, the principle of the state, which in the period of organized capitalism functioned very much as the structuring ground for the operation of both the principle of the market and the principle of the community, seems now on the retreat, as if only fit for a secondary role vis-à-vis these two principles. The retreat of statism is combined with changes in the world system of states and particularly with the decline of the American empire and the reemergence of the Soviet Union as a large field of social experimentation in which the principle of the market and the principle of community are given new prominence. These trends do not necessarily point to the end of statism or to a final crisis of the welfare state; they do change the political debate in such a way as to make room for a more intelligent and particularized welfare state or, rather, for a renewed articulation between the welfare state and what we may call the welfare society, that is to say, a new and more polyphonic community consciousness.

Are these signs enough to make for the emergence of a new paradigm? The truth of both a negative and a positive answer to this question are probably equivalent. We live in a period of paradigmatic transition, and as Koyré has taught us in his study of the scientific revolution of the sixteenth century, in such periods this question cannot be answered in terms of truth claims, precisely because the criteria that ground such claims are themselves under question.[33] What is at stake is not a decision over the validity of new findings but, rather, the emergence or not of a new perception of reality. Thus

---

33. A. Koyré, *Estudos Galilaicos* (Lisbon: D. Quixote, 1986); T. Kuhn, *The Structure of Scientific Revolutions*, 2d ed. (Chicago: University of Chicago Press, 1970).

the question will ultimately be decided in terms of the relative strength—a pragmatic and rhetorical strength—of the groups that will favor one or another global perception.

This fact has a double implication for the argument I will present in the following. First, it accounts for the critique of modernist epistemologies, which Rorty calls foundationalist epistemologies, and of the truth concept in which they are based, a critique diversely present in the work of Rorty himself, Gadamer, Feyerabend, and Morin.[34] Second, it accounts for the reemergence of James's and Dewey's version of pragmatism, and for the renewed interest in Greek and medieval rhetoric, which can be dated back to 1967, the date of publication of Perelman's *New Rhetoric*.[35] Finally, the fact that, in a period of paradigmatic transition, the question of truth can only be solved in pragmatic and rhetorical terms explains why all the attempts to define postmodernism in abstract categories have failed. In a sense, such attempts represent a modern way of capturing the postmodern, they are nets that don't hold the fish. This is even true of the most sophisticated catalogs of the postmodern characteristics, such as the one proposed by Ihab Hassan, which includes: indeterminacy, fragmentation, decanonization, selflessness, depthlessness, the unpresentable unrepresentable, irony, hybridization, carnivalization, performance, participation, constructionism, and immanence.[36]

In my view, this and similar other lists are still presented in modernist terms, in that they leave out the hermeneutic and the existential context that should underlie the combination and concretization of these categories; furthermore, the pragmatic and rhetorical strength that they carry to build a new intellectual mood and a new common sense is also left out. For my part, I would prefer to tell three short stories or, rather, scripts for stories that could be told and

---

34. Richard Rorty, *Philosophy and the Mirror of Nature* (Princeton: Princeton University Press, 1980); H. G. Gadamer, *Wahrheit und Methode*, 2d ed. (Tubingen: J. C. B. Mohr, 1965) and *Reason in the Age of Science* (Cambridge, Mass.: MIT Press, 1983); Paul Feyerabend, *Against Method* (London: New Left Books, 1978) and *Realism, Rationalism, and Scientific Method* (Cambridge: Cambridge University Press, 1981) and *Science in a Free Society* (London: Verso, 1985); Edgar Morin, *Science avec Conscience* (Paris: Fayard, 1982).

35. Chaim Perelman, *The New Rhetoric: A Treatise on Argumentation* (Bloomington: Indiana University Press, 1971).

36. Ihab Hassan, *The Postmodern Turn* (Columbus: Ohio State University Press, 1987), 167

THE POSTMODERN TRANSITION

performed in educational communities. Each story is a partial story very much in the sense that, according to William James, "the world is full of partial stories that run parallel to one another, beginning and ending at odd times."[37] From each story a rhetorical topos can be drawn, but the persuasive or argumentative power of each one of them derives, above all, from the rhetorical chain or sequence in which it is integrated.

The Known and the Unknown

The first story tells us that modern knowledge is a strange bird with wings that don't match. One of the wings, called complicity, flies low, touching the roofs of government offices and business head-quarters; the other, called critique, flies high, half hidden by the clouds. It is not surprising that such a misshapen bird should collide in the mountains of our reflexivity. As we inspect the ruins, we are persuaded that we are still alive by collecting the following topoi in the rubble.

The first topos goes like this: *"Don't touch. This is human."* Our present epistemological situation is a dilemmatic one: ignorance is still unpardonable, but knowledge is sometimes unbearable. Let's take the example of research in genetics and genetic engineering. We must reasonably suspect that, as we know more in this field, it will become more likely that human beings will be the next, and the ultimate commodity. If so, then perhaps we need a guard to shout in favor of the human, much in the same way that the guard of the exhibition of postmodern art in Kassel shouted in favor of the auton-omy of art when Huyssen's child ran his fingers over the surfaces of one of the works in the exhibition: "Nicht berühren. Das ist kunst" ["Don't touch. That is art"].[38]

Second topos: *It doesn't matter if it is not real, provided that it is near.* Modern knowledge in general (modern science as well as mod-ern art, modern ethics, and law) is based on representation, that is, on the creation and isolation of the other, called object, which the self, called subject, then describes as being what it is independent of any creative intervention by the self. Representation thus creates a

37. William James, *Pragmatism* (Cleveland: Meridian Books, 1969), 98.
38. Huyssen, *After the Great Divide*, 179.

distance, the greater the distance, the more objective the knowledge. In a recent analysis of seventeenth-century Dutch painting, Susan Sontag emphasized the way the artist combines "the atmospherics of remoteness with accuracy of depiction, depiction of a real church from a real viewpoint, though never from a near one."[39] Indeed the real and the near have always been antagonistic in modern knowledge. Postmodern knowledge, in its turn, favors the near to the detriment of the real. To be pragmatic is to approach reality from James's "last things," that is, from consequences, and the shorter the distance between acts and consequences, the greater the accuracy of the judgment on validity. On the other hand, because it is rhetorical, postmodern knowledge longs for oral, face-to-face communication, which, as Walter Ong has shown, is situational, close to the human life-world, empathetic and participatory rather than objectively distanced.[40] Postmodern knowledge is thus local, but being local it is also total. The localism involved is the localism of context, not the localism of static spaces and immemorial traditions. It is an internationalist localism, without a solid genius loci, very much like the localism of the new generation of U.S. (or rather New York) objectistic artists, the "new objectistics," according to Bonito Oliva's interpretation of their work.[41]

Finally, the third topos: *From affirmation to critique through alternatives.* Modern critical theory affirms itself by negating the world, by confronting it or by escaping from it, but always possessed by the anxiety of contamination. This posture is premised upon two conditions: the distance effect produced by the representation view of knowledge; and the conception of social reality as a monolithic present. I have already criticized the first condition. As to the second, its untenability becomes more evident as we enter an age of instantaneous social time, of high-speed reality, of televisual experience, of images governed by an aesthetic of disappearance, as Paul Virilio puts it.[42] It becomes now clear that there are generations of reality

---

39. Susan Sontag, "The Pleasure of the Image," *Art in America*, November 1987, 125.

40. Walter Ong, *Orality and Literacy* (London: Methuen, 1982), 36.

41. A. Bonito Olivia, "Neo-America," *Flash Art* 138 (1988): 62.

42. Paul Virilio, "Interview with Paul Virilio," *Flash Art* 138 (1988): 57.

as there are generations of images. There are emergent realities as there are testimonial, transplanted, or residual realities. The specific existential situation of the emergent realities is that the last layers of reality have a surplus of meaning that necessarily spills over them. Thus, the emergent reality cannot help being affirmative before being critical. How is it then possible to be affirmative without being accomplice, critical without being escapist? Through the constant production of alternatives, one assumes the risk of absorption by constantly renewing and recycling reality. Postmodern critical theory is positive in this sense, tirelessly looking for genuine shreds of content in manipulation and domination, putting them to the alternative use of creating new spaces of emancipation. It then assumes the dive into reality in search of a new common sense. Postmodern critical theory is thus both polyphonic and agonistic: against knowledge it creates knowledges, and against knowledges, counterknowledges.

The Desirable and the Possible

The second script deals with the new situation of discrepancy between the desirable and the possible that we are living in. When the desirable was impossible it was handed over to God; when the desirable became possible it was handed over to science. Now that part of the desirable is again impossible, and part of the possible is undesirable, we cannot count on either God or science. We can only count on ourselves. And because everything is in our hands, it is not surprising that we have become increasingly interested in language (hence the second Wittgenstein), in persuasion and the power of knowledge (hence Nietzsche, Foucault, and the New Rhetoric), and, finally, in human communication and interaction (hence the revival of U.S. pragmatism).

To cultivate our new interests I imagine a new kind of school offering two classes: in the first class, where the consciousness of excess is taught, we learn not to desire everything that is possible just because it is possible; in the second class, where the consciousness of deficit is taught, we learn to desire the impossible. The students of reactionary postmodernism attend only the first class; the students of progressive postmodernism attend both classes at the same time. The aim of the communication going on in these classes is not to obtain consensus, as Habermas would have it, but rather to formulate new radical needs in agonistically toned ways, as Agnes Heller would suggest.[43]

However, this description does not suffice to distinguish postmodern critical theory from modern critical theory. After all, both Habermas and Heller subscribe to the latter. What distinguishes postmodern critical theory is that the radical needs are not to be formulated by another radical philosophy; they will, instead, arise out of the socio-aesthetic imagination lodged in emancipatory everyday practices. Only the embeddedness in the near, even if it is a new, unfamiliar near, can achieve the reenchantment of the world. Some emergent social conditions seem to point in this direction. In a recent paper, Ernst Gellner declares himself, even if with some misgivings, disenchanted with the disenchantment thesis. As we know, the thesis states that the modern world's "Faustian purchase" of cognitive, technological, and administrative power forced us to exchange our previous, meaningful and humanly responsive world for "a more predictable, more amenable, but coldly indifferent and uncosy world."[44] This is the well-known iron cage to which Weber has condemned us. Gellner, however, argues that the iron cage only applied to the emergence of industrial society. Today, as the working week shrinks and leisure expands and as the activities requiring Cartesian thought diminish, we are leaving the iron cage and entering a rubber cage. In my view, the rubber cage is still a cage, and so it will remain if the desirable and the possible are not redefined in postmodern times. As much as the modernization theory, modern critical theory converted the desirable and the possible into functional values; the difference between the two theories lies in the way they identify the functions and the social groups that benefit from them. For postmodern critical theory, the desirable and the possible are also aesthetic values and their functionality cannot be separated from their beauty. In this, as in many other instances, postmodern thought innovates by quotation, by recuperating and recycling degraded forms of modernity. We are used to considering Saint-Simon as the father of modernization theory, and of the idea of converting science

43. For a comparison between Heller's and Habermas's thought, see Sandor Radnoti, "A Critical Theory of Communication: Agnes Heller's Confession to Philosophy," *Thesis Eleven* 16 (1987): 104.

44. Ernest Gellner, *Culture, Identity, and Politics* (Cambridge: Cambridge University Press, 1987), 153.

and technology into the great engine of progress, thereby gradually replacing politics by the administration of things. However, if we look at the way he conceived the new political system in 1819–20, it becomes clear that, for him, the desirable and the possible were both inseparably useful and beautiful. In his vision, the first chamber of the House of Commons, called the Chamber of Invention, would consist of 300 members, among whom there would be 200 civil engineers, 50 poets and other literary inventors, 25 painters, 15 sculptors and architects, and 10 musicians. This chamber would be in charge of presenting public projects, the most important of which would be what we would call today physical infrastructures. But he adds that "the roads and canals to be built should not be conceived only as a means of facilitating transport; their construction should be planned so as to make them as pleasant as possible for travelers."[45] As if fearing that this might not be totally clear or deemed important, he adds in a footnote:

> Fifty thousand acres of land (more, if it is thought right) will be chosen from the most picturesque sites crossed by roads or canals. This ground will be authorized for use as resting-places for travellers and holiday resorts for the inhabitants of the neighbourhood. Each of these gardens will contain a museum of both natural and industrial products of the surrounding districts. They will also include dwellings for artists who want to stop there, and a certain number of musicians will always be maintained there to inspire the inhabitants of the canton with that passion whose development is necessary for the greatest good of the nation.[46]

Interest and Capacity

According to the third script, modern men and women used to live in a frontier city whose dynamic transformation was based on the equation *interest* = *capacity*. Whoever had an interest in the processes of transformation also had the adequate capacity to carry them on.

45. Henri Saint-Simon, *Henri Saint-Simon (1760–1825): Selected Writings on Science, Industry, and Social Organization*, ed. K. Taylor (London: Croom Helm, 1975), 203.
46. Ibid., 203.

The greater the interest, the greater the capacity. Liberal political thought was premised upon the idea that the bourgeoisie was among the different classes the most interested in the development of capitalism and, hence, the most capable of bringing it about. Similarly, Marxist theory was premised upon the idea that the working class was the most interested in overcoming capitalism and, as such, the most capable of doing it. With unsurpassable eloquence, the *Communist Manifesto* of 1848, without any doubt one of the great texts of our modernity, links the privileged historical role of the working class in carrying out the social revolution to the fact that this class, contrary to all the others, had nothing to lose except its chains.

As the years went by, modern men and women moved to a Euro-American suburb, and there the equation *interest = capacity* seems to have collapsed. Even assuming that the working classes still have an interest in overcoming capitalism, they most patently lack the capacity to do it. And if, as a theoretical hypothesis, we argue that the capacity, though dormant, is still there, it then appears that they have lost interest in putting their capacity to work.

In the meantime, the last two decades have witnessed the emergence of broadly based social groups interested in the so-called postmaterialist struggles: peace, the defense of the environment, the struggle against the nuclear holocaust, and the fight against sexual and racial discrimination. Such struggles are faced with three major problems. The first one can be formulated in dilemmatic terms: the broader the interest (for instance, the interest in peace or ecology when compared with the interest in sexual and racial equality), the greater the difficulty in identifying the historical subject most capable of leading the social struggle. The second problem is that the difficulty in matching interest and capacity is further complicated by the difficulty in knowing, in advance, which of such interests and struggles can be fought for successfully in capitalist societies and which of them can only succeed if and when capitalism is overcome and replaced by socialism. In the latter case, many people find themselves in the inverted position of that described by the *Communist Manifesto*: they have a great interest in the success of the struggle but, at the same time, feel that they have a lot to lose with the transformations that will thereby occur. To the extent that such struggles can succeed within capitalism, a third problem arises: provided that the struggles succeed and deliver the goods they are supposed to deliver, how to avoid the social devaluation of such goods. In the past, capitalism has been able to devalue such goods either by turning them into new opportunities for profitable enterprise or by circumscribing them to a separate and segregated sector of social action, called the political.

Politics and Law in the Postmodern Transition

The central thesis of this section is: A new theory of subjectivity is needed to account for the fact that we are an increasingly complex network of subjectivities. Out of the ruins of social collectivism, the collectivism of the self is emerging. The struggle against the monopolies of interpretation must be conducted in a way that leads to the proliferation of political and legal interpretive communities. The controlled dispersal of the legal realm will contribute to decanonize and to trivialize law. The end of legal fetishism will mark the emergence of a new legal minimalism and of microrevolutionary practices.

I will now try to justify this thesis by bringing my scripts to bear on a postmodern and critical understanding of law and politics. The last script (interest and capacity) shows that a discrepancy has been growing between the scale of interests in social transformation and the organization of capacities to struggle for them. As some interests become global, the enemy to fight against seems to vanish, which, contrary to what might have been expected, has not facilitated the organization of those wanting to get actively involved in the struggles. This has aggravated the impasse of modern critical theory and, in particular, of orthodox Marxist theory, an impasse that has crystallized in a double reification: the reification of the historical subject and the reification of the political mediation for the deployment of social capacities. The emergence of postmodern critical theory is premised upon the supersession of this double reification.

The reification of the historical subject consists of the a priori historical privilege granted to class and to class politics, that is, and to use Laclau's and Mouffe's words, "the idea that the working class represents the privileged agent in which the fundamental impulse of social change resides."[47] The critique of this reification has been bril-

---

47. Ernesto Laclau and C. Mouffe, *Hegemony and Socialist Strategy: Towards a Radical Democratic Politics* (London: Verso, 1985), 177.

liantly made by Laclau and Mouffe. But, contrary to their view, it is
neither necessary nor correct to go to the other extreme and conclude
that "society has no essence," that is, that it is impossible to account
in sociotheoretical terms for the problem of historical determination.[48] In my view, the most important task for social theory today is
combining global contingency with local determinisms, structure
with agency. If essence is to be conceived in monolithic terms, be it
the society, in all versions of holism (starting with Durkheim), or the
individual, in the recent theories of methodological individualism, it
is only correct to be antiessentialist. But between the essence conceived as a monolithic ontological entity and the nonessentialism of
infinite contingencies, there is the middle ground of a pluralist view
of essences, of a controlled dispersal of social structures.[49]

As far as the question of the historical subject goes, I think that
instead of fixing the a priori priority of a historical subject, as orthodox Marxism did, or instead of sweeping the question of the subject
under the carpet of social knowledge, as both structuralists and
poststructuralists have done, the task ahead consists of analyzing, in
concrete terms, our historical trajectories as subjects both at the bio-
graphical and the macrolevel. Modern men and women are configurations or networks of different subjectivities, and, even though the
internal differentiation of the self is a historical variable, as Agnes
Heller has rightly pointed out, I submit that the differentiation is
neither infinite nor chaotic.[50] As I have proposed elsewhere, contemporary capitalist societies consist of four structural places to which
four structural subjectivities correspond: the subjectivity of the family
corresponds to the *householdplace;* the subjectivity of the class corresponds to the *workplace;* the subjectivity of the individual corresponds
to the *citizenplace;* and the subjectivity of the nation corresponds to
the *worldplace.*[51]

This is not the occasion to provide a full explanation of this
analytical framework. It should merely be mentioned that modern

48. Nico Mouzelis, "Marxism or Post-Marxism," *New Left Review* 167 (1988): 107.
49. My paper on modes of production of law and social power is an attempt to
present such a pluralistic view of structures (Santos, "On Modes of Production").
50. According to Agnes Heller, "the internal differentiation of the Self is itself a
variable . . . it is not only a historical, but also a 'personal' variable" ("The Human
Condition," *Thesis Eleven* 16 [1987]: 4).
51. Santos, "On Modes of Production."

men and women are configurations of these four basic subjectivities. Of course, they are also many other subjectivities (for instance, male/ female, black/white) but all of them are grounded in the four basic ones. On the other hand, the specific configuration of subjectivities varies according to different historical conditions, according to different periods of our lives, or even according to daily routines or circumstances. We attend the meetings of our children's schools as members of a family, go shopping or read the newspaper as individuals, attend the match of our national team as nationals. In all these occasions or situations we are all four, and perhaps even other subjectivities, at the same time, but as the occasions or situations vary, one different basic subjectivity gets the privilege of organizing the specific configuration of subjectivities that accounts for our behavior and attitudes. In this respect, the social and scientific construct of a postmodern critical theory is based on the idea that out of the ruins of social collectivism the collectivism of the self is emerging.

The second reification of critical modern theory, the reification of the political mediation for the deployment of social capacities, consists of the reification of the state. This reification is indeed central to liberal political theory, from which critical theory borrows, and consists of reducing the political to a segregated sector of social action, and in conceiving the latter as action of and/or through the state. This reification gained great prominence in the period of organized capitalism and found its most accomplished expression in the political form of the welfare state.

The crisis of this conception is now apparent. Postmodern critical theory is based on two ideas. First, the hyperpoliticization of the state is the other side of the depoliticization of civil society. Confined to a specific sector of social action, the public sphere, the democratic ideal of modern politics has been neutralized or strongly limited in its emancipatory potential.[52] Second, freedom is not a natural human good that has to be preserved against politics as liberal political theory claims.[53] On the contrary, the broader the political realm the greater the freedom. The end of politics will always mean, in one way or another, the end of freedom.

Based on these two ideas and following Foucault, I suggest that

---

52. Ibid., 306.

53. A critique of the liberal conception of freedom as a prepolitical essence can be read in Hannah Arendt, *Between Past and Future* (Cleveland: Meridian Books, 1963), 149.

there is politics wherever there are power relations. But again I think, and now contrary to Foucault, that we cannot go to the extreme of giving up the task of structuring and grading power forms and power relations. If power is everywhere, it is nowhere. In my view, the four structural places I mentioned before are the loci of four major power forms circulating in our society.[54] These power forms are: patriarchy, corresponding to the householdplace; exploitation, corresponding to the workplace; domination, corresponding to the citizenplace; and unequal exchange, corresponding to the worldplace. There are other forms of power, but these are the basic ones. None of these forms of power is political in itself. It is the combinations among them that make them political, each one, then, political in its own way. Of all four forms of power, only one, domination, is democratic, and even so in a limited degree and in a small group of countries in which the advanced capitalist societies are included. The political aim of postmodern critical theory is to extend the democratic ideal to all other forms of power. Socialism is but the tireless continuing expansion and intensification of democratic practices. This aim, because it has no limit itself, will inevitably show the limit of capitalism, the point at which capitalist social relations will have to block the further expansion of democratic emancipation.

The global but not indiscriminate politicization of social relations will mark the end of the monopolies of political interpretation at the same time that it will ensure that renunciation of interpretation, typical of mass consumption societies, will not follow. While for modern critical theory, the radical democratization of social and personal life had only one enemy, the monopolies of interpretation (be they religion, the state, the family, or the party), for postmodern critical theory there are two enemies, both equally fierce: the monopolies of interpretation and the renunciation of interpretation. To fight against both of them there is only one alternative: the proliferation of political interpretive communities. Softly structured by the specific combinations of subjectivities and of forms of social power, such communities are the social basis of a new political common sense, a new political commitment based on old and new civic virtues in Dewey's sense, that is, virtues that are not poured on us as the metaphysical overflows of any deus ex machina but that, rather, emerge from the

---

54. Santos, "On Modes of Production," 309.

familiar and the near. In this sense, Charles Jencks is right when he includes among postmodernist values the idea that "the human presence is back even if it's on the edge."[55] The human presence is back but not as an unreflexive identity dissolved in deep-rooted traditions. Our roots are on permanent display; they are the rhizome that proliferates on the deep surface and on the momentary eternity of our meaningful encounters. Traditional communities in advanced capitalist societies would be of as little use for us as the medieval guilds were for Durkheim when he proposed the reconstruction of the *corps intermédiaires* (between the state and the individual), the lack of which accounted (in his view) for the rampant anomie in French society at the turn of the century.[56]

The proliferation of political interpretive communities represents the postmodern way and, indeed, the only reasonable way of defending the accomplishments of modernity. I mentioned earlier, among such accomplishments, a fairer distribution of economic resources and a significant democratization of the political system in the conventional sense. As with all processes of transition, the postmodern transition also has a dark side and a bright side. The dark side is that, as the reification of class and of state are further exposed, the modern tools used until now to fulfill and consolidate those promises, that is, class politics and the welfare state, become less reliable and less efficient. The proliferation of political interpretive communities will broaden the political agenda in two convergent directions. On the one hand, it will emphasize the social value of extraeconomic or postmaterialist goods such as ecology and peace; on the other hand, it will expand the concept and the practice of democracy in order to incorporate direct participatory (or base) democracy. The success of the struggle for extraeconomic goods will be conditioned by the success of the struggle for economic goods and for a fairer distribution of economic resources. The struggle for participatory democracy will prevent the emasculation of representative democracy. It is in this sense that the promises of modernity can only be defended, from now on, in postmodern terms.

The postmodern understanding of law starts from here. I will

---

55. Jencks, *Post-Modernism*, 11.

56. Emile Durkheim, *The Division of Labor in Society* (New York: Free Press, 1964), preface to the 2d ed.

concentrate on the topics that, from my point of view, will be most crucial in constructing a new legal common sense.

The End of the Monopolies of Legality

The movement toward a postmodern understanding of law began in the 1960s with the studies of legal pluralism in complex societies, followed by the focus on the informalization of justice. The theoretical and normative claims behind these studies could be traced back to some of the debates in the continental legal philosophy of the nineteenth century, but they were new to the extent that they were sociologically grounded and informed by a progressive political stance. These studies were also very much part of the dominant sociolegal paradigm, that is, the critical analysis of the discrepancy between law in books and law in action with the purpose of contributing positively to the greater efficiency of the official legal system.

The problem with these studies was that these two dimensions, the critical and the positive, did not quite match. Explicitly or implicitly, such studies contained a devastating critique of the official legal system, but they were content to contribute to some minor improvements in the operations of the system. With the privilege of hindsight we can say today that, to the extent that these studies addressed themselves to legislators or state bureaucracies, they were bound to fail.[57] The current disenchantment with this scientific agenda, with the co-optation of its critical potential and with the perverse consequences of some of its proposals, expresses that sense of failure. To my mind, such failure could have been avoided if, instead of addressing itself to the state bureaucrats, this scientific agenda had spoken to the people in general or to specific social groups (i.e., different addresses of legal discourse) and tried to generate a new legal common sense in them. The genuine shred of utopian content of these studies lies in the verification that, in the same geopolitical space, there are not one but many different legal orders and that, accordingly, the claim of the state to a monopoly on the production and

---

57. Austin Sarat and Susan Silbey, "The Pull of the Policy Audience" *Law and Policy* 10 (1988): 97.

distribution of law is absurd. As much as we are networks of subjectivities and enter social relations in which different combinations of
forms of power are present, we also live in different and overlapping
legal orders and legal communities. Each one of them operates in a
privileged social space and has a specific temporal dynamic. Since the
social spaces interpenetrate and the different legal orders are nonsyn-
chronic, the particular stocks of legal meanings that we activate in
specific practical contexts are often complex mixtures, not only of
different conceptions of legality but also of different generations of
laws, some old some new, some declining some emerging, some
native some imported, and some testimonial some imposed.

Corresponding to the four basic subjectivities and forms of
power, I identify four basic forms of law that circulate in society:
domestic law, that is, the native law of the family; production law,
which includes the factory codes and internal regulations of corporations; territorial law, which is the law in the conventional and official
sense; and finally, systemic law that regulates the relations among
the nation-states and that extends far beyond the domain of international law.[58] There are many other legal orders in society, but these
are the basic ones in that they structure the ways in which all the
others operate. This controlled dispersal of legal orders has two important implications for the postmodern understanding of law: first,
of the four forms of law only one, territorial law, is democratic, even
if not completely so. The democratic content of this form of law can
only be expanded or merely secured if the democratization of the
other forms of law becomes central to the participatory political
agenda. Second, relativized in this way, law in general and most
particularly state law is trivialized and decanonized (and, accordingly, the distinction between "high law" and "low law" tends to
disappear). The emancipatory social value of a given legal order lies
in its capacity to secure and expand individual and collective rights
(in the last instance, rights are forms of social competence). The modern understanding of law made law sacred and trivialized rights. The
postmodern understanding of law trivializes law and makes rights
sacred.

---

58. Santos, "On Modes of Production," 309.

From Modeling to Repetition: Toward a New
Legal Minimalism

Modern state law has undergone many changes in the three periods of the development of capitalism. In the first period, the major legal developments aimed at expanding and consolidating the principle of the market. In the period of organized capitalism, state law was specifically characterized by the consolidation and expansion of the principle of the state and the principle of the community. In the current period of disorganized capitalism, the trends carried over from the previous period seem, on the surface, to go on undisturbed. At a deeper level, however, some important changes are taking place. I summarize them as the relative cancellation of the symbolic value of law occurring in the transition from maximal law to minimal law.

In the first and, even more so, in the second period, modern state law was typically a maximal law. The political construction of legal reformism as the hegemonic mode of social transformation endowed state law with imperialistic powers that were used to declare the death of a double enemy: social revolution on the one hand and all kinds of popular, nonstate, nonofficial law on the other. The death rituals were performed in different ways in different periods. Out of them emerged state law as a unique, autonomous, and auratic law. The aura, which as in modern art was inscribed from the start in its uniqueness, was further amplified by the prestige of legal science, particularly in continental Europe, and by the social power of law schools both in Europe and in North America. Fixed in the solid sculptures of legal codes, high court decisions, and leading articles in leading scientific journals, modern state law was allowed to make Comte's slogan of "order and progress" come true, and to plan the future sometimes as a repetition of the present, sometimes as modeling of controlled social innovation. Grounded on the persistence of its building materials, modern state law, as much as modern art, adopted an aesthetic of appearance and permanence in which the dynamics of an eternal present contrasted both with the ephemeral past and the trivial future.

In recent years two complementary changes have occurred that undermine the pedestal upon which this legal posture stands. First, the growth of the regulatory state and the high speed of legal repetition and legal modeling have led to the increasing obsolescence of state law. Its solid fixity seems to be melting away as if possessed, like the televised images, by an aesthetic of disappearance rather than by an aesthetic of appearance. Second, both at the infrastate level and at the suprastate level, there have been emerging forms of law that are explicitly liquid, ephemeral, ever negotiable, and renegotiable, in sum, disposable. Among many examples I cite two, one at the level of the infrastate, the other at the level of the suprastate. They are respectively the regulations of subcontracting, that is, the particularistic laws and contracts that regulate the relations of production among corporations and the legislation of the European Community.[59] In their very different ways, both examples bear witness to the emergence of a contextual legality, finely tuned to the momentary interests of the parties involved and to the power relations among them.

For these emerging forms of law, the *hic et nunc* becomes a categorical imperative. The hyperproductivity of the social context is not only tolerated but celebrated. Like some U.S. postmodern art, the "new objectistics" I mentioned before, this postmodern legality "deliberately lowers the level of its own traditional atmosphere in order to reestablish for it a function suited to the times."[60] It is an antiauratic law, an interstitial, almost colloquial law, which repeats social relations instead of modeling them, and in such a way that the distinction between professional and nonprofessional legal knowledge (as much as the discrepancy between law in books and law in action) ceases to make sense. Confronted with this new legal minimalism, the sociologist of law is at pains to even identify and isolate the legal dimension of social relations, a situation that echoes that of legal anthropologists in the so-called primitive societies. The real books of the law are more and more the changing images of social relations. But this explains why the situation of the legal sociologist is very different from that of the legal anthropologist. The new minimalism is only possible on the basis of a preexistent tradition of auratic, autonomous, highly professionalized law; indeed minimal law is oftentimes developed by professionals trained in the tradition of maximal law. The hyperproductivity of the social context is a complex

---

59. Maria M. Marques, "A Empresa, o Espaço e o Direito," *Revista Crítica de Ciências Sociais* 22 (1987): 69; Francis Snyder, "New Directions in European Community Law," *Journal of Law and Society* 14 (1987): 167.

60. Olivia, "Neo-America," 66.

phenomenon because the latter is to a great extent saturated by modern legality and has been molded by it. In other words, the contextualization of postmodern legality is a two-way process: as law approximates social reality, social reality approximates law.

This emergent and still very marginal postmodern legality coexists peacefully with modern legality, but as it gains ground it corrodes the symbolic stance of modern legality by forcing it to descend into the materiality of the *hic et nunc*. Slowly but steadily, modern law transits from modeling to repetition, from duration to copresence, and concomitantly from generality to particularism, from abstraction to rematerialization.

Law, Microrevolutions, and Neo-Luddism

The transition from modeling to repetition, from planning to ratification, does not mean that law will disappear completely in the social relations it regulates. Law will go on performing an intensification function through which social relations are rerouted from an ordinary chain of being toward a higher chain of being. The difference will lie in the ways in which such a function will be performed. As law, through its many operators, reaches the understanding that its false utopia is coming to an end, the world as it is becomes more recognizable in the process of its legal intensification. As this occurs, two related phenomena will take place: on the one hand, the limits of social transformation through law will become more apparent; on the other hand, other forms of emancipatory practice will gain or regain social credibility.

Among the limits of law and legal reformism the following will become most prominent. First, state law is one among many forms of law circulating in society, even if it is the most important one. Indeed, it became more and more important in the period of organized capitalism, since the objectives and strategies of reformism and democratization concentrated on state law. In this process, all the other forms of law existing in society were left out of the legal picture and were thus allowed to go on reproducing status quo and undemocratic social relations. As this historical process of reduction and occultation is further exposed, the undemocratic nature of law as a whole is unveiled and even the democratic content of state law is put into question. Since the law of the state, while regulating social relations, is forced to interact and negotiate with other forms of law, its reformist and democratic claims must be contextualized and relativized, particularly in view of the hyperproductivity of the social context diagnosed above. A very recent illustration of this can be found in Kristin Bumiller's brilliant analysis of the ways in which antidiscrimination laws may have, in fact, contributed to perpetuating the victimization of the people they were intended to benefit.[61]

The second limit of law and legal reformism is that authentic legal reformism is hard to achieve and that, whenever achieved, it does not sustain its social meaning for very long. Assuming that the undemocratic content of a given network of legal orders is socially exposed, this exposure will, by itself, contribute to the empowerment of those social groups more victimized by the former occultation. The fairer the distribution of power among groups interested in legal reforms, the harder the negotiations to produce reformist laws and the narrower the scope of the reforms. The laws will accordingly become more particularistic and complex. The idea of the simplification of social reality through law that Weber and most prominently Niklas Luhmann celebrated as the genius of modern law[62] will come to an end, and this is not in itself a bad thing. But it will definitely decanonize and trivialize law in general and the state law in particular. In an age of audiovisual speed and social acceleration, these effects are likely to be intensified by the constant and ever-stronger pressure to renegotiate regulatory agreements or impositions. Under these circumstances, law will be easily trapped in the dilemma: either to remain static and be ignored, or to keep up with social dynamics and be devalued as a normative reference.

The third limit of modern state law has to do with the scale (in cartographic terms) used by law to represent and distort social reality. I have dealt with this topic elsewhere.[63] Here it will suffice to mention that the specific scale used in the representation of reality accounts for the type of phenomena that can or cannot be adequately regulated by law. There are phenomena that, no matter how impor-

---

61. Kristin Bumiller, *The Civil Rights Society* (Baltimore: Johns Hopkins University Press, 1988).

62. Niklas Luhmann, *Legitamation durch Verfahren* (Darmstadt: Luchterhand, 1969).

63. Boaventura de Sousa Santos, "Law: A Map of Misreading," *Journal of Law and Society* 14 (1987): 279.

tant in social terms, cannot be adequately dealt with by law because they fall outside the regulation threshold defined by the scale at which that particular law operates. To give examples, we live in a world of Chernobyl and AIDS. In spite of their seriousness, it seems that neither of these problems can be dealt with adequately by state law, one because it is too public or too collective (Chernobyl), the other because it is too private or too individual (AIDS). As these types of limits become more readily identified, the following question will inevitably emerge: if law cannot adequately deal with some of our most serious problems, why should we treat it so seriously?

The principle of the recognizability of the world that presides over the postmodern understanding of law is not confined to the negative function of identifying the limits of law. It opens up to new positivities. On the one hand, the identification of limits maps, by contrast, social spaces in which nonlegal (illegal or alegal) emancipatory practices may take place. On the other hand, since the identification of the limits goes hand in hand with the expansion of the concept of law and its internal fragmentation in a plurality of legal orders, the ideological claim of legal fetishism becomes more untenable and the alternatives to it correspondingly more credible. Such alternatives can be summarized by the concepts of *microrevolutions* and *neo-Luddism*.

If we closely analyze the reform/revolution debate at the turn of the century, we will conclude that the debate was about different strategies to achieve basically the same goal, that is, socialism. As reformism got the upper hand, the social transformation to be brought about under its name was gradually scaled down and state law was the instrument used to achieve that objective. It can even be argued, in favor of the relative autonomy of the law, that law reconstructed the scale of social transformation to a level that would maximize the efficacy of legal regulation. From then on, a discrepancy was created between the scale of legal reformism and the much larger scale of revolution, a discrepancy that further discredited the revolution.[64] This created no serious problem in advanced capitalist societies as long as legal reformism kept its ideological hegemony intact. In recent years, however, the situation has been changing.

---

64. I speak of social revolution on the large scale for the sake of intelligibility. In cartographic, technical terms, one should speak of the small scale: the larger the real space to be represented in the confined space of the maps, the smaller the scale. See Santos, "Law: A Map of Misreading," 283.

The gradual cancellation of the symbolic aura of law will open a gap in our social imagination. After a century of small-scale legal reformism it is, however, impossible to fill such a gap with the old concept of a large-scale social revolution. A postreformist social revolution can only be a network of microrevolutions to be carried out locally, inside political communities whenever and wherever they are created. To conceptualize such microrevolutions is not an easy task. It may help to proceed by quotation—indeed, a very postmodern way—and try to recuperate, recycle, and reinvent degraded forms of social resistance against oppression. Hence the concept of neo-Luddism. It evokes the destruction of mechanical looms in the first decades of the nineteenth century by English weavers confronted with the introduction of new technologies that would eliminate their autonomy in the work process and further degrade their already wretched life conditions. For many decades, such outbreaks of protest were dismissed as foolish, romantic, and reactionary resistance against the inevitability of progress. In recent times, however, and not altogether by coincidence, the Luddite movement has been reevaluated. The pioneering work of Eric Hobsbawm, followed by others,[65] has contributed to changing the Luddite symbol and converting it into the only rational collective action available to workers before the age of unionization. What is coming into the new political agenda is not the specific means of resistance used by the Luddites but, rather, the invention of forms of social innovation that, like those of the Luddites, confirm and intensify the capacity of autonomous subjectivities to free themselves from the prejudices of legal fetishism.

In the technological age, neo-Luddism will certainly be less violent and naive, but it shall equally bear witness to the intensity of civil engagement and political mobilization only obtainable when the objectives of the struggle are transparent, and the results to be expected are as close as possible to the world of everyday life. Only under these conditions will the struggles be lived as rational, as a minirationality that is only total insofar as it is local. Interpretive and transformative communities will generate these struggles through

---

65. Eric Hobsbawm, *Laboring Men* (New York: Weidenfeld and Nicolson, 1964); Jeffrey Wasserstrom, "Civilization and Its Discontents: The Boxers and Luddites as Heroes and Villains," *Theory and Society* 16 (1987): 675.

processes of rhetorical persuasion that get their argumentative am-
munition from the topoi that can be squeezed out of the scripts of
partial stories about knowledge, desire, and capacity that I referred
to previously. It does not matter if such minirationalities are light-
weight, portable, or even pocket rationalities, provided that they explode in our pockets.

Disciplines, Subjectivity, and Law

Robin West

Professor Sarat has asked that I address this question: Given the modern and postmodern disillusionment with reason, how should we criticize or evaluate a law? How should we go about criticizing law, if not by reference to general principles derived from reason? What does it mean, given the "death of reason," to ask whether a particular law—say, a statute outlawing "surrogacy contracts," or a judicial decision requiring the busing of schoolchildren to achieve integrated schools, or a law criminalizing sexual sodomy, or a constitutional provision or constitutional interpretation invalidating state statutes that criminalize abortions on demand—is a *good* law or a *bad* law, a *just* law or an *unjust* law, a moral law or an amoral law? How are we to evaluate laws, constitutions, judicial decisions, statutes, or legal interpretations, if we have lost faith in the Enlightenment ideal of holding acts of power up to the critical light of reason? What does it mean to question the justice or morality or wisdom of a legal decision, or a particular law, or of the idea of law, or of the rule of law, or of a legal system, if it does not mean to question it against general principles of morality or justice culled from the dictates of reason? If, as the Enlightenment ideal holds, our moral norms are (or should be) the products of pure reason, and if, as the postmodern critics of reason insist, the products of reason we call knowledge, including moral knowledge, are themselves products of power, then how do we, or can we, criticize the law, which is, itself, indisputably, a product of power?

By exposing the purportedly apolitical or neutral Enlightenment standards of reason, morality, generality, and justice as themselves intensely and inevitably political, the modern critics of reason may indeed have liberated legal criticism from a false straitjacket of disingenuous neutrality. But have they also rendered *all* forms of criticism of both law and extant positive morality incoherent? And if they have, is not the almost certain ultimate political consequence of this gigantic unmasking of reason *not* popular liberation, or anything even remotely like it but, rather, a political stagnation, moral complacency, and muting of the critical voice such as we may never have previously encountered? Does not the possibility of moral progress depend entirely on the possibility of moral criticism, and does not the possibility of moral criticism depend entirely on the difference, and on their being a difference, between the power that is the object and the reason that is the method of criticism? Have we won freedom from one false savior—the method of reason—at the cost of all criticism, and hence at the cost of moral, societal, and political progress? If we give up on reason, have we given up on criticism?

Before going on to consider answers to Austin's question—how do we criticize, or morally evaluate, law, if not by reference to reason—let me specify more precisely what I take to be excluded by the postmoderns' exclusion of "reason" as a possible answer. The postmodern critique of reason, as it relates to legal discourse, has sought to explode two particular rationalist faiths. First, it has exploded the philosophical notion that we can articulate, in some sort of Kantian fashion, noncontingent, categorical, abstract moral principles that are discernible through reason alone, and that can then be used as a standard against which to evaluate contingent, particular, and utterly concrete legal commands.[1] The postmodern critique of reason renders incoherent what used to be called (in a more rational-

---

1. For the most general statement of the postmodern and pragmatic critique of traditional Kantian philosophy, see Richard Rorty, *Philosophy and the Mirror of Nature* (Princeton: Princeton University Press, 1979). For applications to legal criticism, evaluation and evolution, see Roberto Unger, *The Critical Legal Studies Movement* (Cambridge, Mass.: Harvard University Press, 1984), and William Joseph Singer, "The Player and the Cards: Nihilism and Legal Theory," *Yale Law Journal* 94 (1984): 1. J. M. Balkin, "Deconstructive Practice and Legal Theory," *Yale Law Journal* 96 (1987): 743.

The most recent defense of Kantian formalism against a postmodern and Ungerian attack is Ernest Weinrib, "Legal Formalism: On the Imminent Rationality of Law," *Yale Law Journal* 97 (1988): 949. Also see Fred Schauer, "Formalism," *Yale Law Journal* 97 (1988): 509.

ist time) deontological arguments about a law or a legal system's moral merit. The deontologist would typically argue that if a law cannot be deductively derived from a categorical moral truth or an abstract principle of justice, then the law is unjust, bad, or unwise. Thus, if, for example, a statute or a judicial decision forbidding surrogacy contracts violates a categorical moral imperative that individuals should be allowed to do as they wish with their bodies so long as those actions do not hurt others, then the law or decision that forbids surrogacy contracts is unjust. The postmodern critics of reason have attempted to show that there simply are no categorical, noncontingent, and nonpolitical "neutral truths" of justice or morality of the sort just described that have sufficient content to serve as a base of criticism. Purportedly neutral truths of justice or morality, according to the modern critics of reason, are themselves inherently political and contingent; they are no more noncontingent, abstract, or categorical than the very concrete and particular legal norms they are being used to judge. Deontological moral criticism of law is at best incoherent and at worst self-serving, if it is true, as the postmodern critics claim, that there are no categorical moral truths that can serve as the major premises of deontological arguments.

The second rationalist faith exploded by the critique of reason is the notion that there are empirical, contingent, but nonetheless universal and knowable "truths," or facts about human nature, that can, in turn, ground a knowable conception of the human good, and that can itself then be used as a standard against which to judge particular laws or particular legal systems. This critique renders incoherent what used to be called teleological arguments about a law or a legal system's morality. The teleologist (or consequentialist) specifies a conception of the moral good by identifying some aspect of "human nature" with which the "good" is identified, and then criticizes a law or legal system by asking whether the law being criticized either furthers or frustrates that good.[2] If, for example, a Supreme Court

2. For an excellent example of teleological legal criticism see William Fisher, III, "Reconstructing the Fair Use Doctrine," *Harvard Law Review* 101 (1988): 1661. Critiques of teleological reasoning within the legal literature have been heavily influenced by deconstructivist methodology, and, consequently, the critique takes a particular form: the critic tries to show that the particular human "attribute" reflected in legal-linguistic constructs is, in fact, one of a paired polarity, such that the "human nature" reflected in legal language is contradictory, and that the side of the pole valorized serves a particular set of socially empowered interests. See, e.g., Mark Kelman, *A Guide to*

decision requiring busing furthers communal diversity, or a constitutional interpretation invalidating antiabortion laws furthers individual autonomy, and if diversity and autonomy are necessary aspects
of the good life because they complement some aspect of our intrinsic
human nature, then that decision and that constitutional interpretation are both good, or just. The second prong of the postmodern
attack on reason shows that such purportedly "universal" facts of
human nature are in fact not general at all, but, rather, are true only
of particular human communities, or subcommunities, or interests,
or cultures, or races, or classes, or genders. The critics have suc-
ceeded through these demonstrations in casting doubt upon the notion that there is any shared "human nature" out there to be discovered at all that can serve as a basis of criticism, much less a human
nature that is knowable. Teleological moral criticism of law is similarly, then, at best incoherent and at worst self-serving, if the critics
are right that the conception of the good and the vision of human
nature used as their foundations are conceptions and descriptions
only of some subcommunity—be it a political, gendered, national,
or cultural subcommunity—and not of the human species as a whole.
The conception of the good, if the critic is right, is serving a particular
political agenda—the ends of power—rather than the ends of reason
or the good of the human community.

Austin's question, then, as I understand it, is whether and how
we can criticize law, if not by reference to reason, by which is meant
either categorical moral truths divined by pure reason or, alternatively, a theory of the good in turn grounded in universal but concrete
truths about human nature, derived through rational methods of
empirical inquiry. Put in terms of disciplines, the question is this: To
what source of wisdom, to what discipline, should the legal critic
turn, if not to traditional moral philosophy—the disciplined study of
abstract truths of morality—and if not to traditional social science—
the disciplined study of empirical truths of human and societal na-

---

Critical Legal Studies (Cambridge, Mass.: Harvard University Press, 1987); Duncan
Kennedy, "Form and Substance in Private Law Adjudication," *Harvard Law Review* 89
(1976): 1685; Claire Dalton, "An Essay in the Deconstruction of Contract Doctrine," *Yale
Law Journal* 94 (1987): 997. For nondeconstructionist critiques that expose the influence
of interest and privilege in attempts to locate a universal nature, see Paul Brest, "In-
terpretation and Interest," *Stanford Law Review* 34 (1982): 765; and Mark Tushnet, *Red,
White, and Blue: A Critical Analysis of Constitutional Law* (Cambridge, Mass.: Harvard
University Press, 1988).

ture? This is the central question, I believe, for the legal academy in our generation, and it is for that reason that I am so grateful to Austin for having finally posed it. I believe that neither mainstream nor progressive legal scholars have managed to answer it, and that the failure has led to what can fairly be called a moral crisis in modern law schools.

The first and shortest section of this essay quickly reviews the major response to the question that has emerged from the legal academy, an answer I will call "legal authoritarianism." The second and major section of this essay will critically examine a far more promising set of responses to Austin's question in greater detail. Those responses are presently being propounded and explored by the developing interdisciplinary movements in U.S. law schools. The various interdisciplinary movements now overtaking the traditional legal academy, I will argue, constitute and even have their genesis in an attempt to answer Austin's question. That attempt, however, has been largely unsuccessful, and the reason for that failure is the main topic of the second section of this essay. The third section, drawing heavily on the lessons to be learned from both the promise and failure of interdisciplinary legal studies, suggests my own response.

Legal Authoritarianism

From the perspective of traditional legal scholarship, Austin's question is both peculiar and dangerous. The peculiarity is this: for the vast majority of both doctrinal and theoretical legal scholars (as well as the vast majority of lawyers and judges) Austin's question is oddly *irrelevant*. For most mainstream legal academics, it is not now and has never been *reason*, meaning either abstract morality or a view of human nature, that does or should constitute the standard against which particular laws, decisions, or doctrines should be judged. For most legal scholars, it is law itself—the legal system taken as a whole—rather than either the dictates of reason, or norms of morality derived from knowable human nature, that is the proper moral standard—or baseline—against which to judge particular legal acts or decisions.[3] Although ultimately bankrupt, this view—which I would

3. The most powerful and sophisticated explanation of this idea comes from Ronald Dworkin. See generally Ronald Dworkin, *Law's Empire* (Cambridge, Mass.: Harvard University Press, 1986), *A Matter of Principle* (Cambridge, Mass.: Harvard

call "legal authoritarianism"—is not incoherent. Law is, after all, a normative and critical system of some subtlety and considerable complexity, with numerous axioms and critical habits of thought. It is surely *possible*, whether or not justifiable, to judge the value of a law by reference to the law's own internal critical and normative apparatus. We can ask, for example, whether the decision in a particular contracts case—say a decision that a surrogacy contract is unenforceable because unconscionable—is or is not in line with the development of contracts principles more largely defined. Furthermore, if we feel that our contract law, taken as a whole, is properly and morally grounded in a respect for individual freedom and dignity, then our legal analysis of the implications of contract law for the particular case might constitute a moral analysis as well. To decide or criticize the legality of the opinion will feel like a critique of the morality of the opinion as well, if we feel confident in the morality of the legal standard that forms the baseline of the legal analysis. Similarly, constitutional theorists typically take it as an article of faith that the Constitution—itself a legal document—constitutes a moral as well as legal criterion against which to judge particular laws. An argument against the *constitutionality* of a law is consequently typically felt by both legal theorist and constitutional lawyer to have moral as well as legal import. This attitudinal stance toward the morality of law dominates mainstream contemporary jurisprudence. For better or worse, most legal scholars hold some form of the view that the total universe of authoritative legal rules and principles constitutes the relevant moral norm against which to judge the morality as well as the legality of particular legal rules or laws.

The effect of the dominance of legalistic authoritarianism in contemporary legal education, pedagogy, and scholarship—despite the occasional intrusions of other disciplines and the growing chorus of dissenting voices—is that, at least in the moral sense, legal theory is decidedly in a pre-Enlightenment stage of development, not Enlightenment, and certainly not post-Enlightenment. The morality of legal power—the morality of law—has rarely been decided, in the legal academy, by reference to norms culled from reason; instead, law is typically judged by reference to the dictates of legalism. More simply,

---

University Press, 1985), and *Taking Rights Seriously* (Cambridge, Mass.: Harvard University Press, 1977).

for the legally trained, particular acts of power are typically criticized by reference to other particular acts of power. Indeed, this nonrationalist, pre-Enlightenment, attitudinal stance toward the moral authority of law is so thoroughly ingrained in legal education and legal scholarship that *it*, rather than the faith in reason so characteristic of the Enlightenment, and so characteristic of other disciplines and professions, may well be the determining characteristic of the "legalistic mind."[4] To put one's faith in the morality of legal authority, rather than in reason, may be what is meant by the phrase "think like a lawyer." To "think like a lawyer," in other words, might *mean* that one has learned to take an essentially authoritarian stance toward the entire enterprise of legal thought and criticism.

That authoritarianism is so entrenched in legal education and scholarship suggests the danger I see in Austin's question. The danger is that the postmodern critique of reason will further entrench the preexisting authoritarian and self-referential instincts of the legal academy. Legal authorities of all sorts—the legal system, legal doctrine, precedent, the rule of law—are bound to become all the more appealing as bases for the moral criticism of particular laws, as the possibility of a critical morality derived from some source other than power (such as reason) comes increasingly under attack. With the postmodern critique of reason, in other words, the preexisting legalistic tendency to view legal authority itself as a sufficient standard against which to criticize particular laws or legal decisions need no longer rest solely on a head-in-the-sand refusal to consider the teachings of philosophical or empirical sciences. It can rest, instead, on a sophisticated skepticism that philosophical studies and empirical sciences have nothing normative to offer.

We see this reinforcement of self-referential authoritarianism, I believe, in the only self-conscious, modern response to Austin's question that has emerged from the academy. An increasing number of pragmatic, Rorty-inspired legal scholars have begun to develop a distinctively postmodern form of "legal neopragmatism" as a self-consciously normative response to the modern attack on reason.[5] The

---

4. Some mainstream legal theorists are more forthright about this than others. See, e.g., Paul Carrington, "Of Law and the River," *Journal of Legal Education* 34 (1984): 222.

5. Examples include Singer, "Player and the Cards"; John Stick, "Can Nihilism Be Pragmatic?" *Harvard Law Review* 100 (1986): 332; Joan Williams, "Critical Legal Stud-

new legal pragmatism can best be understood, I think, as yet another attempt to ground the criticism of law in preexisting legal materials, but this time the legal self-referencing is justified not by a belief in the omnipotence or benevolence of law, but rather by the brute force of necessity. Thus, the argument of the modern legal pragmatists seems to be that the modern critique of reason leaves us with no choice. For at least these scholars, the critique of reason that now preoccupies the humanistic and social-scientific disciplines has made the preexisting and relatively unthinking legalistic tendency to shy away from a reasoned critique of law—an attitude we ought to be ashamed of—entirely respectable. In other words, it is now intellectually acceptable for pragmatic, modern legal academics and judges, of either the progressive left or right, to criticize particular laws by reference to more general norms culled from law, or, to put the point more baldly, to criticize acts of power by reference to norms drawn from other acts of power. If the postmodern critique of reason is right, the argument goes, there simply is no alternative. Power is all there is.

For reasons I have elaborated upon elsewhere,[6] I think that this pre-Enlightenment authoritarian attitudinal stance of the legal academy is deeply mistaken, whether implicitly endorsed by the centrist mainstream or explicitly embraced by the progressive left or right. Authority of any sort, including legal authority, simply cannot be the basis of criticisms of power. We have no more reason to assume the morality of the "holder in due course doctrine," or "contract law," or the "Constitution," or the "First amendment," or any other of our most general legalistic principles than we have to assume the morality of the particular law or decision we are criticizing. Therefore, we have no reason to simply employ general legal principles, laws, or systems as the baseline of moral critique of more particular acts of law. If, as Austin's question seems to assume, we cannot criticize law by reference to norms culled from reason, then we must, indeed, look elsewhere for the basis of legal criticism. But we should not look

ies: The Death of Transcendence and the Rise of the New Landells," *New York University Law Review* 62 (1987): 429; Stanley Fish, "Anti-Professionalism," *Cardozo Law Review* 7 (1986): 645; Richard Posner, "The Jurisprudence of Skepticism," *Michigan Law Review* 86 (1988): 827.

6. Robin West, "Adjudication Is Not Interpretation," *Tennessee Law Review* 54 (1987): 203.

to authoritative legal materials themselves. Authority, particularly legal authority, is not an alternative to reason.

The Interdisciplinary Movement

The modern attraction to "interdisciplinary work" in U.S. law schools today stems in large part, I believe, from the hope that in other academic disciplines we will find what we have not found in either law or traditional moral philosophy, namely, normative standards external to both power and abstract reason with which we might criticize law. Interdisciplinary work is largely motivated, in other words, by the hope that in other disciplines we will find the answer to Austin's question. Thus, the interdisciplinary scholars operate on the not unreasonable assumption that other disciplines might supply answers to the questions "how ought we lead, legislate, judge, or advocate"; "how should we use law to do good"; "how do we criticize law"; and "how can we improve upon it."

Thus, to be more specific, both of our two major interdisciplinary movements—the thirty-year-old law and economics movement and the much newer law and humanities movement—have their genesis, at least in part, in attempts to provide a basis for criticism of law that is itself freed of the influence of either traditional moral philosophy or professional legalistic norms. The law and economics movement, most notably, is firmly grounded in the recognizably postmodern skeptical conviction that, for various reasons, neither general legal norms themselves nor philosophical verities can be usefully employed as the basis of evaluation of particular laws. Rather, the only knowable baseline of normative criticism, and hence the only source of value, is the desires, preferences, and choices of particular individuals. The value of a law should therefore be judged by reference to its conduciveness to the creation of opportunities for individuals to create value by acting on their preferences. Consequently, economics—the systematic study of preferences—rather than law or philosophy, is the discipline that must be at the heart of the moral criticism of law. Although predating the arrival of philosophical postmodernism and politically anathema to its most prominent representatives, the law and economics scholars were and are motivated by skeptical convictions that are strikingly similar to those that move the postmodern theorists. According to the law and economics

scholar no less than the postmodern critic of reason, neither philosophy nor law can provide the baseline for the normative criticism of
law. The legal critic must look elsewhere, and for the legal economist,
that means to the preferences of individual consumers.

The law and humanities movement similarly has its genesis in a
recognizably—and this time self-consciously—postmodern attempt
to provide a basis for moral criticism and thinking about law, legal
practice, and the profession, that is freed of the blinding constraints
and biases of the false universals of both traditional moral philosophy
and professional law and legalism. Indeed, it is worth stressing that,
despite the dramatic and obvious differences between the positivistic
methodology of economics and the interpretive and hermeneutic
methods of the humanities, both movements take as their point of
departure the same set of skeptical convictions, themselves commonly rooted in the skepticism that has given rise to the postmodern
critique of reason. For the legal humanist, no less than the legal
economist, agrees with the postmodern critic that neither abstract
truth nor general legal norms can or should constitute the basis for
criticism of positive law. Whereas the economist turns to individual
preferences as the source of value, and hence the basis of criticism,
the legal humanist instead turns to the wisdom encoded in a culture's
texts and explicated by their interpreters—in general, we might say,
to a culture's "canonical and interpretive community"—as the source
of value, and hence the basis of criticism of its positive law. The value
of a law, then, according to the legal humanist, should be judged not
by reference to its conduciveness to the creation of opportunities for
individual consent, as for the legal economist, but, rather, by reference to its conduciveness to the creation of opportunities for meaningfully free participation in the culture's canonical and interpretive
community. Neither philosophy nor law, according to the law and
humanities movement no less than the postmodern critique of reason, can provide the baseline for normative criticism of positive law.
Only the interpretive community—the subcommunity engaged in
dialogic and equal interpretive practices—can provide a standard or
source of moral value.

And yet—and this is the central paradox I wish to explore—in
spite of their genesis in undeniably critical impulses, both the law and
economics movement, and increasingly, I fear, the (newer) law and
humanities movement, are rightly known in legal academia not for

their critical stance toward law, but for their celebration of it. Whatever might have been their initial critical impulse—or better, *in spite*
of their initial critical impulse—both interdisciplinary movements, at
least according to their critics, have come to embrace and reflect
conservative if not reactionary or regressive politics, a general acquiescence in the order of things, and a sometimes quite explicit tendency to establish themselves as apologists or celebrators of the current legal order. Thus, the law and economics movement is known
not for its individualist, pluralist, or anarchic critical edge, but for its
adoring and noncritical attitude toward economic markets and the
individual preferences those markets both produce and satisfy. Similarly, the law and humanities movement, at least according to a growing chorus of critics, is constituted not by a communitarian critical
perspective but by an adoring and noncritical attitude toward the
dominant perspectives and needs of the literate, pontificating "interpretive community" and a respectful deference toward the canonical
texts—both legal and literary—that support that perspective. Law,
of course, is a central structural support of both economic markets
and canonical culture, so the interdisciplinary scholars' adoration of
markets, classics, and their dominant interpretations, respectively,
is quickly translated into a complacent, acquiescent, accepting, or
simply noncritical stance toward law. Despite their original critical
impulse, and despite healthy dissenting wings of both movements,
both the law and economics movement and the law and humanities
movement seem to have succumbed to the authoritarian impulse that
dominates the mainstream legal academy.[7] If we believe the charge
of complacent conservatism made by the critics of the interdisciplinary scholars, then we should conclude that the hope that other
disciplines might provide a source of critical insight about the morality of law, legalism, or particular laws has turned out to be illusory.

The criticism of both movements, of course, is somewhat over-

---

7. For a critique of the conservative bias in law and economics, see Kelman, *Guide
to Critical Legal Studies*. For criticisms of the emerging conservatism of the law and
humanities movement, see David Kennedy, "The Turn to Interpretation," *Southern
California Law Review* 58 (1985): 251; Susan Mann, "The Universe and the Library: A
Critique of James Boyd White as Writer and Reader," *Stanford Law Review* 41 (1989):
959; and Robert Weisberg, "The Law-Literature Enterprise," *Yale Journal of Law and
Humanities* 1 (1988): 1.

stated: there are at least a few progressive legal economists,[8] and there are more than a few profoundly critical, even radical, legal humanists.[9] Nevertheless, there is enough easily demonstrated truth in the charge that it deserves explanation. The question I want to pose, then, is not *whether* both of these movements tend toward conservatism and complacency (which I will take as a given), but rather *why*: why has the critical weight of both of these two particular interdisciplinary movements gravitated toward celebration rather than criticism of legal culture; acquiescence in, rather than dissent from, professional norms and life? Why have both the law and economics movement and the law and humanities movement become conservative, rather than critical, movements in the contemporary legal academy? In both cases, I will submit, the answer lies in the story of each movement's profoundly ambivalent relationship to its moral and philosophical origins, and a similarly ambivalent response to the postmodern critique of reason that has put that philosophical base into doubt. Each movement's story, however, is quite distinctive. Let me start with the law and economics movement.

As is now fairly well understood, the law and economics movement had its inception in a partial embrace and a partial rejection of the politics, moral values, and methods of classical utilitarianism. The moral standard against which all acts of power should be judged, according to the classical utilitarian, is the *individual*, and more specifically, the individual's subjective happiness. Lawmaking, of course, is one realm of power, and should therefore be subject to the same evaluative standard as any other act of power. According to the nineteenth-century classical utilitarians, then, if a law promotes individual happiness, it is a good law; if it promotes pain, misery, suffering, or unhappiness, it is a bad law. Laws should be criticized or praised, quite simply, by reference to their conduciveness to the happiness of the lives of the individuals they effect.

By the early twentieth century, classical utilitarianism had splintered into a bewildering range of utilitarian-inspired theories, one of which turned out to have critical importance for the rise of the law

---

8. See generally Bruce Ackerman, *Reconstructing American Law* (Cambridge, Mass.: Harvard University Press, 1984).

9. See, e.g., Robert Cover, "Nomos and Narrative," *Harvard Law Review* 97 (1983): 4; Richard Weisberg, *The Failure of the Word: The Protagonist as Lawyer in Modern Fiction* (New Haven: Yale University Press, 1984).

and economics movement. From the general utilitarian criterion developed by Bentham, James Mill, and the other classical liberals, at least a few of the English classical liberals of the late nineteenth century and a much larger number of the legal realists and pragmatists of the early twentieth century went on to develop a powerful method of legal criticism that might best be called "ideal-utilitarian." That method had two steps. First, by reasoning inductively on the basis of judgments about the relative subjective happiness of different sorts of lives lived under differing conditions, the legal realists and some of the English liberals reasoned, one should be able to formulate a conception of the ideally happy—or, to use a modern term, an ideally "flourishing"—life. After comparing the subjective happiness incident to a sufficient number of sorts of lives, a critic should be able to say with some confidence, for example, that some degree of personal autonomy, the opportunity to engage in meaningful work, the opportunity to forge and pursue one's own life project, intellectual stimulation, provision for minimal physical needs, involvement in the community's political and cultural life, and the protection of intimate relationships, are all essential components of a subjectively happy individual life. One should be able to determine, in other words, that the ideally happy life is constituted by particular, knowable (although debatable), contingent, relatively general, but nevertheless nonuniversal attributes, and the conditions under which such lives would be most likely to thrive. From such general, tentative, and pragmatically grounded descriptions of the content of the "good life," the early twentieth-century legal realists and pragmatists hoped eventually to forge an ideal of individual life and happiness against which not only particular laws, but also legal systems, constitutions, and forms of government could then be criticized.[10] The second, critical step would then readily follow: a law or legal system that contributes to the conditions necessary to the facilitation of the ideal life—some measure of autonomy, social involvement, privacy, meaningful work, security against want and need, etc.—is a good law. A law or legal system that frustrates such lives is bad.

---

10. The literature here is vast. For a representative sampling see Morris Cohen and Felix Cohen, *Readings in Jurisprudence and Legal Philosophy* (New York: Prentice-Hall, 1951). See generally, John Dewey, *Individualism, Old and New* (New York: Minton, Bach and Co., 1930); and John Stuart Mill, *On Utilitarianism* (New York: Dutton, 1951), for examples of ideal-utilitarianism accounts of the good and the good life.

The modern legal economist's response to the legal realists' utilitarian method of legal criticism was and is strikingly ambivalent. The legal economist (unlike the modern liberal legalist) continues to embrace the classical utilitarian *ideal* of individual subjective happiness as the goal of law. Law should indeed, as classical utilitarians and the legal realists after them held, maximize individual well-being. The legal economist, however, sees an insurmountable "problem of knowledge" with the ideal utilitarian's use of any particular, idealized conception of the good life as a guiding critical norm. The problem with the legal realists' ideal-utilitarian standard of the good life as a measure of the value of law is not so much political—its valorization of one form of life over another—as it is *epistemological*. The ideal-utilitarian mandate to maximize individual happiness by ascertaining its necessary conditions and then criticizing law by reference to whether it impedes or facilitates those conditions, according to the modern legal economist, requires the moral critic to perform the impossible: namely, to specify an ideal conception of happiness that is in turn based on information gleaned from a comparison of the pure subjectivity of other individuals. Thus, the legal realist wanted to posit, on the basis of comparisons of different lives, that an autonomous life is subjectively happier, as well as morally better, than an enslaved one, or that a politically engaged life is similarly happier as well as better than an atomistic one, or that an educated life is more stimulating then one lived in ignorance—that Socrates unhappy, to paraphrase Mill, is happier than a pig satisfied. But these sorts of comparisons, from the demanding, skeptical, and (in retrospect) postmodern perspective of the legal economist, simply cannot be done. We cannot *know* anything about the subjective state of other individuals and, hence, the relative feel of autonomy to slavery, or education to ignorance; we cannot "crawl inside" A or B's skin and see how either of them is "feeling" under divergent life conditions. Knowing that something pains me will not help me determine whether something pains you, since I am me and you are you. Knowing that I am made happy by meaningful work, intellectual stimulation, or political involvement tells me nothing at all about what makes you happy, and hence nothing at all about the nature of happiness itself. It is therefore impossible—whether or not politically wise—to generate the sorts of general, inductive judgments about the conditions of a subjectively happy life necessary to meaningful ideal-utilitarian criticism.

To generalize the point, individual happiness—the realists' utilitarian goal of law—according to the modern economist, is an utterly subjective, idiosyncratic, and individualist quality and is therefore utterly unknowable. We do not have and cannot rationally acquire the kind of data we need to apply the standard of criticism for which the ideal-utilitarian argued. There is no way, then, according to the legal economist, that we can criticize the merits of particular laws by reference to their conduciveness to the components of a happy or "flourishing" life because there is no way we can meaningfully specify the content of such a life. The classical utilitarian was right to put forward the individual's subjective happiness as the goal of law, but the utilitarian-inspired legal critics of the early twentieth century were wrong to assert the possibility that one could specify the necessary conditions of happiness, and then use those specifications as the *standard* for the rational moral criticism of law. The legal critic cannot rationally do what the ideal utilitarian urges.

I want eventually to question whether the legal economists are right to be so skeptical of our ability to know the subjectivity of others and, hence, skeptical of the ability of the legal critic to specify a fairly general account of the content of happiness and then ascertain whether and how much a law impedes or furthers the conditions that foster happy lives. But first I want to stress that it is precisely this claim, that there is an insurmountable epistemological problem with critical ideal-utilitarianism, that defines, unifies, and distinguishes the modern "law and economics movement" from its utilitarian and legal realist predecessors. The legal economist typically endorses the classical utilitarian's conviction that our legal system ought, indeed, maximize the subjective happiness of effected individuals. That is a proper legal goal. But because we cannot perceive, understand, measure, gauge, or in any other way *rationally* compare the subjective lives of other individuals, according to the legal economist, we cannot rationally evaluate or criticize laws by whether or not they foster or promote the necessary conditions for subjective, individual happiness. The goal of law—individual happiness—cannot become an objective standard of legal criticism, because its constituent components—autonomy, political engagement, stimulating

work, etc.—can never be known. Happiness, in short, cannot be an
"object of rational knowledge." Individual subjective welfare is the
goal of law, but because it is essentially unknowable, it cannot serve
as the standard for rational criticism of law.[11]

What, then, should we do? It is here that the "science" of economics enters the picture, and solves the legal economist's epistemological dilemma. We need to forgo the search for the "nature" or
"content" of human happiness, the legal economist argues, but it
does not follow that we should relinquish either the goal of happiness
itself or, more importantly, the method of rational inquiry. Rather,
what we need to do is replace the utilitarian's nonquantifiable, non-
comparable, and essentially unknowable standard of subjective happiness with a standard that *is* knowable, quantifiable, and comparable and, hence, subject to rational inquiry—namely, the preferences,
choices, and consensual transactions of particular, individual consumers. We cannot know what makes someone "happy," but even
given postmodern skepticism and doubts about the value of traditional philosophy's claims of abstract knowledge and social-scientific
empirical claims about "human nature," we can know what each
particular individual wants. More concretely, given the vast differences between people, we cannot know that autonomy, work, or
social engagement will, as a rule, contribute to individual happiness,
but we can know what any particular individual chooses, prefers,
and will pay for. The solution, then, to the epistemological problems
posed by utilitarianism and legal realism is straightforward: we need
to displace unknowable "happiness" with knowable objective
wealth. Rather than maximize happiness, we should aim to maximize
wealth, and we should criticize a law by whether or not it does so.
Thus, Richard Posner, the most committed proponent of the value
of wealth maximization, is led to sharply distinguish the modern
legal economist's interest in value and wealth from the utilitarian's
use of happiness as a guiding critical norm.

The most important thing to bear in mind about the concept of
value is that it is based on what people are willing to pay for

---

11. See, for an example of a legal-economic attack on the subjectivity, irrationality, and idiosyncrasy of classical utilitarian legal criticism, Posner's discussion of Bentham in Richard Posner, *The Economics of Justice* (Cambridge, Mass.: Harvard University
Press, 1981), 31–48.

something rather than on the happiness they would derive from having it. Value and happiness are of course related. . . . But while value necessarily implies utility, utility does not necessarily imply value. The individual who would like very much to have some good but is unwilling or unable to pay anything for it—perhaps because he is destitute—does not value the good in the sense in which I am using the term *value*.

Equivalently, the wealth of society is the aggregate satisfaction of those preferences (the only ones that have weight in a system of wealth maximization) that are backed up by money, that is, that are registered in a market.[12]

Economics, we might say—with its minimalist claims about "human nature"—is the quintessentially postmodern science, and law and economics—with its minimalist claims about what is or is not desirable—is the quintessentially postmodern system of value.

It is, then, a continuing commitment to the Enlightenment ideal of the possibilities and values of rational inquiry, *combined with* distinctively postmodern doubts that there is any such knowledge about "happiness" that can be rationally acquired through philosophy or social science generalities that can meaningfully guide action, that define the methodology of the law and economics movement. A lingering Enlightenment commitment to rational method combined with postmodern doubt that its traditional disciplines—philosophy and social science—produce rational knowledge, requires, for the legal economist, that legal criticism be grounded in the objective "discipline" of economics rather than in the politics, irrationality, and ethical indeterminacy of idealism, philosophy, or the social sciences. For although we cannot "know," through either philosophical investigation or scientific inference, the nature of happiness itself, through the methods of economics we *can* rationally know—even within the constraints of postmodern skepticism—and can objectively quantify, compare, and maximize the preferences, choices, and wealth of other individuals. Such knowledge requires neither abstract truth and deduction, nor universal claims of "human nature." Preferences, wealth, and choices, unlike happiness, are objective, measurable, observable, quantifiable phenomena. Since we cannot objectively and

---

12. Posner, *Economics of Justice.*

rationally "know" the nature of another's happiness, but can know his or her objective, behavioral preferences and choices, we should then seek to maximize not his or her subjective well-being but, rather, his or her preferences, choices, and wealth. Preferences and choices are preferred standards of criticism not only because they are good evidence of the individual's subjective happiness but also, and more importantly, because they are knowable. It is only by maximizing wealth that we can hope to fulfill the mandate of utilitarianism.

It is also, however, precisely this commitment to preferences, choices, and wealth—grounded, importantly, not in utilitarian ethics but in an independent and postmodern skepticism regarding the possibility of attaining knowledge about the subjectivity of others—that ultimately unhinges legal economists from their traditionally classically liberal and individualistic base, and steers them instead toward modern conservatism. By substituting particular instances of objectively manifested "consent," "preferences," and "wealth" for the general conditions of subjective flourishing, happiness, pleasure, or well-being, to say nothing of the autonomy, meaningful work, social engagement, and intellectuality that, according to the legal realists, might comprise it, in order to make the entire enterprise more "reasonable," the law and economics movement has converted ideal-utilitarianism—at its inception, a potentially profoundly critical ethic—into first libertarianism and then conservatism. For, as countless critics—modern, postmodern, and otherwise—of the law and economics movement have now pointed out, our "preferences" and our "consensual transactions" no less than our "markets" are themselves the products of hierarchies of power that are, in turn, in large part constructed by law.[13] Our "preferences," our choices, and the transactions to which we give our consent reflect both our individual and social histories, including present distributions of wealth and power, the prejudices of our upbringing, the pettiness or cramped mean spiritedness of our social peers, the xenophobia of our society, and the current state of our law, to name just a few distorting influences on those ephemeral, knowable "objects" in which the legal

13. See, e.g., Kelman, *Guide to Critical Legal Studies*, 151–85; Cass Sunstein, "Legal Interference with Private Preferences," *Chicago Law Review* 53 (1986): 1129; Robin West, "Authority, Autonomy, and Choice," *Harvard Law Review* 99 (1985): 384; Robin West, "Taking Preferences Seriously," *Tulane Law Review* 64 (1990): 659; Margaret Radin, "Market Inalienability," *Harvard Law Review* 100 (1987): 1849.

economists have placed such tremendous normative faith. They hardly constitute an Archimedean point freed of the influences of power from which we can rationally criticize law. To the extent that preferences, choices, and consensual transactions reflect preexisting distributions of power and wealth, the criticism of law by reference to our choices is no less political than the criticism of law by reference to constructed ideals. It is also, to that extent, an inherently and inevitably conservative enterprise.

It is, then, not all that surprising that the law and economics movement has emerged not as the voice of radical individualism, or liberalism, or even ideal-utilitarianism, but instead as the voice of conservatism in the legal academy. Both our private preferences reflected in the market and our public preferences reflected in participatory politics are a product of the orderings of our present world, including our legal world. The preferences, choices, consensual transactions, and existing desires of the individual in which the legal economist puts such faith do not provide a basis for moral criticism of law that is independent of the "authority of law" itself. Those preferences and choices are themselves the products of power, including legal power. To criticize power by reference to preference is ultimately to hold up power to power. Holding power up to power—the familiar authoritarian response—is no alternative to the Enlightenment scholar's illusive quest to hold power to the critical light of reason.

A strikingly parallel story can be told of the emergence of the much newer, 1980s law and humanities movement, and its unfolding transformation into yet another voice of conservatism in the legal academy. Although the law and humanities movement is far more diffuse than the law and economics movement, the story of the legal humanist's attempt to answer Austin's question is nevertheless in many ways analogous to that of the legal economist's. Like the legal economist's ambivalent ties to classical and ideal-utilitarianism, the law and humanities scholars are also ambivalently both attracted to and repelled by an underlying ethical and political philosophy. The participants in the modern law and humanities movement, for the most part, partially embrace and partially reject the modern civic republican's ideal of communitarian happiness, health, well-being, or virtue, just as the law and economics movement partially embraces, and partially rejects, the utilitarian's ideal of individual happi-

ness, health, well-being, or flourishing. The conservatism that is now
characteristic of so much law and humanities scholarship has its
genesis in that ambivalence.

Modern civic republicanism, as a normative ideal, is a far more
contemporary ethic than utilitarianism, but the two movements nevertheless have noteworthy structural similarities. The modern civic
republican holds that the standard against which all acts of power
should be judged is not *individual* health or happiness, as the utilitarian holds, but rather *communitarian* well-being, health, or happiness.[14] Like the utilitarian's individualism, the modern republican's
communitarian normative goal is subjective in a sense: it is the subjectively felt happiness, or well-being, of the community (rather than
the individual) that the lawmaker should seek to maximize. At the
same time, and again like the utilitarian, the civic republican's
method aims at some objectivity: just as the ideal-utilitarians developed various objective conceptions of the ideally happy individual
life, civic republicans have developed "objective" or ideal conceptions
of what constitutes a happy community. Communitarian happiness,
for most modern republicans, is constituted by particular, knowable,
contingent, culturally variable, but nevertheless specifiable attributes
just as, for the ideal-utilitarian, individual happiness is constituted
by particular, knowable, contingent, nonuniversal, but nevertheless
fairly general characteristics. A "good" community, according to various modern republican conceptions, is a diverse, vibrant, self-governing, nonoppressive, deliberative, respectful, egalitarian, and caring community and, if a law promotes it, then it is a good law. A
"bad" community, correlatively, is a homogenous, intolerant, deadened, oppressive, disrespectful, hierarchical, violent, and uncaring
community and again, if a law promotes it, then it is a bad law.

From such general descriptions, republicans have begun to forge
an account of ideal community life from which not only laws and
legal systems, but also political systems and constitutions can be
criticized. Laws, legal systems, and community judgments that generate, foster, or promote communities that are relatively diverse,
equal, tolerant, deliberative, self-governing, and vibrant can be presumed to be promoting communitarian well-being, while those that

---

14. See, e.g., Cass Sunstein, "Beyond the Republican Revival," *Yale Law Journal*
97 (1988): 1539; Frank Michelman, "Law's Republic," *Yale Law Journal* 97 (1988): 1493;
Tushnet, *Red, White, and Blue.*

foster hegemony, intolerance, hierarchy, xenophobia, and conformity—such as antisodomy or miscegenation laws—do not, and are
properly criticized on that account.[15] Now, although it is considerably
more murky and less self-conscious than the relationship of the law
and economics movement with classical utilitarianism, the law and
humanities movement can also be understood as grounded in a fundamentally ambivalent reaction to the communitarian standard of
value embraced by civic republicanism. Thus, many of our most
prominent modern legal humanists—including thinkers as diverse
as Stanley Levinson, Owen Fiss, and James Boyd White—agree with
the civic republicans that the subjective health and well-being of the
community, rather than the subjective happiness of the "atomistic
individual," ought be the goal of law. In fact, the humanistic thinkers
tend to locate the common thread that connects them with their rejection, on this basis, of economic patterns and methods of thought.[16]
But the sharp differences in patterns of thinking between the legal
economists and the legal humanists may have blinded us to some of
their similarities. One such similarity is simply that the relation of
legal humanism to civic republicanism is more similar than dissimilar
to the relation between economic legalism and utilitarian individualism. For, just as the legal economist sees a "problem of knowledge"
with the ideal-utilitarian's insistence that one can meaningfully compare different subjective experiences and construct an objective standard of the good life on the basis of such comparisons, the legal
humanist similarly sees a problem of knowledge with the civic republican's parallel claim that one can meaningfully compare the worth
of different conceptions of communitarian good, and construct an
objectively knowable standard of community value. How are we to
know, asks the skeptical legal humanist, particularly the legal humanist most influenced by postmodern developments, whether participation, equality, tolerance, diversity, oppression, respect, care, hierarchy, or violation are criteria of a good or bad, healthy or unhealthy,
happy or unhappy community? What is good for one community,
after all, may obviously be bad for another. How are we to know,
then, whether a particular community or a particular description of an

---

15. Thus, Michelman criticizes antisodomy laws on the basis of civic republican
ideals in Michelman, "Law's Republic."

16. See Owen Fiss, "The Death of Law," *Cornell Law Review* 72 (1986): 1; James
Boyd White, "Law and Economics," *Tennessee Law Review* 54 (1987): 203.

ideal community is an intersubjectively good or bad community? How are we to make these "intercommunitarian" judgments of utility?

Thus, just as the economists objected to ideal-utilitarian standards of criticism on the ground that the individualistic ideals it constructed required an inaccessible knowledge of the subjective lives of individuals, so the legal humanists fear that the communitarian ideals of civic republicanism require an inaccessible intercommunitarian knowledge of the well-being of other communities.[17] What has been drastically obscured by what are undoubtedly profound differences between these two movements is that the objection in both cases to the creation of objective standards from comparisons of subjective experience of others stems from precisely the same source. Like interpersonal knowledge, the kind of intercommunitarian knowledge required by republicanism can neither be derived from "abstract principles of moral truth," nor from empirically sound "general truths of human or social nature." Neither form of knowledge—the interpersonal kind demanded by utilitarianism nor the intercommunitarian kind demanded by republicanism—can be derived from reason. Therefore, the kind of knowledge critical republicanism requires, like the kind of knowledge ideal-utilitarianism requires, is not possible. The law and humanities movement, like the law and economics movement, has its genesis in its response to precisely this problem of knowledge. Participation in the law and humanities movement, for many if not most, is primarily motivated by a search for a more public, and hence more knowable, criterion of communitarian value than that propounded by traditional political theorists, just as the law and economics movement begins with a search for a more public, and hence more knowable, criterion of individualistic welfare than that put forward by classical and ideal-utilitarian philosophers.

How is the problem solved? Like the legal economist (and unlike the postmodern theorist), the legal humanist remains committed to the general ideal of knowledge freed of the influence of power as the Archimedean point of reference from which meaningful criticism can proceed, and rational inquiry as the method by which such knowl-

---

17. See, generally, James Boyd White, "Is Cultural Criticism Possible?" *Michigan Law Review* 84 (1986): 1373, and "Thinking about Our Language," *Yale Law Journal* 96 (1987): 1960, 1974.

edge can be obtained. Thus, the legal humanist needs a disciplined "proxy" for the unwieldy and politicized notion of "community value," just as the legal economist sought out a proxy for individual well-being. At this point, the disciplines of literature and modern critical literary theory, respectively, enter the picture, and solve the problem of knowledge—albeit in somewhat differing ways. Law and humanities, very roughly, splits into a procedural and substantive wing, each influenced by a different humanistic subdiscipline.

First, the procedural wing of the law and humanities movement (sometimes called interpretivism), heavily influenced by critical literary theory, finds the proxy for communitarian well-being in the community's "interpretive" health and prowess. Just as the process of "choosing" and the preference that is its product serve as an objectively knowable proxy for subjective individual happiness for the modern legal economist, so the procedural legal humanists find their criterion of subjective, communitarian value in the process of interpretation. The mere presence of an interpreted text evidences, for the procedural legal humanist, the presence of minimal communitarian values, in a sense that strikingly parallels the legal economist's insistence that a fulfilled "preference," or a choice, evidences an increase in individual personal well-being. For the existence of an interpreted text—a produced, heard, understood, and interpreted communication—at least evidences whatever equality and tolerance between speaker and listener is required for communication and interpretation to have successfully occurred. That may well be a considerable degree of equality and openness, and equality and openness are certainly components of subjective community health. A community that vigorously produces, reads, discusses, interprets, and criticizes central and unifying shared "texts" is, therefore, a good community.

The procedural legal humanist is thus moved to displace the civic republican's subjective, unknowable "good, healthy, community" and the participation, egalitarianism, diversity, and tolerance that are its constituent parts, as the standard of legal criticism, with the notion of the "interpretive community": a community that is actively engaged in criticism, interpretation, and debate of its central, unifying texts is a good community, while one that is not so engaged, is not. The procedural notion of the interpretive community, after all, does not produce the problem of knowledge that plagues the subjective values behind the republican's criterion of communitarian well-being: interpretation is almost by definition a public, knowable, accessible process, and can be studied in a disciplined way, namely through the various disciplines of the humanities, just as objective, public, accessible preferences can be studied by economics. A law that facilitates the interpretive community—a law that furthers dialogic and interpretive values—is, therefore, a good law, and a law that frustrates such values is bad.

Thus, the procedural legal humanist typically endorses the procedural values of unimpeded dialogue, communication, and fair hearing. In a representative passage, James Boyd White explains:

> [Law and Humanities studies] teaches us that we should continue to do what we have always done, which is to engage in the kind of conversation in which disagreements and misunderstandings are addressed, always imperfectly and always incompletely but not always without accession of understanding. Of course not all conversations go equally well. Implied in what I have said is that our attention must continuously be given to the quality of the conversational process: to our openness to the views of another, to our willingness to revise our own terms, to our readiness to learn more fully the degree to which, whenever we speak, we say more than we mean or know. Who am I to you, and you to me? With what attitude toward each other and toward our languages do we speak. What are our voices? If we can get these things right, the rest of what we care about, or ought to care about, will follow.[18]

Law, then, should be judged by whether it facilitates this interpretive and textual conversation. Judged by that standard, White concludes, Anglo-American legalism scores quite highly:

> As for law, it too partakes of the radical uncertainty of the rest of life, the want of firm external standards. But it is also a special way of living on these conditions, a way of making standards internally, out of our experience, as we make ourselves in our talk. The law is in fact a method of cultural criticism and cultural transformation, as well as cultural preservation. . . . [T]he law

---

18. White, "Cultural Criticism," 1384.

has been by far the best and most powerful method of cultural criticism American society has had. . . . The main reason for this . . . is that the law is in structure multivocal, always inviting new and contrasting accounts and languages.[19]

The second wing of the law and humanities movement is substantive and is inspired not by critical legal theory, but by literature itself. Substantive or cultural legal humanists find their proxy for communicative value not in the process of interpretation but, rather, in the content of the culture's canonical great texts. The substantive legal humanist, like the proceduralist, is skeptical of any individual's ability to ascertain the nature of the communitarian good, but confident that, through the method of the humanities, the great canonical texts can be fruitfully combed for their collective wisdom. James White, the foremost proponent of substantive as well as procedural legal humanism, explains:

> [Through the method of the humanities] we can learn to participate in a cross-cultural conversation about the relationship between mind and language, between self and culture, and do so with minds often vastly superior to our own. It is to maintain the possibility of such a conversation that we preserve the works of our past and seek to educate our minds to understand and respond to them.
>
> To put it in a phrase, I think that the study of the humanities is the central activity by which the responsive and critical mind can best be formed and tested, that it offers the ground upon which cultural criticism can rest. . . . One function of cultural tradition . . . is that of a collective and selective memory, the preservation of the best we have done, which can serve to set standards by which to measure contemporary achievements and attempts. The tradition . . . can be taken as establishing a set of presumptions that can serve as a comprehensive and practical spur to our own education, individual and collective.[20]

Legal criticism, then, like all cultural criticism, should be grounded neither in abstract philosophy nor social science, but in the collective

---

19. Ibid., 1386.
20. Ibid., 1378–82.

images of community life culled from canonical culture. Unsurprisingly, White's understanding of what those images require of us
converge with the communitarian ideals of civic republicanism. For
White, though, the authority of those ideals stem not from their
conduciveness to flourishing communities but, rather, in their en-
shrinement in canonical culture.

> To turn at the end from process to substance, from the way we
> make our standards to what they ought to be, we can ask: What
> do we learn when we turn to the experience of the past and the
> present and seek to discover ultimate standards of value? To
> answer that question by performance has been the object of my
> other work, which I can sum up by saying that for me the voice
> of our tradition is plain and plainly right. The object of human
> community, we have always known, is the recognition of the
> value of each person as a center of worth and meaning, as living
> in the kind of perpetual process of reciprocal interaction with
> nature, language, and other people through which each of us
> makes himself. In this we are at once the same and different: the
> same in the essentials of our situation—in our dependence on
> culture and our need to make it, in the creative center of our
> lives—but different in what we make, for each of us is ultimately
> unique. It is in fact upon this double truth that our equality rests:
> if we were wholly the same or wholly different we could disre-
> gard one another. As it is, our deepest obligation and highest
> hope is to create a world in which each person is recognized, in
> which each may achieve as fully as possible the realization of his
> or her capacities for life.[21]

My claim, then, is that the law and humanities movement has its
inception in an attempt to transform the civic republican's critical
communitarian standard from something unknowable—community
happiness, health, or well-being—into something objective and
knowable. Like the republican, the legal humanists remain committed to the proposition that a law should promote community values
(such as openness, equality, diversity, and tolerance), but go on to

---

21. Ibid, 1386.

argue that law ought to be criticized not directly by reference to its tendency to create morally worthy, egalitarian, open, and tolerant communities but, rather, either by comparison of the sort of community it will create with the images of communal life propounded by our great canonical cultural texts or, alternatively for the procedural-ist, by reference to whether or not it creates opportunities for textual production, readings, interpretation, conversation, and dialogue. The "canonical community" and the interpretive community become the lodestar of a good community, just as, for the economist, well-functioning markets and individual preferences and consensual transactions become the lodestar of individual well-being. Hence, for the legal humanist, the critical test of law is its capacity to create either values that accord with those of canonical culture or conditions conducive to the flourishing of the interpretive community: a com-munity actively engaged in the production and interpretation of com-municative texts. The legal humanist substitutes a commitment to canonical culture and interpretive practices as the criteria of value against which we should criticize law for the communitarian's inter-subjective and unknowable healthy community, just as the economic legalist substitutes a commitment to preference, choice, and markets for the utilitarian's unknowable standard of individual happiness.

Again, I will ultimately question whether the legal humanist is right to be skeptical of the civic republican's ability to compare differ-ent communities' intersubjective well-being, and hence to construct ideals of communitarian well-being. But first I want to stress that it is precisely this skepticism—this doubt that we can know the commu-nity directly—that defines and unifies modern legal humanism, and distinguishes it from contemporary civic republicanism, no less than the parallel skepticism regarding the accessibility of individual well-being distinguishes the law and economics movement from utilitari-anism. The legal humanist, like the civic republican, ultimately values community, and holds to a communitarian standard of legal criticism: a law is a good law if it makes a good community. Unlike the republi-can, however, and clearly reflecting the influence of postmodern the-ory, the legal humanist is skeptical of our ability to know or specify the nature of the good community (as well as our ability to know and specify the nature of anything else), just as the legal economist is skeptical of our ability to know or specify the content of individual happiness. Since we cannot know what constitutes the intersubjective well-being of a community, we should seek instead either to mirror the lessons of canonical culture or to maximize the community's textual and interpretive productivity. If a law creates conditions that either serve the values propounded by the literary canon, or furthers the production, interpretation, and criticism of texts, it thereby furthers communitarian values. Laws should be criticized, then, by reference to their tendency to encourage or frustrate the well-being of the interpretive and canonical community. The interpretive and canonical community jointly solve the problem of knowledge that plagues republicanism, no less than individual preference and markets solve the problem of knowledge that plagues utilitarian individualism.

It is also, however, precisely by substituting the canonical and interpretive community for the good community, that the legal humanist—both procedural and substantive, theoretical and canonical—not only makes communitarian value susceptible to the reasoned critical attention of the humanities, but also converts it first into cultural traditionalism, and then to conservatism. Let me begin with procedural legal humanism. As numerous postmodern and poststructuralist critics of humanism have argued, a high degree of textual interpretive activity is no more indicative of the presence of an egalitarian or tolerant or healthy community than is the existence of a fulfilled preference reflective of an increase in individual well-being. To put the same point slightly differently, writers and readers or speakers and listeners can communicate across, create, reify, and reinforce conditions of oppression, conformity, xenophobia, and hierarchy, just as individuals can contractually or freely consent within conditions of extreme inequality. Abstractly to value textual and interpretive productivity is ultimately to value whatever matrix of power is conducive to that particular form of productivity.[22] To value or criticize a law by reference to its capacity to generate interpretive and textual productivity within the interpretive community it creates and from which it derives is ultimately to criticize one act of power by references to others.

The substantive, cultural prong of the law and humanities movement even more obviously collapses in conservatism. A culture's

---

22. This is a central insight of modern critical social theory. See generally Michel Foucault, *Discipline and Punish*, trans. Alan Sheridan (New York: Pantheon, 1977), and *The History of Sexuality*, trans. Robert Hurley (New York: Pantheon, 1978).

great texts and their dominant interpretations reflect and constitute the values of the community from which the texts come, and back into which they will be submerged. It is disastrously circular to criticize law by reference to the values and standards of the great texts and dominant interpretations of the canonical community: great texts no more give us an objective, humanistic basis for communitarian criticism of law than preferences or consensual transactions give us an objective, economic basis for individualistic criticism of law. Both the perceived greatness of the text itself and the knowledge, the images, and the values it contains are products of power. To hold the law to the critical standard of the values and perspectives of the great texts is similarly to simply criticize acts of power by acts of power. The canonical text, no less than the individualistic preference, is no solution to the critical dilemma posed by the omnipresence of power.

My hypothesis, then, very generally, is that in spite of the vast differences between these two movements—one is committed to libertarian and individualist goals while the other is committed to republican and communitarian goals; one is generally identified with the political left and the other with the political right; and one is allied with the humanistic disciplines of literature and critical theory and the other with the social scientific discipline of economics—both the law and humanities movement and the law and economics movement have gone through similar patterns of development, crisis, reformulation, critique, and capitulation, and the end result in both cases has been a reversion to the authoritarian legal complacency that both movements were initially well poised to avoid. Let me review that cycle. First, both movements are initially defined by their endorsement of overtly subjective or intersubjective goals, coupled with a rejection of the use of idealistic descriptions of the objective content and conditions of those goals as standards of legal criticism. Thus, the law and economics movement endorses the classical utilitarian's insistence that subjective individual well-being is the goal of law, but rejects the related legal realist's ideal-utilitarian claim that one can specify the nature of individual well-being in a way that can then serve as an evaluative standard for legal criticism. Rather, preference and choice, according to the legal economist, must serve as critical stand-ins. We should aim to maximize preference and choice (and criticize law by reference to whether or not it does so) rather than well-being, because preference and choice, unlike well-being, are measurable, quantifiable, knowable, and, hence, susceptible to the rationalist tools of the economic discipline. Similarly, the law and humanities movement endorses the civic republican's identification of subjective communitarian well-being as the goal of law, but rejects the republican's insistence that one can identify the nature of communitarian well-being in a way that can serve as the standard of legal criticism. Rather, communitarian interpretivism and canonical culture must serve as the critical standards instead. We should aim to realize the wisdom of the canon or nurture the community's textual and interpretive productivity (and criticize law by reference to whether or not it does so) because a culture's texts and interpretive practices, rather than communitarian well-being, are susceptible to the critical and knowable standards of humanistic discourse. In both cases, it is the combination of partial endorsement and partial rejection of overtly subjective critical standards that define the movements.

Second, both movements reject the use of individual and community happiness (or well-being) as the *standard* of legal criticism for much the same reason. In both cases, the interdisciplinary legalist is skeptical that the critic can attain or articulate any meaningfully general knowledge of the nature, content, or conditions of individual or community well-being. The result is that in both cases, the criterion of criticism—individual well-being on the one hand, communitarian well-being on the other—raises, in the eyes of the interdisciplinary scholar, a "crisis of rationality." If we understand *rationality* to mean a commitment to the knowledge obtained through deductively sound and empirically verifiable propositions, then both the utilitarian and the republican standards require a sort of knowledge that cannot be rationally acquired. The ideal-utilitarian standard of the good life requires an unattainable knowledge of the comparative subjective well-being of individuals, and the civic republican ideal of the good community requires intersubjective knowledge of the comparative well-being of communities. Neither sort of knowledge, however, can be obtained through deductive inferences or empirically verifiable propositions. The sort of knowledge required for the moral standard against which the law is to be judged for both the ideal-utilitarian and the modern communitarian is not attainable.

Both modern interdisciplinary movements—law and economics and law and humanities—have their interdisciplinary inception in a response to this perceived epistemological crisis. Both endorse a particular goal—individual and communitarian well-being—as the goal of legalism. But both have come to view that goal as incapable of rational assessment or description. Neither individual nor communitarian well-being can be an object of rational knowledge, and consequently neither can serve as an Archimedean standard against which law should be criticized, even though they constitute the goal toward which law should strive. Both movements, then, displace the original ideal as the basis against which law should be criticized with a more public standard that can be rationally "knowable." The legal economist substitutes happiness with objectively knowable individual preferences, choices, and opportunities for consent. Under the legal economist's standard, whatever law maximizes one's preferences and one's consensual transactions (rather than one's well-being) is a good law, and whatever minimizes fulfillment of one's preferences or opportunities for consent is a bad law. Similarly, the legal humanist displaces the republican commitment to communitarian well-being with a substantive commitment to canonical culture and a procedural commitment to the promulgation of texts and interpretations. Under the legal humanist's standard, whatever law promotes the values of the canon or maximizes the opportunity for dialogic participation in communitarian textual conversation is a good law, and whatever law frustrates such textual communication is a bad law. The community's great texts and interpretive productivity, unlike the worth of the community's values, can be objects of rational knowledge—it is possible, at least humanistically if not scientifically, to study a community's texts, even if we can never know that community's inner life.

In both cases, it is this displacement of the unknowable ideal of individual or community happiness with an object of rational knowledge—generated in turn by both a profound skepticism about the possibility of rational understandings of the nature of happiness, and continuing commitment to the Enlightenment ideal of rationality and discipline as the means by which knowledge is acquired—that defines the interdisciplinary legal movement. By substituting the purportedly unknowable ideals of individualistic and communitarian well-being with objective, quantifiable preferences and consensual transactions on the one hand, and communicative texts on the other, the scientific discipline of economics became central to the critical task of liberalism, and the humanistic disciplines of literature and literary theory became central to the critical work of communitarianism. Subjective, irrational ethics became tamed by disciplined knowledge. It is also, however, precisely this displacement of subjective ethics with objects of rational knowledge, that proved to be fatal to both interdisciplinary movements' critical potential. In an effort to avoid irrationalism, both movements, at their inception, moved toward a standard amenable to disciplined rational inquiry as the benchmark of legal criticism. The legal economist moved away from individual subjective well-being and to wealth maximization; the legal humanist moved away from intersubjective communitarianism and toward textualism. But neither preferences—the lodestar of value to the legal economist—nor great texts and interpretive productivity—the lodestar of value for the legal humanist—can survive the postmodern critical assault on reason. Preferences, canonical texts, and interpretations, no less than the worldly and transcendental knowledge that is the product of empirical and philosophical inquiry, are products of power, including legal power. Neither a community's interpretations, its canonical texts, nor our individual preferences are any more moral than the politics that produce them. When the economic and humanistic interdisciplinary scholars criticize law by reference to individualistic preferences on the one hand, and canonical culture or communitarian textual productivity on the other, they have both embraced a version of legalistic authoritarianism that their political forebears set out explicitly to avoid.

Sympathy, Intersubjectivity, and Intercommunitarianism

Is there any way that this circle can be broken? Put in terms of politics, the circle is this. In an attempt to escape the apparent irrationality of utilitarian and republican critique, the interdisciplinary scholars moved toward normative standards that they hoped would be more susceptible to disciplined analysis—preferences and markets for the legal economist; cultural texts and interpretations for the legal humanist. Those standards themselves, however, are no less hopelessly politicized by virtue of their rationality as the overtly political base from which each movement fled. Put epistemologically the circle is this. Both movements are conceived as attempts to provide alternatives to the impossibility of certain types of knowledge: the impossibility of knowing what utilitarianism requires—the conditions and contents of individual happiness—and the impossibility of knowing what republicanism requires—the conditions and content of community well-being. Both were then led by the force of that conviction to the development of more knowable standards and, hence, to interdisciplinary methods and commitments. The apparent objectivity of those standards, however, no less than the reasonableness and rationality of those interdisciplinary commitments, have quickly come to be understood as entirely dependent upon the extent to which the standards and disciplines in question recreate, reify, and legitimate existing hierarchy. Whether viewed epistemologically or politically, the outcome of the circle of subjectivity, irrationality, knowledge, discipline, and regression has been the same. Both movements have come to represent, in the modern legal world, a legal conservatism that may be culturally or economically sophisticated, but that is, at core, indistinguishable from the legal authoritarianism of the traditional, unidisciplinary legal scholar. Both movements moved from openly political, liberatory, and critical analysis to an apparently neutral, reasonable, disciplined, nonpolitical methodology, and both have wound up with a purportedly apolitical but, in fact, intensely conservative commitment to the values and mainstays of the status quo.

I want to suggest one possible way out of the circle of irrationality to discipline to regression, and that is that we reexamine the crisis of knowledge that in each case started the circle rolling. We need to put back into question the initial skepticism toward the possibility of knowledge of the subjectivity of both the individual and the community, which constituted, in turn, the basis of the ideals against which law was to be criticized. It is that skepticism toward the possibility of knowing the nature of another individual's or community's subjective life that prompted first the legal economist and then the legal humanist to abandon individual and community well-being in favor of markets and texts as the standard against which law should be critically measured. But it is worth noting that the turn to alternative disciplines in each case was driven not only by postmodern doubt about philosophy and empirical science, but also by an Enlightenment-based faith in the methods of rationality: the interdisciplinary scholars insisted not only that individual and community happiness were, by their nature, not subject to rational inquiry, but that we should *therefore* substitute in their stead standards that would be susceptible to rational inquiry—wealth, for the economists; texts and interpretations, for the humanists. Thus it was faith in rationality no less than skepticism toward claims of philosophical and scientific knowledge that drove the legal humanist and legal economist toward the interdisciplinary positions that now seem themselves to be so riddled with the politics of regression. That faith, however, may have been misplaced—the basis of it has now surely been put into doubt by postmodern scholars—and, if so, then that arguably misplaced faith might suggest a way out of the circle. If we have truly come to doubt the purifying moral power of rational inquiry, then surely we ought also to reexamine the rationalism-inspired doubts that led us to the conviction that it is not possible to know another's subjective welfare, or what it is to inhabit another's community. Rather than reject the criteria of individual and community well-being as standards of evaluation because they cannot be objects of rational inquiry, we might, instead and more profitably, question the insistence on rationality as our standard of what is and is not knowable.

Thus, it may indeed be true that we cannot rationally know the subjective feel of another individual's welfare or a community's health, and cannot therefore rationally specify the nature of the good individual and communitarian life. If we are committed to rational methods of inquiry as the exclusive route to knowledge, then we will have to displace those objects of knowledge with something else. But if, as now seems to be the case, we are no longer convinced of the virtues of rationalism, then we ought to begin to consider the possibility that there may be nonrational, irrational, or arational ways of knowing the subjectivity of individuals or of communities that are worthy of attention and respect. Our relentless and apparently failed quest for rational knowledge might have blinded us to other ways of knowing.[23] Rather than despair the failures of rational inquiry, we should explore those possibilities. In other words, the insistence on rational knowledge and, hence, on *objects* of rational knowledge, may have blinded us to the possibilities within the human spirit for arational and arationally acquired forms of undisciplined knowledge and insight.

---

23. Feminist studies are beginning to open up this possibility. See Mary Belenky, et al., *Women's Ways of Knowing* (New York: Basic Books, 1986).

Furthermore, and finally, it may be *that* knowledge and *those* insights—arationally acquired—that lie at the heart of an answer to Austin's question. It may be, in other words, that arational knowledge is at the root of the ideals—individual autonomy, communitarian tolerance, and the like—that should and can constitute the standards against which we should judge legal and political acts of power. If we truly have come to realize, or believe, or suspect, that reason does not and cannot provide us with an independent standard against which to judge acts of power, then we ought at least to consider the possibility that other human attributes, capacities, and abilities might do or provide what reason cannot.

Let me give a couple of specific examples of what I mean by the claim that arational knowledge might constitute the real basis of a moral criticism of law and then make a couple of general concluding observations. First, the legal economist may be right to doubt that we can rationally know the subjectivity of other individuals, and thus formulate an ideal conception of the good life on the basis of information rationally acquired through comparisons of those lives. But it does not follow from this doubt, even if well founded, that we cannot know and compare the subjectivity of others, and construct individualistic ideals on the basis of those comparisons. The source of our knowledge of the subjectivity of the other may not be rationality, either understood as general norms of reason or as empirical claims about nature. Rather, the source of our knowledge of this subjectivity may not be our capacity for rationality at all, but rather our utterly arational capacity for *sympathy*.[24] When we sympathize with the other, we open our hearts to his or her subjective predicament, rather than our minds to his or her behavioral choices and preferences. We sympathetically come to know the feel of his or her subjective pain, or the quality of his or her subjective pleasure. The knowledge we acquire through sympathetic sensitivity to the subjectivity of the

---

24. This is, of course, an old as well as a new claim. Adam Smith, among other thinkers of the Scottish Enlightenment, was impressed by the role of sympathy in the acquisition of moral knowledge. See Adam Smith. *The Theory of Moral Sentiments* (Oxford: Clarendon, 1971). Recently, feminist legal theorists have explored the role of sympathy and empathy in legal judgment. See Lynne Henderson, "Legality and Empathy," *Michigan Law Review* 85 (1987); 1574; Martha Minow, "Foreword: Justice Engendered," *Harvard Law Review* 101 (1987): 10. I have explored the connection between this stand of feminist legal theory and radical legal critique in Robin West, "Literary Woman and Economic Man," *Mercer Law Review* 39 (1988): 867.

other cannot, indeed, be quantified or calculated. It cannot become an object of rational knowledge. But that does not mean that such knowledge does not exist. It does exist. We can and do sympathize with the other. We can, do, and should use our knowledge of the subjectivity of others, sympathetically and arationally acquired, in forming our ideals about what life should be like, and hence in forming our normative judgments about law.

Similarly, the legal humanist may be right to insist that we can never rationally know the quality of a community's life, but wrong to believe that it follows from that that we cannot know, and hence compare, the quality of communitarian life, and form ideals on the basis of such knowledge. Again, it may have been wrongheaded to think that this sort of knowledge is rationally acquired. We know the qualitative feel of oppressive, tyrannical, violent communal living, and we know the qualitative feel of liberating, tolerant, egalitarian, robust, nurturing, caring, and vibrant community life, and we know that the first is a bad way to live in communities and that the second is a good way to live. We can judge a community's subjective well-being in the same way that we can judge an individual's. We open our hearts to the quality of the community members' lives. We can know more about the quality of a community's values than whether or not they are conducive to the production of public, communicative texts and interpretations, just as we can know more of the subjectivity of an individual's life than whether or not he or she has and acts on his or her preferences. Our communitarian life extends well beyond that which we textually express, just as our individual subjective life is far richer than that which is embodied in our preferences, and we can acquire an appreciation of that nontextual life, just as we can understand, to some degree the quality of an individual's subjective life that is not reflected in his or her preferences. The knowledge we sympathetically acquire of the quality of nontextual life in particular communities might not be capable of rational, humanistic, literary analysis. But it does not follow that it does not exist.

In U.S. legal culture, we use this knowledge of the subjectivity of the individual and collective other when we argue that an unconscionable contract ought not be enforced, even though both parties consented to it, or that a community's or majority's textual moral commitment—enacted in law—ought not be honored, even though it fairly represents its will. We use this knowledge of the subjectivity of the individual or community life when we argue the merits of paternalistic legislation, or of judicial intervention into markets, or of nontextual constitutional protection of fundamental interests in which the majority of the public at any given time seem to have no perceived stake. Indeed, we must have considerable faith in our irrational knowledge of the subjectivity of the other. We rely on such knowledge when we conclude that the "other's" expressed individual preference, or the community's articulated textual belief, is ill advised, and that the contract or statute to which it gave rise ought not be enforced, by reference to our sense of the true, subjective welfare of the individual or communitarian other—even, at times, a quite distant other.

Thus, we use arational, sympathetic knowledge of the other not only when we criticize acts of power of distant lawmakers, but also acts of power that emanate from "others" themselves, such as a contractual commitment or a majoritarian preference. If this is a worthwhile thing to do—if our arational critical practices can indeed by justified—then the legal economist and the legal humanist are wrong to deny the practicability of the methods of criticism made possible by individualistic utilitarianism and communitarian republicanism. The legal economist and legal humanist turned away from subjective criteria of criticism because of their skeptical conviction that such criteria could ever become objects of rational knowledge. But maybe that skepticism was not, after all, well grounded. Perhaps subjective goals—individual happiness and a healthy community—can also be standards of criticism even if they can never be objects of rational knowledge. Perhaps, as the postmodern critics urge, our insistence on rationality was ill conceived. If it was, then we should reexamine the viability of overtly political and subjectivist criticism of the sort propounded by classical utilitarianism and modern civic republicanism. Moral criticism of law might be properly grounded not in abstract reason, nor in general truths, nor in the dictates of preexisting law, nor in naked power, but, rather, in the sympathetic judgments of the heart.

I do not mean to deny that our capacity for sympathy, no less than our subjective experiences of pain, are not themselves heavily influenced by the hierarchical and political structures in which we find ourselves. Our ability to sympathize will obviously be, in large part, determined by our upbringing, our sense of commonality or differentness, and the generosity we have been taught to grant or withhold to others. But nevertheless, once we see the politics in our disciplined knowledge and methods of reason, we should no longer feel compelled by the dictates of rationalism to shun ways of learning that depend upon arational insight or intersubjective connection with others. Whether or not "socially constructed," we do, in fact, use our sympathetic understanding of the subjective plight of others to formulate ideals against which to criticize both the social reality in which that subjectivity is lived and the law, as well as the cultural traditions that uphold it. The arationality of such knowledge should not detract from its moral authority.

Once we recognize this capacity for sympathy, and the role it plays in our capacity for moral knowledge, we will also, perhaps, better appreciate its distinctive failings—most notably the perverse dependence of our capacity to build sympathetic feelings of solidarity, community, and wholeness with some, upon principles and practices of exclusion of others. With an understanding of the extent to which our moral commitments, ideals, and, hence, critical judgments about law are grounded in sympathy for the others in our lives, we might consequently better appreciate the failings and limits of that capacity and thereby improve the quality of our moral lives themselves. Ideally we might learn to use the tools of sympathetic identification and learning to counter the limitations of our moral sentiments. The end result could be a far richer, even if no less "constructed," moral understanding of the impact of our law on the quality of the subjective lives of the individuals and communities it may, indeed, in part "construct," but which it no doubt affects. We should not be deterred from the project by the perceived irrationality of the human capacity at its core.

Those of us in the nonmainstream interdisciplinary legal academy who have tried to answer Austin's question—how should we criticize the law, if not by reference to reason, and if not by reference to the law itself—have gone wrong, I believe, in our conviction that we should look to other academic disciplines for normative guidance. We should, indeed, be looking for guidance outside the legal academy, and it is surely true that other disciplines have much to offer. But we have relied too heavily on other disciplines, and on the idea of *discipline* that underlies them, for an articulation of our ideals. We should instead look to our sympathetic understandings both of the ideal community central to civic republicanism and the ideal individual central to liberal utilitarianism and the commitments to freedom, welfare, tolerance, nurturance, egalitarianism, individualism, and communitarianism that compete within and between them. No doubt if we do so, we will quickly realize that other academic disciplines are indispensable to our ability to achieve, articulate, enrich, and defend our moral convictions. We do indeed, most emphatically, need stories and metaphors to understand the subjectivities of lives not our own, particularly of those silenced lives that, for whatever reason, find themselves outside the perimeters of the dialogic interpretive community but not outside the reach of the law's coercive force. Similarly, we do indeed need economics to appreciate the far-flung and invisible consequences of our policies and desires, and we do indeed need theories of interpretation to come to grips with the inevitable limits of our understanding. But our moral beliefs and ideals *themselves* must come from the politics and struggles of the heart, not the disciplines of the mind. It is those moral convictions, grounded not in reason but in love, nurtured not in the head but in the heart, borne not in discipline but in the bonds of community, and realized not in the constraint of rationality but in the work of free individuals, that should inform our critical—and particularly our radically critical—sensitivities.

The Law Wishes to Have a Formal Existence

Stanley Fish

Achieving Plain and Clear Meanings

The law wishes to have a formal existence. That means, first of all, that the law does not wish to be absorbed by, or declared subordinate to, some other—nonlegal—structure of concern; the law wishes, in a word, to be distinct, not something else. And second, the law wishes in its distinctness to be perspicuous; that is, it desires that the components of its autonomous existence be self-declaring and not be in need of piecing out by some supplementary discourse; for were it necessary for the law to have recourse to a supplementary discourse at crucial points, that discourse would be in the business of specifying what the law is, and, consequently, its autonomy would have been compromised indirectly. It matters little whether one simply announces that the principles and mechanisms of the law exist ready-made in the articulations of another system or allows those principles and mechanisms to be determined by something they do not contain; in either case, the law as something independent and self-identifying will have disappeared.

In its long history, the law has perceived many threats to its autonomy, but two seem perennial: morality and interpretation. The dangers these two pose are, at least at first glance, different. Morality is something to which the law wishes to be related, but not too closely; a legal system whose conclusions clashed with our moral intuitions at every point so that the categories *legally valid* and *morally right* never (or almost never) coincided would immediately be sus-

159

pect; but a legal system whose judgments perfectly meshed with our moral intuitions would be thereby rendered superfluous. The point is made concisely by the Supreme Court of Utah in a case where it was argued that the gratuitous payment by one party of the other party's mortgage legally obligated the beneficiary to repay. The court rejected the argument, saying "that if a mere moral, as distinguished from a legal, obligation were recognized as valid consideration for a contract, that would practically erode to the vanishing point the necessity for finding a consideration."[1] That is to say, if one can infer directly from one's moral obligation in a situation to one's legal obligation, there is no work for the legal system to do; the system of morality has already done it. Although it might seem (as it does to many natural law theorists) that such a collapsing of categories recommends itself if only on the basis of efficiency (why have two systems when you can make do with one?), the defender of a distinctly legal realm will quickly answer that since moral intuitions are notoriously various and contested, the identification of law with morality would leave every individual his or her own judge; in place of a single abiding standard to which disputing parties might have recourse, we would have many standards with no way of adjudicating between them. In short, many moralities would make many laws, and the law would lack its most saliently desirable properties, generality and stability.

It is here that the danger posed by morality to law, or, more precisely, to the rule (in two senses) of law intersects with the danger posed by interpretation. The link is to be found in the desire to identify a perspective larger and more stable than the perspective of local and individual concerns. Morality frustrates that desire because, in a world of more than one church, recourse to morality will always be recourse to someone's or some group's challengeable moral vision. Interpretation frustrates that desire because, in the pejorative sense it usually bears in these discussions, interpretation is the name for what happens when the meanings embedded in an object or text are set aside in favor of the meanings demanded by some angled, partisan object. Interpretation, in this view, is the effort of a morality, of a particular, interested agenda, to extend itself into the world by inscribing its message on every available space. It follows then that,

---

1. Manwill v. Oyler, 11 Utah 2d 433, 361 P.2d 177 (1961).

in order to check the imperial ambitions of particular moralities, some point of resistance to interpretation must be found, and that is why the doctrine of formalism has proved so attractive. Formalism is the thesis that it is possible to put down marks so self-sufficiently perspicuous that they repel interpretation; it is the thesis that one can write sentences of such precision and simplicity that their meanings leap off the page in a way no one—no matter what his or her situation or point of view—can ignore; it is the thesis that one can devise procedures that are self-executing in the sense that their unfolding is independent of the differences between the agents who might set them in motion. In the presence (in the strong Derridean sense) of such a mark or sentence or procedure, the interpretive will is stopped short and is obliged to press its claims within the constraints provided by that which it cannot override. It must take the marks into account; it must respect the self-declaring reasons; it must follow the route laid down by the implacable procedures, and if it then wins it will have done so fairly, with justice, with reason.

Obviously then, formalism's appeal is a function of the number of problems it solves, or at least appears to solve: it provides the law with a palpable manifestation of its basic claim to be perdurable and general; that is, not shifting and changing, but standing as a point of reference in relation to which change can be assessed and controlled; it enables the law to hold contending substantive agendas at bay by establishing threshold requirements of procedure that force those agendas to assume a shape the system will recognize. The idea is that once a question has been posed as a *legal* question—has been put into the proper *form*—the answer to it will be generated by relations of entailment between that form and other forms in the system. As Hans Kelsen put it in a book aptly named *The Pure Theory of Law*,

> The law is an order, and therefore all legal problems must be set and solved as order problems. In this way legal theory becomes an exact structural analysis of positive law, free of all ethical-political value judgments.[2]

Kelsen's last clause says it all: the realms of the ethical, the political, and of value in general are the threats to the law's integrity. They are

2. P. 192. Trans. Max Knight from the 2d (rev. and enl.) German ed. (Berkeley: University of California Press, 1967).

what must be kept out if the law is to be something more than a
misnomer for the local (and illegitimate) triumph of some particular
point of view.

There are at least two strong responses to this conception of law.
The first, which we might call the "humanistic" response, objects
that a legal system so conceived is impoverished, and that once you
have severed procedures from value, it will prove enormously difficult, if not impossible, to relink them in particular cases. Since the
answers generated by a purely formal system will be empty of content (that, after all, is the formalist claim), the reintroduction of content will always be arbitrary. The second response, which we might
call "radical" or "critical," would simply declare that a purely formal
system is not a possibility, and that any system pretending to that
status is already informed by that which it purports to exclude.
Value, of both an ethical and political kind, is already inside the gate,
and the adherents of the system are either ignorant of its sources or
are engaged in a political effort to obscure them in the course of
laying claim to a spurious purity. In what follows, I shall be elaborating a version of the second response, and arguing that however much
the law wishes to have a formal existence, it cannot succeed in doing
so, because—at any level from the most highly abstract to the most
particular and detailed—any specification of what the law is will already be infected by interpretation and will therefore be challengeable. Nevertheless, my conclusion will not be that the law fails to
have a formal existence but that, in a sense I shall explain, it always
succeeds, although the nature of that success—it is a political/rhetori-
cal achievement—renders it bitter to the formalist taste.

We may see what is at stake in disputes about formalism by
turning to a recent (July, 1988) opinion delivered by Judge Alex Kozinski of the United States Court of Appeals for the Ninth Circuit.[3]
The case involved the desire of a construction partnership called
Trident Center to refinance a loan at rates more favorable than those
originally secured. Unfortunately (or so it seemed), language in the
original agreement expressly blocked such an action, to wit that the
" '[m]aker shall not have the right to prepay the principal amount
hereof in whole or in part' for the first 12 years."[4]

---

3. Trident Center v. Connecticut General Life Insurance Company, 847 F.2d 564
(9th Cir. 1988).
4. Ibid., 566.

Trident's attorneys, however, pointed to another place in the writing where it is stipulated that "[i]n the event of a prepayment resulting from a default . . . prior to January 10, 1996 the prepayment fee will be ten percent"[5] and argued that this clause gives Trident the option of prepaying the loan provided that it is willing to incur the penalty as stated. Kozinski is singularly unimpressed by this reasoning, and, as he himself says, dismisses it "out of hand,"[6] citing as his justification the clear and unambiguous language of the contract. Referring to Trident's contention that it is entitled to precipitate a default by tendering the balance plus the ten percent fee, Kozinski declares that "the contract language, cited above, leaves no room for this construction,"[7] a judgment belied by the fact that Trident's lawyers managed to make room for just that construction in their arguments. It is a feature of cases like this that turn on the issue of what is and is not "expressly" said that the proclamation of an undisputed meaning always occurs in the midst of a dispute about it. Given Kozinski's rhetorical stance, the mere citation (his word, and a very dangerous one for his position) of the contract language should be sufficient to end all argument, but what he himself immediately proceeds to do is argue, offering a succession of analyses designed to buttress his contention that "it is difficult to imagine language that more clearly or unambiguously expresses the idea that Trident may not unilaterally [more is given away by this word than Kozinski acknowledges] prepay the loan during its first 12 years."[8] If this were in fact so, it would be difficult to imagine why Kozinski should feel compelled to elaborate his opinion again and again. I shall not take up his points except to say that, in general, they are not particularly persuasive and usually function to open up just the kind of interpretive room he declares unavailable. Thus, for example, he reasons that Trident's interpretation "would result in a contradiction between two clauses of the contract" whereas the "normal rule of construction . . . is that courts must interpret contracts, if possible, so as to avoid internal conflict."[9] But it is no trick at all (or at least not a hard one) to treat the two clauses so that they refer to different anticipated

5. Ibid.
6. Ibid.
7. Ibid., 567.
8. Ibid., 566.
9. Ibid.

situations and are not contradictory (indeed that is what Trident's lawyers do): in the ordinary course of things, as defined by the rate and schedule of payments set down in the contract, Trident will not have the option of prepaying; but in the extraordinary event of a default, the prepayment penalty clause will then kick in. To be sure, Kozinski is ready with objections to this line of argument, but those objections themselves trace out a line of argument and operate (no less than the interpretations he rejects) to fill out the language whose self-sufficiency he repeatedly invokes.

In short (and this is a point I shall make often), Kozinski's assertion of ready-made, formal constraints is belied by his efforts to stabilize what he supposedly relies on, the plain meaning of absolutely clear language. The act of construction for which he says there is no room is one he is continually performing. Moreover, he performs it in a way no different from the performance he castigates. Trident, he complains, is attempting "to obtain judicial sterilization of its intended default,"[10] and the reading its lawyers propose is an extension of that attempt rather than a faithful rendering of what the document says. The implication is that *his* reading is the extension of nothing, proceeds from no purpose except the purpose to be scrupulously literal. But his very next words reveal another, less disinterested purpose: "But defaults are messy things and they are supposed to be. . . . Fear of these repercussions is strong medicine that keeps debtors from shirking their obligations. . . ."[11] And he is, of course, now administering that strong medicine through his reading, a reading that is produced not by the agreement, but by his antecedent determination to enforce contracts whenever he can. The contrast then is not (as he attempts to draw it) between a respect for what "the contract clearly does . . . provide"[12] and the bending of the words to an antecedently held purpose, but between two bendings, one of which by virtue of its institutional positioning—Kozinski is after all the judge—wins the day.

Except that it doesn't. In the second half of the opinion there is a surprise turn, one that alerts us to the larger issue Kozinski sees in the case and explains the vehemence (often close to anger) of his

---

10. Ibid., 568.
11. Ibid.
12. Ibid., 567 n.1.

language. The turn is that Kozinski rules for Trident, setting aside the district court's declaration that the clear and ambiguous nature of the document leaves Trident with no cause of action and setting aside, too, the same court's sanction of Trident for the filing of a frivolous lawsuit. In so doing Kozinski is responding to Trident's second argument, which is that "even if the language of the contract appears to be unambiguous, the deal the parties actually struck is in fact quite different" and that "extrinsic evidence" shows "that the parties had agreed Trident could prepay at any time within the first 12 years by tendering the full amount plus a 10 percent prepayment fee."[13] Kozinski makes it clear that he would like to reject this argument and rely on the traditional contract principle of the parol evidence rule, the rule (not of evidence but of law) by which "extrinsic evidence is inadmissible to interpret, vary or add to the terms of an unambiguous integrated written instrument."[14] He concedes, however, that this rule has not been followed in California since *Pacific Gas & Electric Co. v. G. W. Thomas Drayage & Rigging Co.*,[15] a case in which the state supreme court famously declared that there is no such thing as a clear and unambiguous document because it is not "feasible to determine the meaning the parties gave to the words from the instrument alone."[16] In other words (mine, not the court's), an instrument that seems clear and unambiguous on its face seems so because "extrinsic evidence"—information about the conditions of its production including the situation and state of mind of the contracting parties, etc.—is already in place and assumed as a background; that which the parol evidence rule is designed to exclude is already, and necessarily, invoked the moment writing becomes intelligible. In a bravura gesture, Kozinski first expresses his horror at this doctrine ("it . . . chips away at the foundation of our legal system")[17] and then flaunts it by complying with it.

> While we have our doubts about the wisdom of *Pacific Gas*, we have no difficulty understanding its meaning, even without extrinsic evidence to guide us . . . we must reverse and remand to

---

13. Ibid., 568.
14. Ibid.
15. 68 Cal.2d 33, 442 P.2d 641 (1968).
16. *Trident Center v. Connecticut General*, 568 (citing 69 Cal.2d 38).
17. Ibid., 569.

the district court in order to give plaintiff an opportunity to present extrinsic evidence as to the intentions of the parties.[18]

That is, "you say that words cannot have clear and constant meanings and that, therefore, extrinsic evidence cannot be barred; I think you are wrong and I hereby refute you by adhering strictly to the rule your words have laid down."

But of course he hasn't. The entire history of the parol evidence rule—the purposes it supposedly serves, the fears to which it is a response, the hopes of which it is a repository—constitutes the extrinsic evidence within whose assumption the text of the case makes the sense Kozinski labels "literal." When he prefaces his final gesture (the judicial equivalent of "up yours") by saying "As we read the rule," he acknowledges that it is *reading* and not simply receiving that he is doing.[19] And to acknowledge as much is to acknowledge that *Pacific Gas* could be read differently. Nevertheless, the challenge Kozinski issues to the Traynor court is pertinent; for what he is saying is that the question of whether or not it is possible to produce " 'a perfect verbal expression' "[20]—an expression that will serve as a "meaningful constraint on public and private conduct"[21]—will not be settled by the pronouncement of a court. Either it is or it isn't; either a court or a legislature or a constitutional convention can order words in such a way as to constrain what interpreters can then do with them or it cannot. The proof will be in the pudding, in what happens to texts or parts of texts that are the repository of that (formalist) hope. The parol evidence rule will not have the desired effect if no one could possibly follow it.

That this is, in fact, the case is indicated by the very attempt to formulate the rule. Consider, for example, the formulation found in section 2–202 of the Uniform Commercial Code.

Terms with respect to which the confirmatory memoranda of the parties agree or which are otherwise set forth in a writing intended by the parties as a final expression of their agreement with respect to such terms as are included therein may not be contradicted by evidence of any prior agreement or of a contem-

---

18. Ibid., 569–70.
19. Ibid., 569.
20. Ibid. (citing 69 Cal. 2d 37).
21. Ibid., 569.

poraneous oral agreement but may be explained or supplemented
    (*a*) by course of dealing or usage of trade (Section 1–205) or by course of performance (Section 2–208); and
    (*b*) by evidence of consistent additional terms unless the court finds the writing to have been intended also as a complete and exclusive statement of the terms of the agreement.[22]

One could pause at almost any place to bring the troubles lying in wait for would-be users of this section to the surface, beginning perhaps with the juxtaposition of "writing" and "intended," which reproduces the conflict supposedly being adjudicated. (Is the writing to pronounce on its own meaning and completeness or are we to look beyond it to the intentions of the parties?) Let me focus, however, on the distinction between explaining or supplementing and contradicting or varying. The question is how can you tell whether a disputed piece of evidence is one or the other? And the answer is that you could only tell if the document in relation to which the evidence was to be labeled one or the other declared its own meaning; for only then could you look at "it" and then at the evidence and proclaim the evidence either explanatory or contradictory. But if the meaning and completeness of the document were self-evident (a wonderfully accurate phrase), explanatory evidence would be superfluous and the issue would never arise. And on the other hand, if the document's significance and state of integration are not self-evident—if "it" is not complete but must be pieced out in order to become what "it" is— then the relation to "it" of a piece of so-called extrinsic evidence can only be determined after the evidence has been admitted and is no longer extrinsic. Either there is no problem or it can only be solved by recourse to that which is in dispute.

Exactly the same fate awaits the distinction between "consistent additional terms" and additional terms that are inconsistent. "Consistent in relation to what?" is the question; the answer is "consistent in relation to the writing." But if the writing were clear enough to establish its own terms, additional terms would not be needed to explain it (subsection [*b*], you will remember, is an explanation of "explained or supplemented"), and if additional terms are needed

22. *Uniform Commercial Code*, 10th ed. (St. Paul, Minn.: West Publishing, 1987), 71.

there is not yet anything for them to be consistent or inconsistent with. The underlying point here has to do with the distinction—assumed but never examined in these contexts—between inside and outside, between what the document contains and what is external to it. What becomes clear is that the determination of what is "inside" will always be a function of whatever "outside" has already been assumed. (I use quotation marks to indicate that the distinction is interpretive, not absolute.) As one commentary puts it, "questions concerning the admissibility of parol evidence cannot be resolved without considering the nature and scope of the evidence which is being offered," and "thus the court must go beyond the writing to determine whether the writing should be held to be a final expression of the parties' . . . agreement."[23]

Nowhere is this more obvious than in the matter of *trade usage*, the first body of knowledge authorized as properly explanatory by the code. Trade usage refers to conventions of meaning routinely employed by members of a trade or industry, and is contrasted to *ordinary usage*, that is, to the meanings words ordinarily have by virtue of their place in the structure of English. The willingness of courts to regard trade usage as legitimately explanatory of contract language seems only a minor concession to the desire of the law to find a public—i.e., objective—linguistic basis, but in fact it is fatal, for it opens up a door that cannot be (and never has been) closed. In a typical trade usage case, one party is given the opportunity to "prove" that the words of an agreement don't mean what they seem to mean because they emerged from a special context, a context defined by the parties' expectations. Thus, for example, in one case it was held that, by virtue of trade usage, the shipment term "June-Aug." in an agreement was to be read as excluding delivery in August;[24] and in another case the introduction of trade usage led the court to hold that an order for thirty-six-inch steel was satisfied by the delivery of steel measuring thirty-seven inches.[25] But if "June-Aug." can, in certain persuasively established circumstances, be understood to exclude August, and "thirty-six" can be understood as

23. Gordon D. Schaber and Claude D. Roher, *Contracts in an Nutshell*, 2d ed. (St. Paul, Minn.: West Publishing, 1984), 243.

24. Warren's Kiddie Shoppe, Inc. v. Casual Slacks, Inc., 120 Ga. App. 578, 171 S.E.2d 643 (1969).

25. Dekker Steel Co. v. Exchange National Bank of Chicago, 330 F.2d 82 (1964).

meaning thirty-seven, then anything, once a sufficiently elaborated argument is in place, can mean anything: "thirty-six" could mean seventy-five, or, in relation to a code so firmly established that it governed the expectations of the parties, "thirty-six" could mean detonate the atomic bomb.

If this line of reasoning seems to slide down the slippery slope too precipitously, consider the oft cited case of *Columbia Nitrogen Corporation v. Royster Company.*[26] The two firms had negotiated a contract by which Columbia would purchase from Royster 31,000 tons of phosphate each year for three years, with an option to extend the term. The agreement was marked by "detailed provisions regarding the base price, escalation, minimum tonnage and delivery schedules,"[27] but when phosphate prices fell, Columbia ordered and accepted only one-tenth of what was specified. Understandably, Royster sued for breach of contract, and was awarded a judgment of $750,000 in district court. Columbia appealed, contending that, in the fertilizer industry,

> because of uncertain crop and weather conditions, farming practices, and government agricultural programs, express price and quantity terms in contracts ... are mere projections to be adjusted according to market forces.[28]

One would think that this argument would fail because it would amount to saying that the contract was not worth the paper it was printed on. If emerging circumstances could always be invoked as controlling, even in the face of carefully negotiated terms, why bother to negotiate? Royster does not make this point directly, but attempts to go the (apparently) narrower route of section 202. After all, even trade usage is inadmissible according to that section if it contradicts, rather than explains, the terms of the agreement, and as one authority observes, "it is hard to imagine a ... 'trade usage' that contradicts a stated contractual term more directly than did the usage in *Columbia Nitrogen Corporation.*"[29] The court, however, doesn't see it that way.

26. 451 F.2d 3 (1971).
27. Ibid., 9.
28. Ibid., 7.
29. Steven Emanuel and Steven Knowles, *Contracts* (Larchmont, N.Y.: Emanuel Law Outlines, 1987), 160.

Although the opinion claims to reaffirm "the well established rule that evidence of usage of trade . . . should be excluded whenever it cannot be reasonably construed as consistent with the terms of the contract,"[30] the reaffirmation undoes itself; for by making the threshold of admissibility the production of a "reasonable construal" rather than an obvious inconsistency (as in 31,000 is inconsistent with 3,100), the court more or less admits that what is required to satisfy the section is not a demonstration of formal congruity but an exercise of rhetorical skill. As long as one party can tell a story sufficiently overarching so as to allow the terms of the contract and the evidence of trade usage to fit comfortably within its frame, that evidence will be found consistent rather than contradictory. What is and is not a "reasonable construal" will be a function of the persuasiveness of the construer and not of any formal fact that is perspicuous before some act of persuasion has been performed.

The extent to which this court is willing to give scope to the exercise of rhetorical ingenuity is indicated by its final dismissal of the contention by Royster that there is nothing in the contract about adjusting its terms to reflect a declining market. "Just so," says the court, there is nothing in the contract about this and that is why its introduction is not a contradiction or inconsistency. Since "the contract is silent about adjusting prices and quantities . . . it neither permits or prohibits adjustment, and this neutrality provides a fitting occasion for recourse to usage of trade . . . to supplement the contract and explain its terms."[31] Needless to say, as an interpretive strategy this could work to authorize almost anything, and it is itself authorized by the first of the official comments on section 202 (and why a section designed supposedly to establish the priority of completely integrated writings is itself in need of commentary is a question almost too obvious to ask): "This section definitely rejects (a) any assumption that because a writing has been worked out which is final on some matters, it is to be taken as including all the matters agreed upon."[32] Or in other words, just because a writing says something doesn't mean that it says everything relevant to the matter; it may be silent on some things, and in relation to those things parol evidence is admissible. But of course the number of things on which a

---

30. Columbia Nitrogen v. Royster Company, 451 F.2d 3 (1971), 9.
31. Ibid., 9–10.
32. *Uniform Commercial Code*, 71.

document (however interpreted) is silent is infinite, and consequently there is no end to the information that can be introduced if it can be linked narratively to a document that now becomes a mere component (albeit a significant one) in a larger contractual context.

One way of doing this is exemplified by the majority opinion in *Masterson v. Sine*,[33] a case in which the attempt of a bankruptcy trustee to exercise an option to purchase a particular piece of property (on the grounds that the right of option belongs to the estate) was challenged by parol evidence tending to show that it was the intention of the drafting parties to keep the property in the family (Mr. Masterson and Mrs. Sine were brother and sister) and "that the option was therefore personal to the grantors and could not be exercised by the trustee."[34] The trial court excluded the evidence, ruling that the written contract was a complete and final embodiment of the terms of the agreement and said nothing about the assignability of the option. The court, in the person of Chief Justice Traynor (the same Traynor who in Kozinski's eyes commits the villainy of *Pacific Gas*), responds by declaring that, yes, "the deed is silent on the question of assignability,"[35] but that this very silence was a reason for admitting the evidence, not as a gloss on the agreement as written, but as proof of a collateral agreement—an agreement made on a related, but adjoining matter—that was entered into orally. The beauty of this recharacterization of the situation is that it manages at once to save the integrity of the integrated agreement and to create another agreement whose honoring has the effect of setting aside what the integrated agreement seems to say. This is all managed by telling another story about the negotiations. The parties conducted not one, but two negotiations; in one, the question of the conveying of the land and the option of the conveyers to repurchase was settled; in another (orally conducted), the question of reserving the option to members of the family was settled. The demands of formalism are at once met and evaded, a result that led two dissenting justices to complain that the parol evidence rule had been eviscerated, that the decision rendered all instruments of conveyance, no matter how full and complete, suspect, and that the reliance one might previously have placed upon written agreements had been materially undermined.

---

33. 65 Cal. Rptr. 545, 436 P.2d 561 (Cal. Sup. Ct. 1968).
34. Ibid., 562.
35. Ibid., 565.

This conclusion might seem to be the one I, myself, was moving toward in the course of presenting these examples, for surely the moral of *Columbia Nitrogen, Warren's Kiddie Shoppe, Dekker Steel, Pacific Gas,* and *Masterson v. Sine* (and countless others that could be adduced) is that the parol evidence rule is wholly ineffective as a stay against interpretive assaults on the express language of contracts and statutes. But the moral I wish to draw goes in quite another direction, one that reaffirms (although not in a way formalists will find comforting) the power both of the parol evidence rule and of the language whose "rights" it would protect, to "provide a meaningful constraint on public and private conduct."[36] It is certainly the case that *Masterson v. Sine*, like *Columbia Nitrogen* and the others, indicates that no matter how carefully a contract is drafted it cannot resist incorporation into a persuasively told story in the course of whose unfolding its significance may be altered from what it had seemed to be. But the same cases also indicate that the story so told cannot be any old story; it must be one that fashions its coherence out of materials that it is required to take into account. The important fact about *Masterson* is not that in it the court succeeds in getting around the parol evidence rule, but that it is the parol evidence rule—and not the first chapter of Genesis or the first law of thermodynamics—that it feels obliged to get around. That is, given the constraints of the institutional setting—constraints that help shape the issue being adjudicated—the court could not proceed on its way without raising and dealing with the parol evidence rule (and this would be true even if the rule had not been invoked by the eager trustee); consequently, the *path* to the result it finally reaches is constrained, in part, by the very doctrine that result will fail to honor.

One sees this clearly in the route the court takes to the discovery that there are not one, but two agreements. It is not enough, the court acknowledges, to observe that if an agreement is silent on a matter, information pertaining to it is admissible, for the official comment to section 2–202 adds that "if the additional terms are such that, if agreed upon, they would certainly have been included in the document in the view of the court, then evidence of their alleged making must be kept from the trier of fact."[37] In other words, the court must

---

36. *Trident Center*, 569.
37. *Uniform Commercial Code*, 72.

determine whether or not the additional terms that would make up a collateral agreement are such that persons contemplating the original agreement would certainly have considered including them; for if they were such and were not included, their exclusion was intentional and the original writing must be regarded as complete. In *Masterson*, the court reasons that the inexperience of the parties in land transactions made it unlikely that they would have been aware "of the disadvantages of failing to put the whole agreement in the deed" and rules that therefore "the case is not one in which the parties 'would certainly' have included the collateral agreement"[38] had they meant to enter into it. Again the point is not so much the persuasiveness of such reasoning (in another landmark case a New York court found the same reasoning unpersuasive),[39] but the fact that it must be produced, and this requirement would have held even if the reasoning had been rejected. It was open to the court (as a note to the case indicates) to find that in a particular instance what the parties would naturally have done was, in fact, not done and that "the unnatural actually happened";[40] but had the court so found, the official comment would have been honored even as it was declared to be inapposite, for that finding (or some other in the same line of country) would have been rendered obligatory by the existence of the comment. It is always possible to "get around" the comment as it is always possible to get around the parol evidence rule—neither presents an absolute bar to reaching a particular result; there is always work that can be done—but the fact that it is the comment you are getting around renders it constraining even if it is not, in the strict sense, a constraint.

In short, the parol evidence rule is of more service to the law's wish to have a formal existence than one might think from these examples. The service it provides, however, is not (as is sometimes claimed) the service of safeguarding a formalism already in place, but the weaker (although more exacting) service of laying down the route by which a formalism can be fashioned. I am aware, of course, that this notion of the formal will seem strange to those for whom a formalism is what is "given" as opposed to something that is made. But, in fact, efficacious formalisms—marks and sounds that declare

---

38. *Masterson*, 731–32.
39. *Mitchill v. Lath*, 247 N.Y. 377, 160 N.E. 646 (1928).
40. *Masterson*, 731n.

meanings to which all relevant parties attest—are always the product
of the forces—desire, will, intentions, circumstances, interpretation—they are meant to hold in check. No one has seen this more
clearly than Arthur Corbin who, noting that "sometimes it is said
that 'the courts will not disregard the plain language of a contract or
interpolate something not contained in it,' "[41] offers for that dictum
this substitute.

> If, after a careful consideration of the words of a contract, in the
> light of all the relevant circumstances, and of all the tentative
> rules of interpretation based upon the experience of courts and
> linguists, a plain and definite meaning is achieved by the court,
> a meaning actually given by one party as the other party had
> reason to know, it will not disregard this plain and definite
> meaning and substitute another that is less convincing.[42]

There are many words and phrases one might want to pause over in
this remarkable sentence (*relevant, tentative, experience, actually*), but
for our purposes the most significant word is *achieved* and, after that,
convincing. Achieved is a surprise because, in most of the literature, a
plain meaning is something that constrains or even precludes interpretation, while in Corbin's statement it is something that interpretation helps fashion; once it is fashioned, the parol evidence rule can
then be invoked with genuine force: you must not disregard this
meaning—that is, the meaning that has been established in the
course of the interpretive process—for one that has not been so established. *Convincing* names the required (indeed the only) mode of
establishing, the mode of persuasion, and what one is persuaded *to*
is an account (story) of the circumstances ("relevant" not before, but
as a result of, the account) in relation to which the words of the
agreement could only mean one thing. Of course, if an alternative
account were to become more rather than less convincing—perhaps
in the course of appeal—then the meanings that followed from *its*
establishment would be protected by the rule from the claims of
meanings to which the court had not been persuaded. As Corbin
puts it in another passage, "when a court says that it will enforce a
contract in accordance with the 'plain and clear' meaning of its

41. Corbin, *Corbin on Contracts*, one-volume edition (St. Paul, Minn.: West Publishing, 1952), 496.
42. Ibid., 497.

words . . . the losing party has merely urged the drawing of inferences . . . that the court is unwilling to draw."[43] That is, the losing
party has told an unpersuasive story, and consequently the meanings
it urges—i.e., the inferences it would draw—strike the court as
strained and obscure rather than plain.

There are, then, two stages to the work done by the parol evidence rule: in the first its presence on the "interpretative scene"
works to constrain the path interpreters must take on their way to
telling a persuasive story (an account of all the "relevant" circumstances); then, once the story has been persuasively told, the rule is
invoked to protect the meanings that flow from that story. The phrase
that remains to be filled in is *persuasive story*. What is one and how is
it, in Corbin's word, *achieved*? The persuasiveness of a story is not the
product merely of the arguments it explicitly presents, but of the
relationship between those arguments, and other, more tacit, arguments—tantamount to already in-place beliefs—that are not so much
being urged as they are being traded on. It is this second, recessed,
tier of arguments—of beliefs so much a part of the background that
they are partly determinative of what will be heard as an argument—
that does much of the work of fashioning a persuasive story and,
therefore, does much of the work of filling in the category of "plain
and clear" meaning. What kinds of arguments or (deep) assumptions
are these? It is difficult to generalize (and dangerous, since generalization would hold out the false promise of a *formal* account of persuasion), but one could say first of all that they will include, among
other things, beliefs one might want to call "moral"—dispositions as
to the way things are or should be as encoded in maxims and slogans
like "order must be preserved" or "freedom of expression" or "the
American way" or "the Judeo-Christian tradition" or "we must draw
the line somewhere." It follows, then, that whenever there is a dispute about the plain meaning of a contract, at some level the dispute
is between two (or more) visions of what life is or should be like.

Consider, for example, still another famous case in legal interpretation, *In Re Soper's Estate*.[44] The facts are the stuff of soap opera.
After ten years of marriage, Ira Soper faked his suicide and resur-
faced in another state under the name of John Young. There he mar-

43. Ibid., 515.
44. 196 Minn. 60, 264 N.W. 247 (1935).

ried a widow who died three years later, whereupon he married another widow with whom he lived for five years when he again committed suicide, but this time for real. The litigation turns on an agreement Soper-Young made with a business partner according to which, upon the death of either, the proceeds of the insurance on the life of the deceased would be delivered to his wife. The question of course is who is the wife, Mrs. Young or the long-since deserted Mrs. Soper, who, to the surprise of everyone, appeared to claim her rightful inheritance.

The majority rules for the second wife, Gertrude, while a strong dissent is registered on behalf of the abandoned Adeline. There is a tendency in both opinions to present the case as if it were a textbook illustration of a classic conflict in contract law between the view (usually associated with Williston) that determinations of the degree of integration and of the meaning of an agreement are to be made by looking to the agreement itself and the view (later to be associated with Corbin) that such issues can only be decided by ascertaining the intentions of the drafting parties, that is, by going outside the agreement to something not in it but in the light of which it is to be read. But, in fact, what the case illustrates is the impossibility of this very distinction. It is the minority that raises the banner of literalism, arguing that since a man can have only one lawful wife and since Adeline was, at the time of the agreement, "the only wife of Soper then living,"[45] the word *wife* must refer to her. The majority replies that by the same standard of literalism, the agreement contains no mention of a Mr. Soper, referring only to a Mr. Young whose only possible wife was a lady named Gertrude; and indeed, observes Justice Olson, the document can only be read as referring to Adeline by bringing in the same kind of oral evidence her lawyers (and the dissent) now wish to exclude. An inquirer merely looking at the document might well conclude "that two different men are involved," for after all,

> in what manner may either establish relationship to the decedent as his "wife" except by means of oral testimony. . . . Adeline, to establish her relationship, was necessarily required to and did furnish proof, principally oral, that her husband, Ira Collins

---

45. Ibid., 433.

Soper, was in fact the same individual as John W. Young, [and] Gertrude by similar means sought to establish her claim.[46]

The moral is clear even though the court does not quite draw it: rather than a dispute between a reading confining itself to the document and one that goes outside it to the circumstances from which it emerged, this is a dispute between two opposing accounts of the circumstances. Depending on which of these accounts is the more persuasive—that is, on which of the two stories about the world, responsibility, and wives is firmly in place—the document will acquire one of the two literal meanings being proposed for it. The majority finds itself persuaded by Gertrude's story and thus can quite sincerely declare that the "agreement points to no one else than Gertrude as Young's 'wife,'"[47] and Justice Olsen with an *e* (I resist the temptation to inquire into the *différance* of this difference) can declare with equal sincerity that "I am unable to construe this word to mean anyone else than the only wife of Soper then living."[48] Indeed he *is* unable, since as someone who subscribes to the moral vision that underlies Adeline's claims—a vision in which responsibilities once entered into cannot be weakened by obligations subsequently incurred—*wife* can only refer to the first in what is, for him, a nonseries; just as, for Justice Olson with an *o*—in whose morality obligations in force at the time of agreement take precedence over obligations recognized by a legal formalism—*wife* can only refer to the person "all friends and acquaintances . . . recognized . . . as his wife."[49]

The majority says that the "question is not just what words mean literally but how they are intended to operate practically on the subject matter,"[50] but its own arguments show that words *never* mean literally except in the context of the intention they are presumed to be effecting, and that rather than being determined by the meanings the words already (by right) have, the intentional context—established when one or the other party succeeds in being convincing—

---

46. Ibid., 431.
47. Ibid.
48. Ibid., 433.
49. Ibid., 431.
50. Ibid., 433 (citing City of Marshall v. Gregoire, 193 Minn. 188, 198–99, 259 N.W. 377, 381–82).

determines the meaning of the words. In short, the issue is not nor
could ever be the supposed choice between literal and contextual
reading, but the relative persuasiveness of alternative contexts as
they are set out in ideologically charged narratives. That is why it is
no surprise to find Justice Olsen's confidence declaration of linguistic
clarity ("I am unable to construe") preceded by a rehearsal of the
moralizing story that produces that clarity:

> Much is said in the opinion as to the wrong done to the innocent
> woman whom he purported to marry. Nothing is said about the
> wrong done to the lawful wife. To have her husband abandon
> her and then purport to marry another, and live in cohabitation
> with such other, was about as great a wrong as any man could
> inflict upon his wife.[51]

The majority thinks that something else (setting aside as of no account the relationship between the deceased and Gertrude) is the
greater wrong and therefore thinks, like the minority, that the meaning of the agreement is obvious and inescapable. Again, my point is
not to discredit the reasoning of either party nor to dismiss the claim
of each to have pointed to a formal linguistic fact; rather, I wish only
to observe once again that such formal facts are always "achieved"
and that they are achieved by the very means—the partisan urging
of some ideological vision—to which they are then rhetorically (and
not unreasonably) opposed.

Contract's Two Stories

That is to say—and in so saying I rehearse the essence of my argument—the law is continually creating and recreating itself out of the
very materials and forces it is obliged, by the very desire to be law,
to push away. The result is a spectacle that could be described (as the
members of the critical legal studies movement tend to do) as farce,
but I would describe it differently, as a signal example of the way in
which human beings are able to construct the roadway on which they
are traveling, even to the extent of "demonstrating" in the course of
building it that it was there all the while. The failure of both legal

---

51. Ibid., 433.

positivists and natural law theorists to find the set of neutral procedures or basic moral principles underlying the law should not be taken to mean that the law is a failure, but rather that it is an amazing kind of success. The history of legal doctrine and its applications is a history neither of rationalistic purity nor of incoherence and bad faith, but an almost Ovidian history of transformation under the pressure of enormously complicated social, political, and economic urgencies, a history in which victory—in the shape of *keeping going*—is always being wrested from what looks like certain defeat, and wrested by means of stratagems that are all the more remarkable because, rather than being hidden, they are almost always fully on display. Not only does the law forge its identity out of the stuff it disdains, it does so in public.

If this is true of the law's relation to interpretation, it is equally true of its relation to morality, as one can readily see by inquiring into the doctrine of consideration. Consideration is a term of art and refers to the "bargain" element in a transaction, what X did or promised to do in return for what Y did or promised to do. It is an article of faith in modern contract law that only agreements displaying consideration—a mutuality of bargained-for exchange—are legally enforceable. The intention of this requirement is to separate the realm of legal obligation from the larger and putatively more subjective realm of moral obligation, and the separation is accomplished (or so it is claimed) by providing *formal* (as opposed to value-laden) criteria of the intention to be legally bound. There are all kinds of reasons why one might make promises or perform actions conferring benefits on another and all kinds of after-the-fact analyses of what the promise signified or what the action contemplated. But if there is something tangible offered in return for something tangible requested, the transaction is a legal one and the machinery of legal obligation kicks in.

> The existence of consideration helps to provide *objective evidence* that the parties intended to make a binding agreement. It helps courts distinguish those agreements that were intended by the parties to be legally enforceable from . . . promises of gifts which neither party expected to be enforceable in court.[52]

---

52. Emanuel and Knowles, *Contracts*, 72.

By demarcating an area of legal obligation that is distinct from and independent of the larger matrix of obligations that make up our social existence, consideration plays a role similar to the role played (if it could be played) by the parol evidence rule. Just as Judge Kozinski says (or wants to say) to *Trident*, "you may not like the agreement you made, you may wish you could have it to do all over again, or that you had employed another negotiating team, but, nevertheless, this is the agreement you signed and this is what it says, and that's all there is to it," so might he or another judge say, "you may repent of your bargain because you know that someone will pay more for the automobile, but you promised to hand it over if he gave you $500; he has given you $500 and you must hand it over." Like absolutely express language (if there could be such a thing), consideration is a device for severing the moment of legal transaction from its surrounding circumstances and reducing it to a form that will stand out over the circumstances in which it is later examined by a court.

Consideration is, thus, a part of the law's general effort to disengage itself from history and assume (in two senses) a shape that time cannot alter. Consideration can be said to be such a shape because it has no content or, rather (it amounts to the same thing), can have any content whatsoever provided that there is an exchange and it is voluntary. That is why courts frequently declare that they will not inquire into the adequacy of the consideration,[53] will not, that is, inquire into whether or not the two parties were equally informed or received equivalent benefits from the exchange or were equally powerful actors in the market. To do so would be to reintroduce the very issues—of equity, of the distribution of resources, of fairness, of relative capacity, of *morality*—that consideration is designed to bracket. (All of those issues will return by routes students of contract law know very well, but the fact that such indirection is required is crucial.) With these issues bracketed, the act of contracting (or so it is claimed) becomes purely rational as the parties play out their formal roles in response to a mechanical requirement, the requirement of consideration. This, in turn, requires the court to be similarly mechanical (formal) lest it substitute for the bargain two free agents rationally made a bargain it would have preferred them to make.

53. *Restatement of the Law Second, Contracts Second*, vol. 1 (St. Paul, Minn.: American Law Institute Publishers, 1981), sec. 79.

> Where a party contracts for the performance of an act...his estimate of the value should be left undisturbed....There is...absolutely no rule by which the courts can be guided, if once they depart from the value fixed by the promisor. If they attempt to fix some standard, it must necessarily be an arbitrary one, and...then the result is that the court substitutes its own judgment for that of the promisor, and, in doing this, makes a new contract.[54]

That is, presumably the parties had reasons for bargaining as they did and the court should not set aside those reasons for reasons that seem to it to be more compelling. The court's responsibility is to "judge" the contract only in a weak sense, to determine whether or not it displays the requisite shape of consideration; were it to exercise judgment in a stronger sense by inquiring into the conditions of the contract, the court would pass from being an instrument of *the* law into an instrument of *a* morality. The result, should this occur, would be exactly the same result that attends the failure to constrain interpretation, the making of a new contract in place of the contract it is the job of the law to enforce. The conclusion is one toward which I have been pointing since the beginning of this essay: interpretation and morality are not simply twin threats to the autonomy and integrity of the law; they are the *same* threat. Interpretation is the name for the activity by which a particular moral vision makes its hegemonic way into places from which it has been formally barred.

If interpretation and morality pose the same threats to the law's self-identity, what is true of one is likely to be true of the other, and, as we have seen, what is true of interpretation is that it is already inside the precincts that would exclude it. The parol evidence rule does not—cannot—work because the integrated agreement it is designed to protect can only come into being—achieve integration—by the very (interpretive) means it stigmatizes. Similarly, the distinction between legal and moral obligation will not work because any specification of a legal obligation is itself already linked with a morality. The large point here is one that I cannot pause to argue (although it has been argued elsewhere by me and by others): that the requirement of procedures that are neutral between contending moral agendas

---

54. Wolford v. Powers, 85 Ind. 294 (1882), 303.

cannot be met because, in order even to take form, procedures must promote some rationales for action and turn a blind eye to others. This is spectacularly true of the procedures built around the doctrine of consideration, a doctrine that finally makes sense not as an alternative to morality, but as the very embodiment of the morality of the market, a morality of arm's length dealing between agents without histories, gender, or class affiliation. Whatever one thinks of this conception of transaction and agency, it is hardly one that has bracketed moral questions; rather it has decided them in a particular way, and, moreover, in a way that is neither necessary nor inevitable. As E. Allan Farnsworth points out, the principle of "direct bilateral exchanges" is not the "only possible basis for an economic system." Other societies have "distributed their resources by sharing, based on notions of generosity, rather than by bargaining, based on notions of self-interest."[55] Historically, the morality of self-interest and with it the requirement of consideration triumphed after a determined effort by Lord Mansfield to make contractual and moral obligations one and the same. The fact that he failed does not mean that morality had been eliminated as an issue in contract law, but that one morality—the morality of discrete, one-shot transactions—became so firmly established that it won the right to call itself "mere procedure" and was able to set up a watchdog—called "consideration"—whose job it was to keep the other moralities at bay.

In a way, this outcome is inevitable given what we have already noted about the law. In order to be law, it must define itself *against* particular moral traditions. It follows then that the first thing a moral tradition must do after having captured the law (or some portion of its territory) is present itself as being beyond or below (it doesn't really matter) morality. This, in turn, dictates the strategy by which any alternative morality will have to make its way: it will have materially to alter the law while maintaining all the while that it is preserving what it alters. Just as the winning interpretation of a contract must persuade the court that it is not an interpretation at all but a plain and clear meaning, so the winning morality must persuade the court (or direct the court in the ways of persuading itself) that it is

55. E. Allan Farnsworth, *Contracts* (Boston: Little, Brown, 1982), 6.

not a morality at all but a perspicuous instance of fidelity to the law's form.

Contract law performs this feat of legerdemain by implanting within consideration theory a number of subversive concepts, chief among which is the concept of "contract implied in law." Nominally, a contract implied in law is a category in the taxonomy of contracts, but in fact it exceeds the taxonomy and threatens to render it incoherent. The category can be best grasped by contrasting it with its two neighbors, the express contract and the contract implied in fact. An express contract is a written or oral agreement whose terms explicitly state the basis for consideration: I will do or promise to do this if you will do or refrain from doing or promise to do or promise to refrain from doing that. Now, it may be that the parties have entered into no formal agreement but comport themselves in relation to one another in ways that could only be explained by the existence of the requisite contractual intentions. If you bring a broken item to a repair shop and leave it, your action and the action of the shop's agent are intelligible only within the assumption that, in return for his professional skill, you have obligated yourself to the payment of a reasonable fee. In short, you and the shop have entered into a contract even though it has not been expressly stated; it is a contract implied in fact, implied, that is, by the behavior of the contracting parties.

Express contracts and contracts implied in fact are thus different ways of signifying an intention to be party to a bargained-for exchange. Contracts implied in law, on the other hand, are not attempts to ascertain and enforce the parties' intentions with respect to a contemplated transaction, but are imposed by a court on persons irrespective of the intentions they had or the actions they performed. Indeed, a contract implied in law is a judgment by a court that a party *ought* to have had a certain intention or performed in a certain way and for the purposes of justice and equity that intention or performance will now be imputed to him along with the obligations that follow. The notion of a contract implied in law springs all the bolts that consideration is designed to secure and provides the means for a court to do what, under contract law, a court is not supposed to do, make a new contract in accordance with its conception of morality. Contract implied in law is a wild-card category inserted into the heart of contract doctrine, and, moreover, courts that employ it often admit as much.

> [A] contract implied in law is not a contract at all, but an obliga-
> tion imposed by law for the purpose of bringing about justice and
> equity without reference to the intent or agreement of the parties
> and, in some cases, in spite of an agreement between the parties.
>   . . . It is a non-contractual obligation that is to be treated proce-
> durally as if it were a contract. . . . [56]

In other words, the notion of implied in law contract does not belong
in contract law, for as Stanley Henderson puts it, "the substantive
right to recover benefits conferred upon another does not respect
legal categories, particularly that of contract."[57]

What, then, is it doing there? The question implies that contract
law would be better off were it not there or were its presence accounted for in ways that could better support a claim to consistency.
Consistency, however, is not a feature of contract law but is its (always precarious) achievement, and it is an achievement whose possibility depends on *not* resolving the conflicts contract doctrine displays. It is *because* it is a world made up of materials that pull in
diverse directions that contract law can succeed in its endless project
of making itself into a formal whole. Rather than being an embarrass-
ment, the presence in contract doctrine of contradictory versions of
the enterprise is an opportunity. It is in the spaces opened by the
juxtaposition of apparently irreconcilable impulses—to be purely formal and intuitively moral—that the law is able to exercise its resourcefulness.

These spaces continue to be opened up even in documents supposedly designed to close them. Here, for example, is section 86 of
Restatement Second, a section that promises to adjudicate the tension
between legal and moral notions of obligation, but ends up reproducing it.

86. Promise for Benefit Received

   (1) A promise made in recognition of a benefit previously
       received by the promisor from the promisee is binding
       to the extent necessary to prevent injustice.

---

56. Continental Forest Products, Inc. v. Chandler Supply Company, 95 Idaho
739, 743, 518 P.2d 1201 (1974), 1205.

57. Stanley Henderson, "Promises Grounded in the Past: The Idea of Unjust
Enrichment and the Law of Contracts," *Virginia Law Review* 57 (1971): 1141.

(2) A promise is not binding under Subsection (1)
    (a) if the promisee conferred the benefit as a gift or for other reasons the promisor has not been unjustly enriched; or
    (b) to the extent that its value is disproportionate to the benefit.[58]

Although the form of the section is straightforward and declarative, its content, as Grant Gilmore has observed, is hesitant and even schizophrenic.[59] By recognizing promises for benefits received, subsection (1) seems to send us firmly in the direction of an expansive notion of legal obligations (in "classic doctrine" such promises are not enforceable because the benefit was unsought and is not part of a bilateral exchange); but wait, "what Subsection (1) giveth, Subsection (2) largely taketh away";[60] such a promise will not be binding if the benefit came to the promisor in the form of a gift, that is, in a form not involved in a mutual transaction, that is, in a form without consideration. As Henderson observes, the requirement of subsection (2) "means that events are to be screened by consideration tests in order to determine which promises are to be included within the category of promises binding without consideration"; and he concludes that the restriction as stated "erodes the policy of growth manifested" in subsection (1).[61] But this is to regard the section as if it were (or aspired to be) a logical statement when, in fact, it is a set of directions for accomplishing a particularly difficult (but essential) task, the task of maintaining the formal basis of contract law while at the same time making room for the substantive concerns formalism desires to exclude. By first opening the door to moral obligation (that is, to promises for benefits received) and then allowing it to enter only if it can be provided with an origin in a bargained-for exchange, section 86 delivers a message, and delivers it not despite but because of its schizophrenia: "Relax the requirement of consideration, but do so in the guise of honoring it." The message is repeated and given a rationale almost charming in its transparency in official comment (a):

---

58. *Restatement Second, Contracts Second*, 233.
59. Grant Gilmore, *The Death of Contract* (Columbus: Ohio State University Press, 1974), 74–75.
60. Ibid.
61. Henderson, "Promises Grounded in the Past," 1127.

Enforcement of promises to pay for benefit received has sometimes been said to rest on "past consideration" or on the "moral
obligation" of the promisor, and there are statutes in such terms
in a few states. Those terms are not used here: "past consideration" is inconsistent with the meaning of consideration stated in
[section] 71, and there seems to be no consensus as to what
constitutes a "moral obligation."[62]

Or in other words, "look, if we want to revise contract doctrine so as
to bring it more into line with our moral intuitions, we would be well
advised to do so in terms that contract doctrine, as presently formulated, will find acceptable. Neither past consideration nor moral obligation are such terms. The first fails because it is too obviously ex
post facto with respect to the moment of exchange that constitutes a
contract; it too nakedly asks us simply to declare that what had not
been bargained for in the past—an unasked-for benefit—was in fact
the basis of a bargain. The second fails because it provides us with
no standard—there seems to be no consensus as to what constitutes
a 'moral obligation'—and too nakedly acknowledges that the basis
of law is variable. It is true that in some precincts these terms have
been used, but the liabilities they present are greater than the advantage of employing them. If we want our moral intuitions to be incorporated into the law we will have to make sure that they look like
what the law wants them to look like."

That is to say, they must be worked into a form that matches the
picture of consideration, the picture of a freely chosen giving up of
something in return for something just as freely proffered. The fact
(as I take it to be) that the notion of choosing one's obligations independently of historical pressures is a fiction, that the "inside" of the
isolated and "free" transaction is always determined by an "outside"
it does not acknowledge, may be philosophically compelling; but the
morality of consideration—of exchanges uninfluenced by anything
except the opportunities offered by the moment of transaction—is too
firmly embedded in contract doctrine to be embarrassed by any
analysis of it. So firmly is it embedded that anticonsideration impulses can be harbored and even nurtured in contract doctrine
where, rather than undermining the orthodox view, they provide it

---

62. *Restatement Second, Contracts Second*, 233–34.

with the flexibility it needs. Henderson notes that "the judicial process, in spite of a consistent adherence to the test of bargain, exhibits a recurring tendency to appeal to a code of moral duties in order to justify enforcement of a particular promise."[63] Henderson calls this a "fundamental inconsistency" that has been "built into contract analysis,"[64] but like most "buildings" this structure is neither accidental nor unproductive. In order to be what it claims to be—something, rather than everything or nothing—contract law must uphold a view of transaction in which its features are purely formal; but in order to be what it wants to be—sensitive to our always changing intuitions about how people ought to behave—contract law must continually smuggle in everything it claims to exclude. I must emphasize again that the so-called formal view of legal obligation was never really formal at all, but was the extension of a social vision from which it was detached at the moment of that vision's triumph. The tension between consideration doctrine with its privileging of the autonomous and selfish agent and the doctrine of moral obligation with its acknowledgment of responsibilities always and already in place is a tension between two contestable conceptions of life; it is just that one of them has won the right to occupy the pole marked *formal* (i.e., unattached to any particular agenda) in a powerful (because constitutive of an institutional space) opposition. Given that victory, the fact that the claim of consideration doctrine to be merely formal cannot finally be upheld is of no practical consequence; it is upheld by the rhetorical structure it has generated, and in order to alter that structure you must appear to be upholding it too. As I have already said, you can only get around consideration doctrine by elaborately honoring it.

And how do you do that? In many ways, including several we have already observed. You develop a taxonomy of contractual kinds, one of which violates the principles of the taxonomy; you produce a document (the *Restatement*) that, in the guise of clarifying the state of the law, presents its contradictions in a form that further institutionalizes them; you announce as a "principle of law" that the improver of another's land has no right to relief, and then in the next sentence you declare this principle "merely . . . technical" (i.e., legal)

---

63. Henderson, "Promises Grounded in the Past," 1122–23.
64. Ibid., 1122.

and dismiss it in favor of "an equitable remedy";[65] you develop and expand notions like promissory estoppel, duress, incapacity, unconscionability, and unjust enrichment and then expand them to the point where there is no action that cannot be justified in their terms; you invoke the distinction between public and private, even as you allow public pressures to determine the distinction's boundaries. In short, you tell two stories at the same time, one in which the freedom of contracting parties is proclaimed and protected and another in which that freedom is denied as a possibility and undermined by almost everything courts do. But in order to make them come out right, you tell the two stories as if they were one, as if, rather than eroding the supposedly formal basis of contract law, the second story merely refines it at the edges and leaves its primary assertions (which are also assertions of the law's stability) intact.

Illustrations of this process are everywhere in the law; indeed, as I have been arguing, the process *is* the law. For a conveniently concise and naked instance of the process at work, we can turn to a classic case of promise for benefit received, *Webb v. McGowin*.[66] Webb was an employee of a lumber company and one of his duties was to clear the upper floor of a mill by dropping pine blocks weighing 75 pounds to the ground below. "While so engaged" he saw McGowin directly below him, in the line of drop as it were, and rather than allowing the block to fall, he diverted its course by falling with it, "thus preventing injuries to McGowin," but causing himself to suffer "serious bodily injuries" as a result of which "he was badly crippled for life and rendered unable to do physical or mental labor." A grateful McGowin, "in consideration . . . [for] having prevented him from sustaining death or serious bodily harm" promised to pay Webb $15 every two weeks for the rest of his life.[67] That sum was paid until McGowin's death, whereupon the payments were discontinued and Webb sued to recover the unpaid installments.

This recital of the facts is taken, the court acknowledges, from the appellant's brief, and therefore it is obvious from the beginning where the court's (moral) sympathies lie. It is also obvious what obstacles stand in the way of transforming those sympathies into a legal remedy. Webb's action seems, on its face, to be a spontaneous

---

65. Pull v. Barnes, 142 Colo. 272, 350 P.2d 829 (1960).
66. 27 Ala. App. 82, 168 So. 196 (1935).
67. Ibid., 196–97.

and gratuitous expression of fellow feeling and, as such, ineligible for a remedy that requires evidence of a transaction of a pecuniary nature. Late in the opinion, however, the court declares that

> [t]he case at bar is clearly distinguishable from that class of cases where the consideration is a mere moral obligation or conscientious duty unconnected with receipt by promisor of benefits of a material or pecuniary nature.[68]

But as the facts are initially encountered, the category of "mere moral obligation or conscientious duty" seem to be the one they clearly instantiate. The clarity to which the court refers is not a clarity it finds, but a clarity it *achieves*, and, accordingly, the story the opinion really tells is of that achievement.

The work is already being done as the facts are rehearsed. Presumably the action that initiates the entire affair took place in a split second, but in the court's presentation of it (or rather, the presentation adopted wholesale from the appellant's brief), that action occurs in slow motion: from the first report that the appellant was "in the act of dropping the block" (a locution that already extends the duration of something that must have occurred in the blink of an eye) to his decision (if that is the word) to drop with it, four long sentences intervene. What these sentences do is transform an instantaneous and instinctive response to an unanticipated situation of crisis into a deliberative and considered act. The first sentence does this by beginning the sequence all over again and further dilating it: "As he started to turn the block loose"—"in the act" now has stages, starting and whatever is the next stage after starting. (Of course starting could itself be further subdivided; there is no end to the process of drawing out process.) This stop action technique then leads to the revelation of what is stopping the action: "he saw J. Greeley McGowin, testator of the defendants, on the ground below and directly under where the block would have fallen." The recital has now become a drama of the "Perils of Pauline" variety. Will the block fall? What will Webb do? The "would have fallen" tells us that it didn't, in fact, fall and provokes in us the desire to know how Webb prevented it from falling; but before that desire is fulfilled two additional sentences inform us, first of what "would have" happened if the block would have fallen

---

68. Ibid., 198.

("Had he turned it loose it would have struck McGowin with such force as to have caused him serious bodily harm or death"), and, second, how (by what deliberative route) Webb arrived at the course of action he finally (by now this is a full-fledged melodrama) took: "The only safe and reasonable way to prevent this was for appellant to hold to the block and divert its direction in falling from the place where McGowin was standing and the only safe way to divert it so as to prevent its coming into contact with McGowin was for appellant to fall with it to the ground below." A teacher of freshman composition might be moved to criticize this sentence and the entire passage for repetition ("to the ground below" or some variant appears five times in almost as few sentences) and prolixity ("so as to prevent its coming into contact"), but such criticism would miss the effect and the intention behind it, to stretch a punctual moment into a sequence long enough to allow the playing out of freely chosen alternatives and consequences, so that when, in the next sentence, we are told (with a brevity whose force is in direct proportion to the prolixity of what comes before it) "Appellant did this," our sense of what he did is complicated enough, has a sufficient number of stages and spaces, so that we can regard it as the action of a rational and free agent.

So far, so good, but the court is only halfway home; conferring rationality and choice on Webb is quite an achievement, but in order to be truly efficacious it has to be matched by another: Webb's rationality and choice must be shown to exist in a reciprocal relation with the rationality and choice of McGowin. After all, on the facts, his promise to compensate occurs *after* the benefit has been received and the element of bargain for a consideration is conspicuously absent. The court deals with this difficulty in two simultaneously performed moves: it quantifies the benefit and it transforms the quantified benefit into one the promisor (McGowin) had requested. The benefit is quantified not by a legal or even an economic argument but by a blatantly moral one (remember that the point of these moves is to disengage the case from the realm of "mere moral obligation"). After all, the court reasons, the preservation of life is something for which physicians charge, and patients willingly pay a price; therefore, "[l]ife and preservation of the body have material, pecuniary values, measurable in dollars and cents."[69] That is to say, since if Webb were a

---

69. Ibid.

physician and McGowin his patient what passed between them would be regarded as a transaction in relation to services rendered, let us so regard it. At the same time that an analogy is thus extended into a legal fact, the present case is related to an earlier one in which "a promise . . . to pay for the past keeping of a bull which had escaped from defendant's premises and had been cared for by plaintiff was valid," on the reasoning that in the circumstances the promise was "equivalent to a previous request."[70] The court conveniently ignores the fact about the case that would distinguish it from the one before it (since the bull is a fungible good, both its value to the owner and the value of the service rendered by the person who cares for it can be monetarized) and seizes the opportunity to exclaim that the service Webb rendered McGowin was "far more material than caring for his bull."[71] In this sentence, the two contradictory strains of the court's argument mesh perfectly: the moral argument that nothing could be more material than the saving of life becomes (through an equivocation on the notion of material) a reason for finding that the present instance of saving a life is both more and less than moral, that is, legal and quantifiable. The moral urgency of the court's desire produces the sleight of hand by which the case is disengaged from moral consideration. It is then that the court can triumphantly declare that "[t]he case at bar is clearly distinguishable from that class of cases where the consideration is a mere moral obligation."[72]

It remains only for the court to consolidate its gains in a final breathtaking move. Since it has now been shown that "the promisor received a material benefit constituting a valid consideration for his promise," we can regard the promise as "an affirmance or ratification of the services rendered carrying with it the presumption that a previous request for the service was made," and the court proceeds immediately to so regard it:

McGowin's express promise to pay appellant for the services rendered was an affirmance or ratification of what appellant had done raising the presumption that the services had been rendered at McGowin's request.[73]

---

70. Ibid., 197.
71. Ibid.
72. Ibid., 198.
73. Ibid.

And when was this request made? Why in that infinitely extended moment when all the alternative courses of action and all the attendant consequences passed through Webb's mind, and now we are told implicitly, passed through McGowin's mind also. The commercial transaction of voluntary and free agents that seemed so obviously lacking in this case is now supplied and given a location in the minds of two parties who never spoke a word to one another.

The conclusion is as inevitable as it is fantastic: "the services rendered by the appellant were not gratuitous." That is, they were bargained for. And how do we know that? Because of "[t]he agreement of McGowin to pay and the acceptance of payment by appellant." In other words, the meaning and shape of what McGowin did on August 3, 1925, becomes clear in the light of what the two parties did later. In "real-life" terms, the reasoning is familiar and uncontroversial; often we only know what we did when subsequent actions provide us with a retrospective understanding of our actions. But the world of contract is not "real life"; it is (or is supposed to be) formal, and in *that* world, events are discrete and discernible in terms of punctual intentions and foreseen (not retroactively constructed) consequences. The court is dangerously close, here, to falling into the language of "past consideration," but the danger is avoided because, in the context of the opinion's story (of which this is the conclusion), what Webb and McGowin did after the event (make a promise and accept a payment) becomes proof of what they actually (not as a matter imposed after the fact) did *in* the event, enter into a transaction. The fact that they never spoke or in any real sense ever met and the fact that the transaction they are said to have entered into is bizarre ("if you will risk being crippled for life I will pay you thirty dollars a month") might give one pause, but pausing is not what the opinion encourages (except in those earlier moments when the space in which this "bargain" will be inserted is being opened up) and the court quickly moves to a brisk exit: "Reversed and remanded."

In a brief but revealing concurring opinion, Judge William H. Samford further pulls back a curtain that had never really been closed. He admits that the opinion he now joins is "not free from doubt" and acknowledges that according to "the strict letter of the rule" Webb's recovery would be barred, but then he simply declares the "principle" the court has been following, a principle whose articulation he attributes to Chief Justice Marshall when he said "I do not think that law ought to be separated from justice."[74] The effect is complex but swift; what Justice Marshall says amounts to a denial of the law's independence, but the fact that he, the most respected jurist in U.S. history, said it makes his pronouncement a *legal* one and therefore one that can be invoked as a legal justification for departing from the rule of law. Once again, and on several levels of constructions supporting constructions (Justice Samford legitimizes the creative work of his brethren by linking it in a narrative to the equally creative work of a now authoritative predecessor), the legal establishment reaffirms its commitment to a formal process it is in the act of setting aside. Once again, the two stories have been told and then made into the single story that assures the continuity of the tradition.

The Amazing Trick

An unsympathetic reader of the previous paragraph, or indeed of this entire essay, might say that what I have shown is that what works in the law is what you can get away with, precisely the observation made by some members of the critical legal studies movement in essays that point, as I have, to the contradictions that fissure legal doctrine. The difference between those essays and this one lies in the conclusions that follow (or are said to follow) from the analysis. The conclusion often (but not always) reached by critical legal studies proponents is that the inability of legal doctrine to generate logically consistent outcomes from rules and distinctions that have a clear formal basis means that the entire process is at once empty and insidious. The process is empty because its results are entirely ad hoc—lacking firm definitions or borders, the concepts of doctrine can be manipulated at will and in any direction one pleases—and the process is insidious because these wholly ad hoc determinations are presented to us as if they had been produced by an abstract and godly machine. Here is a representative statement from a well-known essay by Clare Dalton that anticipates many of my own arguments.

> ... we need ... to understand ... how doctrinal inconsistency necessarily undermines the force of any conventional legal argument, and how opposing arguments can be made with equal

---

74. Ibid., 199.

force. We need also to understand how legal argumentation disguises its own inherent indeterminacy and continues to appear
a viable way of talking and persuading.[75]

By "doctrinal inconsistency" Dalton means (1) the inability of doctrine to keep itself pure—as she points out, the poles of supposedly
firm oppositions are defined in terms of one another and thus cannot
do the work they pretend to do—and (2) the presence in doctrine of
contradictory justificatory arguments that are deployed by lawyers
and jurists in an ad hoc and opportunistic manner. That is why "opposing arguments can be made with equal force": given the play in
the logic of justification, the facts of a case can, with equal plausibil-
ity, be made to generate any number of outcomes, no one of which
is deduced from a firm base of principle. Nevertheless, Dalton's com-
plaint continues, the law's apologists present these outcomes as if
they issued from a procedure that was as determinate as it was impersonal.

To this I would reply, first, that doctrinal inconsistency undoes
conventional argument only when the arguments are removed from
the local occasion of their emergence and then put to the test of fitting
with one another independently of any particular circumstances. But
since it is only in particular circumstances that arguments weigh or
fail to weigh, the inconsistency Dalton is able to document is not fatal
and is embarrassing only if the context is not law and its workings,
but philosophy and its requirements. Law, however, is not philosophical (except when it borrows philosophy's arguments for its own
purposes) but pragmatic, and from the pragmatic standpoint, the
inconsistency of doctrine is what enables law to work. Dalton inad-
vertently says as much when, in the same sentence, she denies force
to conventional argument because of its inconsistency, and then complains that conventional argument, again because of its inconsistency, has too much force. This is not so much a contradiction as it
is a distinction (not quite spelled out) between two kinds of force,
one good and one bad. The good force is the force of determinate
procedure, and that is what the law lacks; the bad force is the force
of rhetorical virtuosity, and that the law has in shameful abundance.
But the rhetorical nature of law is a shameful fact only if one requires

75. Clare Dalton, "An Essay in the Deconstruction of Contract Doctrine," *Yale Law Review* 94 (1985): 1007.

that it operate algorithmically, and that is the requirement (of which there are hard and soft versions) of the position Dalton rejects. By stigmatizing the law's rhetorical content, she makes herself indistinguishable from her opponents for, like them, she measures the law by a standard of rational determinacy; it is just that where they give the law high marks, she finds it everywhere failing.

My point is that while Dalton's description of the law is exactly right, it is a description of strengths rather than weaknesses. When Dalton observes that the law's normative statements are so vaguely formulated ("fairness," "what justice requires," "good faith") that the moment of "normative choice" is deferred "until an individual judge is required to make an individual decision,"[76] all she means is that while the law's normative formulations specify the vocabulary and conceptual "neighborhood" of decision making, they set no limits to what a judge can do with that vocabulary on the way to reaching a plausible (in the sense of recognizably legal) result. In the absence of a mechanical decision procedure there is ample room for judicial maneuvering (although, as I have shown, that maneuvering is itself far from free), and if the "individual decision" is strong enough—if the story it tells seems sufficiently seamless—it will have constituted the norm it triumphantly invokes as its justification. That is the trouble, Dalton might respond: the law is at once thoroughly rhetorical and engaged in the effacing of its own rhetoricity. Exactly, I would reply, and isn't it marvelous (a word intended nonevaluatively) to behold. It may be true that "we have no reliable, and therefore no legitimate, basis for allocating responsibility between contracting parties,"[77] but while the legitimacy is not ready-made in the form of some determinate system of rules and distinctions, it is continually being achieved by the very means Dalton rehearses in such detail.

Consider, for example, her discussion of the interplay between the doctrines of consideration and reliance. She has been retelling the story of *Second Restatement* sections 71 and 90 (one defining contract obligation in terms of consideration, the other concerning "Contracts Without Consideration") and notes the avoidance both in the *Restatement* and in the cases that invoke it of "the knotty questions of how their coexistence should be imagined."[78] The mechanisms of avoid-

76. Ibid., 1035.
77. Ibid., 1066.
78. Ibid., 1084.

ance, as she describes them, include the sequential application of the doctrines so that each of them seems to be preserved and a clash between them is forever deferred; the stipulating of different measures of recovery in a way that suggests a distinction that an analysis of the cases does not support; and the elaboration of different vocabularies that cause "reliance rhetoric to sound different from consideration rhetoric," although when the occasion demands, the two vocabularies can draw together and begin "to appear indistinguishable."[79] Impressive as this is, it is only a partial catalog of the mechanisms at the law's disposal, mechanisms that allow a distinction that cannot finally be maintained to be reinforced and, at other times, relaxed and, at still other times, conveniently forgotten. The story is an amazing one, and Dalton accurately characterizes it as "the story of how what appears impossible is made possible."[80]

It is, in short, the story of rhetoric, the art of constructing the (verbal) ground upon which you then confidently walk. Reviewing a case that displays the law's virtuosity at its height, Harry Scheiber exclaims

> One is reminded . . . of a dazzling double-feint, backhand flying lay-up shot by a basketball immortal. Only in slow motion replay does one comprehend the whole move; and only then does one realize that defiance of gravity is an essential component of it![81]

Scheiber calls this the law's "amazing trick," the trick by which the law rebuilds itself in mid-air without ever touching down. It is a trick Dalton and others decry, but it is the trick by which law subsists and it is hard to imagine doing without it. The alternatives would seem to be either the determinate rationality that every critical legal analysis shows to be impossible, or the continual exposure of the sleights of hand by means of which the "amazing trick" is performed. But if the latter alternative were followed, and every legal procedure turned into a debunking analysis of its enabling conditions, decisions would never be reached and the law's primary business would never get done. Perhaps this is the result we want, but somehow I doubt it,

---

79. Ibid., 1091.

80. Ibid., 1087.

81. Harry Scheiber, "Public Rights and the Rule of Law in American Legal History," *California Law Review* 72 (1984): 236–37.

and therefore I tend to think that the law's creative rhetoricity will survive every effort to deconstruct it.

It need hardly be said that I am not the first to declare that the operations of law are rhetorical. That is, in fact, Dalton's point, although she makes it as an indictment, and it is the point of others who (in the tradition of Cicero) see the law's rhetoricity more positively. Under the rubric of "rhetorical jurisprudence," Steven J. Burton has elaborated a description of the law that accords on many points with the one presented here. His basic thesis is that the "local law of a society represents a possible organization of human relations, and a public commitment to bring it into empirical being"; each application of the law "brings that imagined world into being in some respect."[82] In this argument, the organization of human relations is not something the law follows or replicates, but something the law produces, and produces by means it invents. Rather than proceeding as science does (at least in pre-Kuhnian characterizations) to adjust its presentation in order "better to fit the world," law is a practical discipline, operating to change the world so as "better to fit the representation."[83] That change is brought about by a discourse that creates the authorities it invokes. "A rhetorical understanding concerns the criteria of evidence implicit in a local legal discourse, and thus the effects of the discourse on what the participants will take seriously as law or legal argument, with or without good reasons."[84] A rhetorical jurisprudence does not ask timeless questions; it inquires into the local conditions of persuasion, into the reasons that *work*; and what it finds interesting about the law's normative claims is not whether or not they can be cashed (in strict terms they cannot), but the leverage one can achieve by invoking them.

Whether such concepts of law are sound or not, they continue in legal discourses to influence the thoughts and actions of many legal actors. Accordingly, they are an important object for rhetorical study within the effort to understand legal practices.[85]

---

82. Steven J. Burton, "Rhetorical Jurisprudence: Law as Practical Reason" (unpublished manuscript), 69.

83. Ibid., 63.

84. Ibid., 9.

85. Ibid., 2.

Not surprisingly, I find this very agreeable. I become nervous only when Burton shifts from describing the law as rhetorical to a claim that this description, if heeded, could have beneficial consequences for legal practice: "A rhetorical criticism draws attention to features of law that are neglected by a legal discourse as a first step toward possibly improving that discourse as *legal*."[86] The course of this improvement is not spelled out, but it seems to follow from the reasoning that once we know the law to be rhetorical we will be better able to function within it, better able to "listen, deliberate and justify action."[87] But knowing that the law is rhetorical could improve it only if we were thereby insulated against that rhetoricity—in which case Burton would be harboring a desire for the scientific jurisprudence his essay rejects—or if that knowledge made the law *more* rhetorical than it already is—a goal that is incoherent since the condition of being rhetorical, of being tied to the exigencies and pressures of the moment, admits of no degree. Once "the law is understood from the practical point of view as a system of reasons for action,"[88] one does not either gain a distance from those reasons or become more compelled by them because one has achieved that understanding. They will still be *local* reasons, as they were before they were so named by Burton, and they will still occur in the context of local pressures rather than in the context of some overall recognition that they are local. The lesson of the law's rhetoricity—the lesson that reasons are reasons only within the configurations of practice and are not reasons that generate practice from a position above it—must be extended to itself. It can no more serve as a master thesis than the formalist theses it replaces. Formalists at least make their mistake legitimately, since it is *their* position that local practices follow or should follow from master principles; it cannot, without internal contradiction, be a rhetorician's position, even when the master principle is rhetoric itself.

Burton's flirtation with what I have elsewhere called "antifoundationalist theory hope" (the hope that by becoming aware of the rhetoricity of our foundations we gain a [nonrhetorical] perspective on them that we didn't have before) is a fully developed romance in the work of James Boyd White. White defines the law (correctly in

---

86. Ibid., 9.
87. Ibid., 69.
88. Ibid.

my view) as "a set of resources for thought and argument."[89] This set, he argues, is open and includes the concepts thought to be basic to the enterprise. As a result, the law is at every level creative, constructing its principles even as it applies them.

> For in speaking the language of the law the lawyer must always be ready to try to change it: to add or to drop a distinction, to admit a new voice, to claim a new source of authority, and so on. One's performance is in this sense always argumentative, not only about the result one seeks to obtain but also about the version of the legal discourse that one uses—that one creates—in one's speech and writing. That is, the lawyer is always saying not only "here is how this case should be decided," but also "here—in this language—is the way this case and similar cases should be talked about. The language I am speaking is the proper language of justice in our culture." . . . in this sense legal language is always argumentatively constitutive of the language it employs.[90]

To this point I am more or less with White, but he loses me when his description of the way the law works leads to a demand for a new form of legal practice: "This means that one question constantly before us as lawyers is what kind of culture we shall have."[91] But the question "before us" is always a legal one, couched in terms of legal categories and possible courses of action. The fact that a legal question can always be shown to have a source in presupposed cultural values does not mean that it is the business of a legal inquiry to discover or revise those values. Of course one could always engage in that business, but to do so would not be to practice law as the institution's members now recognize it. White himself makes the point when he observes again and again that the workings of the law are local; "it always starts in a particular place among particular people," and therefore "one cannot idealize" it by saying "here is how it should go in general."[92] But here is White, idealizing it and saying

89. James Boyd White, *Heracles' Bow: Essays on the Rhetoric and Poetics of the Law* (Madison: University of Wisconsin Press, 1985), 33.
90. Ibid., 34.
91. Ibid., 42.
92. Ibid., 39.

how it should go in general: it should provoke a continuing philosophical discussion of the society's values and goals. But were it to
do that, it would not be law but moral philosophy; the irremediably
local perspective of the law—its rootedness in particular disputes
requiring particular, and timely, solutions—leaves no room for the
extended reflections White recommends and indeed brands them as
inappropriate. The judge who was always stopping to "put his (or
her) fundamental attitudes and methods to the test of sincere engagement with arguments the other way"[93] would not be doing his or her
job as a judge, but would be doing something else, something valuable no doubt but, in legal terms, something inept and even irrespon-
sible (unless the exercise were preliminary, strategically, to the an-
nouncing of a conclusion, in which case the practice of testing one's
attitudes against alternatives would not be engaged in for its own
sake—as an effort to expand one's consciousness—but for the sake
of a goal to which a limited consciousness was precommitted).

White's mistake is to conflate the perspective from which one
might ask questions about the nature of law (is it formal or moral or
rhetorical?) with the perspective from which one might ask questions
in the hope that the answers will be of use in getting on with a legal
job of work. It is from the first perspective (the perspective of metacritical inquiry) that one might decide that the law is a process in which
"we, and our resources, are constantly remade by our own collective
activities,"[94] but those who are immersed in that process do not char-
acteristically act with the intention of furthering that remaking, but
with the intention either of winning or deciding. With respect to that
intention, an account of the law's rhetoricity will either be irrelevant
(i.e., it does not touch on the issues the case raises) or dangerous
(introducing it could weaken the position you are defending) or, in
some circumstances, marginally helpful (as when you remind yourself and your fellows that the law is not an exact science and is less
severe than science in its demand for proof). But even in this last
instance, the thesis of the law's rhetoricity will not have generated a
new way of practicing law; it will merely have added one more resource to a practice that will still be shaped, in large measure, by the
goals the law will continue to have, the goals of winning an argument

---

93. Ibid., 47.
94. Ibid., 45.

or crafting an opinion. These are result-oriented activities, and to engage in them seriously is to have already foreclosed on the openness to alterity that White would have us adopt.

White doesn't see this because he thinks that if openness to alterity characterizes the law (as opposed to the more closed characterizations offered by formalist theorists), then legal actors should themselves be open; since history shows that the law "provides a ground for challenge and change,"[95] it is with the motives of challenge and change that we should act. But while challenge and change are often the by-products of the resourcefulness legal actors display, they are not the motives for which legal action is usually taken. It may be, as White contends, that, as a rhetorical process, the law can never be closed to the interpretive pressures of alternative conversations and displays a "structural openness,"[96] but it does not follow that those who practice the law do so with the intention of being thus open. That is the intention of those who would practice a form of critical self-consciousness. As it turns out, this is precisely the future White envisions for the law: the legal agent will continually "doubt the adequacy of any language, and seek to be aware of the limits of her own forms of thought and understanding"; she will be committed to "'many-voicedness'" and be "profoundly against monotonal thought and speech, against the single voice, the single aspect of the self or culture dominating the rest."[97] White calls this vision "rhetorical," but it is a strange rhetoric that imagines conflict finally dissolved in the wash of a many-voiced pluralism. The truth is that White's hopes for the law are not rhetorical, but transcendental; he regards the scene of persuasion as only temporary, and, like Habermas, he looks forward to a time when all parties will lay down their forensic arms and join together in the effort to build a new and more rational community. This "commitment to openness,"[98] this determination to "be tentative and poetic,"[99] may be admirable, but it is hard to see what place it could have in a process that *demands* single-voiced judgments, even if that voice can be shown to be plurally constituted.

---

95. Ibid.
96. Ibid.
97. Ibid., 124.
98. Ibid.
99. Ibid., 125.

White may begin by acknowledging and celebrating difference, but in the end he cannot tolerate it.

The same can be said of Peter Goodrich, a British-style critical legal scholar who, in books and essays of enormous erudition and sophistication, elaborates "a concept of a rhetoric of legal language" that emphasizes "the rhetorical, sociolinguistic and loosely pragmatic dimensions and contexts of any communicational practice."[100] Goodrich begins by observing that a "defining feature of all formalism" is the "rejection of history,"[101] that is, of the circumstantial background that informs the supposedly self-sufficient and self-declaring rule or doctrine. He then finds the source of the formalist dream in "the distinction between logic and rhetoric,"[102] a distinction that produces the traditional categories of the philosophy of language with a pure semantic kernel at their center and the meanings generated by social and political conditions on the stigmatized periphery. Of course, Goodrich insists, this pure center is a "mythology,"[103] "palpably more rhetorical than actual,"[104] a device for diverting attention away from "the actual 'social facts' or historical and particular 'forms of life' that determine the substantive meaning of legal rules."[105] Once we realize that meaning is "the product or outcome of communication between socially organized individuals and groups," we will see that there could not possibly be any "self-articulated unities of discourse" because every text, no matter how apparently autonomous "implies other meanings, other texts, other discourses, and will constantly exceed the boundaries of any given instance of discourse."[106]

Once again I find myself in agreement both with the analysis and its conclusion: rather than a formal mechanism applying determinate rules to self-declaring fact situations, the law is "preeminently the discourse of power,"[107] that is, a discourse whose categories, distinc-

100. Peter Goodrich, *Legal Discourse: Studies in Linguistics, Rhetoric, and Legal Analysis* (New York: St. Martin's Press, 1987), 5–6.
101. Ibid., 27.
102. Ibid., 61.
103. Ibid., 77.
104. Ibid., 58.
105. Ibid., 57.
106. Ibid., 147.
107. Ibid., 88.

tions, and revered formulas are extensions of some political program that does not announce itself as such. Goodrich supports and extends this conclusion by analyzing cases in which, as he shows, it is "the persuasive function of particular rhetorical techniques"[108] rather than any independent logic that generates decisions, even though the decision will always be presented as one that reinforces "the distinction between the formal normative character of the legal process and the substantive content . . . of a dispute."[109] The law, in short, is continually engaged in effacing the ideological content of its mechanisms so that it can present itself as "a discourse which is context independent in its claims to universality and reason."[110] In this way it rhetorically establishes its independence from the very social and political values that are its content, exercising a "constant, centripetal, endeavor to maintain itself by differentiation and by exclusion of the discourses and languages which surround it."[111] By "avoiding or excluding the . . . implications of its own institutionalization," its status as a historical and contingent discourse, and "by treating legal problems of syntax or of a lexico-grammatical kind . . . the law manages and controls . . . the hierarchy of social and political relations . . . while apparently doing no more than prohibiting and facilitating certain generic and inherently uncontroversial, legally specific, activities and functions."[112]

Except for the somewhat inflated vocabulary, this is precisely my account of the law as a discourse continually telling two stories, one of which is denying that the other is being told at all. The difference is that for Goodrich this account amounts to a scandal, whereas for me it simply brings to analytical attention the strategy by which the law fashions out of alien materials the autonomy it is obliged to claim. Were the law to deploy its categories and concepts in the company of an analysis of their roots in extralegal discourses, it would not be exercising, but dismantling its authority; in short it would no longer be law. Goodrich quite correctly sees that one can become an adept in the law only by forgoing an inquiry into the sources of the norms you internalize: "the entire process of socializa-

108. Ibid., 90.
109. Ibid.
110. Ibid., 175.
111. Ibid.
112. Ibid., 176.

tion into the legal institution is a question of learning deference and obedience, a question of explicit and implicit education into the requisite modes of interaction—the forms, procedures and languages—of the different levels, functions and topics of the legal system."[113] But he thinks that we can and should undo this education and bring into the foreground everything it labored to occlude. We must "challenge the hermetic security ... of substantive jurisprudence";[114] we must make visible the "alternative meanings"[115] that legal meanings ignore:

> In reading the law, it is constantly necessary to remember the compositional, stylistic and semantic mechanisms which allow legal discourse to deny its historical and social genesis. It is necessary to examine the silences, absences and empirical potential of the legal text, and to dwell upon the means by which it appropriates the meaning of other discourses and of social relations themselves, while specifically denying that it is doing so.[116]

Now, it may be that "in reading the law"—that is, in subjecting it to a sociological or deconstructive analysis—one must remember everything forgotten in the course of its self-constitution, but the practice of law requires that forgetting, requires legal discourse to "appropriate the meaning of other discourses ... while specifically denying that it is doing so." And if you reply that a practice so insulated from a confrontation with the contingency of its foundations is unworthy of respect, I would reply, in turn, that every practice is so insulated and depends for its emergence as a practice—as an activity distinct from other activities—on a certain ignorance of its debts and complicities. As I have put the matter elsewhere,

> "Forgetfulness," in the sense of not keeping everything in mind at once, is a condition of action, and the difference between activities ... is a difference between differing species of forgetfulness.[117]

---

113. Ibid., 173.
114. Ibid., 132.
115. Ibid., 183.
116. Ibid., 204.
117. Stanley Fish, *Doing What Comes Naturally* (Durham, N.C.: Duke University Press, 1989), 397.

This is true even of the practice of remembering what other practices have forgotten, for in order to engage in that practice, Goodrich must himself forget (or at the very least bracket) the empirical conditions that give rise to law and constrain its operation, conditions including the need for procedures to adjudicate disputes, and the pressure for prompt remedies and decisions. I am not criticizing Goodrich, only pointing out that his project is no more free of forgettings than the project he excoriates. His mistake is to think that it could be so free, and he thinks *that* because he believes in the possibility of a general discourse that takes account of everything and excludes nothing. There is no such discourse, only the particular discourses that gain their traction by the very means Goodrich laments. And, indeed, it is more than a little ironic that Goodrich finally scorns the material setting of the law's exercise and seeks to set it, instead, in the leisurely precincts (no less material but differently so) of a philosophy seminar. The law, however, is not philosophy; it is law, although, like everything else it can become the object of philosophical analysis, in which case it becomes something different from what it is in its own terms. To be sure, the phrase "in its own terms" refers to the very construct Goodrich would expose, and exposing it as a construct is a perfectly respectable thing to do. That is not, however, what the law can do and still remain operative as law. It is certainly true, as Goodrich both asserts and demonstrates, that the law is not "best read in its own terms,"[118] but that does not mean that the law is best not *practiced* in its own terms, for it is only by deploying its own terms confidently and without metacritical reservation that it can be practiced at all. Goodrich ends his book with a call for the "interdisciplinary study of law . . . aimed . . . at breaking down the closure of legal discourse."[119] This is a worthy project and one that (with his help) is already succeeding; but it is an academic project determined in its shape by norms of academic inquiry (themselves forms of closure): once the seminar is over and the grip of philosophy's norms has been relaxed, legal discourse will once again be closed (although the shape of its closure will be endlessly revisable) and the law will resume the task of simultaneously declaring

---

118. Goodrich, *Legal Discourse*, 212.
119. Ibid.

and fashioning the formal autonomy that constitutes its precarious, powerful being.

I cannot conclude without speaking briefly to three additional points. First of all, my account and defense of the law's rhetoricity—of the strategies by which it generates outcomes from concerns and perspectives it ostentatiously disavows—should not be taken as endorsing those outcomes. Although much of legal theory is an effort to draw a direct line between some description of the law's workings and the rightness (or wrongness) of particular decisions, it has been my (antitheoretical) point that "rightness" is automatically conferred on any decision the system produces, that is to say, any decision that follows from the persuasive marshalling of certain arguments. As soon as an argument has proven to be persuasive to the relevant parties—a court, a jury—we say of it that it is right, by which we mean that it is now the law (nothing succeeds like success), that it is *legally* right. Of course, we are still free to object to the decision on other grounds, to find it "wrong" in moral terms or in terms of the long-range health of the republic. In that event, however, our recourse would not be to an alternative form of the legal process but to alternative arguments that would be successful—that is persuasive—within the same general form. In my view, the legal process is always the same, an open, though bounded, forum where forensic battles are contingently and temporarily won; therefore, preferred outcomes are to be achieved not by changing the game but by playing it more effectively (and what is and is not "more effective" is itself something that cannot be known in advance). In short, even if the cases I discuss were to be decided differently, were to be reversed or overturned, the routes of decision would be as I have described them here.

This brings me to my second point. It might seem that, by saying that the legal process is always the same, I have made the law into an ahistorical abstraction and endowed it with the universality and stability my argument so often denies. However, this objection (which I raise myself because others will certainly raise it) turns on a logical quibble and on the assumption that one cannot at the same time be true to history and contingency and make flat categorical statements about the way things *always* are. But what I am saying is that things always are historical and contingent; that is, I am privileging history by refusing to recognize a check on it—a determinate set of facts, a monumentally self-declaring kind of language—and it is only a philosophical parlor trick that turns this insistence on historicity into something ahistorical. The alternative to my account would be one in which the law's operations were grounded in a reality (be it God or a brute materiality or universal moral principles) independent of historical process, and it seems curious to reason that, because I do not allow for that reality, I am being unhistorical. To be sure, the possibility that such an independent reality may reveal itself to me tomorrow remains an alive one, but it is not a possibility that can weigh on my present understanding of these matters, nor would it be the case that the act of ritually acknowledging it (as Dalton, Burton, White, and Goodrich urge) would be doing anything of consequence. Nevertheless, there is a sense in which the present essay is not historical: it doesn't do historical *work;* that is, it does not chart in any detail any of the differently contingent courses the law has taken in the areas it has marked out for its own. That work, however, is in no way precluded by my thesis and, indeed, the value of doing it is greatly enhanced once that thesis is assented to; once contingency (or ad-hocness or makeshiftness or rhetoricity) is recognized as constitutive of the law's life, its many and various instantiations can be explored without apology and without any larger (that is, grandly philosophical) rationale.

This brings me to my final point. Assuming, for the sake of argument, that I am right about the law and that it is in the business of producing the very authority it retroactively invokes, why should it be so? Why should law take *that* self-occluding and perhaps self-deceiving form? The short answer is that that's the law's job, to stand between us and the contingency out of which its own structures are fashioned. In a world without foundational essences—the world of human existence; there may be another, more essential one, but we know nothing of it—there are always institutions (the family, the university, local and national governments) that are assigned the task of providing the spaces (or are they theaters) in which we negotiate the differences that would, if they were given full sway, prevent us from living together in what we are pleased to call civilization. And what, after all, are the alternatives? Either the impossible alternative of grounding the law in perspicuous and immutable abstractions, or the unworkable alternative of intruding that impossibility into every phase of the law's operations, unworkable because the effect of such

intrusions would be so to attenuate those operations that they would
finally disappear. That leaves us with the law as it is, something we
believe in because it answers to, even as it is the creation of, our
desires.

A Journey Through Forgetting: Toward a Jurisprudence of Violence

Austin Sarat and Thomas R. Kearns

Leviathan, a sea monster symbolizing evil in the Old Testament and in Christian literature generally,[1] was the figure famously chosen by Thomas Hobbes to symbolize the State. Still under Hobbes's influence, we might today—perhaps in a fitful, nightmarish sleep—conjure up similar images of law as a frightening, bloodthirsty beast, but with this difference: the modern Leviathan would be as intent on concealing its bloodletting activities, on covering its bloody tracks, as on slaking its deadly thirst. That these images seem to apply to contemporary law, that law seems intent on (and is largely successful at) threatening violence while denying or making invisible the violence it inflicts, is the subject of this essay. What is the point of brandishing the sword and gaining submission by fear and then, as it seems, lessening that fear by denying or concealing the sword's use? How did such seemingly conflicting practices come about? By what devices are they sustained? What ends do they serve? These are the questions taken up as we try, in a preliminary way, to understand the appalling absence of anything even approximating a jurisprudence of violence in contemporary legal theory.

It is, of course, a commonplace that violence of all kinds is done everyday with the explicit authorization or tacit acquiescence of legal

We are grateful for the helpful comments of Marianne Constable, Tom Dumm, Peter Fitzpatrick, Joel Handler, and Susan Silbey.

1. See Psalms 74:14, "Thou didst crush the heads of. . . ."

institutions and officials.[2] Some of this violence is done directly by legal officials,[3] some by citizens acting under a dispensation granted by law, and some by persons whose violent deeds are retroactively condoned.[4] Moreover, the violence that law produces or protects is not just inscribed on bodies subject to incarceration or execution; it includes, as well, the suffering imposed, say, on a welfare mother when her benefits are reduced or on a homeless man when he is branded a loiterer and told to "move along."[5]

Some, no doubt, would want to resist these as further examples of law's violence; in these cases, it will be said, there is no intent to punish or to cause pain. But this misses the point. Law's violence is not coextensive with law's malevolence; rather, it is inflicted wherever legal will is imposed on the world, wherever a legal edict, a judicial decision, or a legislative act cuts, wrenches, or excises life from its social context.[6] So conceived, law's violence is hardly separable from the rule of law itself, from the deadening normalcy of bureaucratic abstractions and routine interpretive acts that claim for law a position beyond positioning and a universality made plausible only by the systematic privileging of some voices and silencing of others.[7] Thus law's interpretive violence is presented as impersonal and even-

---

2. As Martha Minow has recently written, "Law is itself violent in its forms and methods. Official power effectuates itself in physical force. . . ." See Minow, "Words and the Door to the Land of Change: Law, Language, and Family Violence" (Manuscript, 1990), 14. See also Jacques Derrida, "Force of Law: The 'Mystical Foundation of Authority,'" *Cardozo Law Review* 11 (1990): 919.

3. For examples of the legal authorization of official violence, one might consider cases on the use of lethal force in law enforcement. See Kortum v. Alkire, 69 Cal. App. 3d 325 (1977), and Tennessee v. Garner, 471 U.S. 1 (1985).

4. Self-defense provides perhaps the best example of such after-the-fact authorization of violence. See People v. La Voire, 155 Colo. 551 (1964); State v. Gough, 187 Iowa 363 (1919); People v. McGrandy, 9 Mich. App. 187 (1967).

5. Whether it be the inmate on death row, the welfare mother, or the homeless man, law's clients and its consumers know that pain very well. See Robert Johnson, *Condemned to Die: Life Under Sentence of Death* (New York: Elsevier, 1981), and Austin Sarat, "'. . . The Law Is All Over': Power, Resistance and the Legal Consciousness of the Welfare Poor," *Yale Journal of Law and the Humanities* 2 (1990): 343.

6. As Derrida says, "To be just, the decision of a judge, for example, must not only follow a rule of law . . . but must also assume it, approve it, confirm its value by a reinstituting act of interpretation, as if nothing previously existed of law. . . . Justice, as law, is never exercised without a decision that *cuts* . . ." ("Force of Law," 961–62).

7. See Martha Minow, "Partial Justice: Law and Minorities." See also Patricia Williams, "Alchemical Notes: Reconstructing Ideals from Deconstructed Rights," *Harvard Civil Rights–Civil Liberties Law Review* 22 (1987): 401.

handed rule following, the crushing consequence of law's inexorable will. Law is first implicated in violence only at the level of interpretation, in the cerebral effort to give voice to law and to make rules work.[8]

But law's violence does not end there. At the point that decisions and words are finally brought to bear on citizens' bodies, law, as it is studied in legal theory and jurisprudence, is nowhere to be found. Yet it is this distinctive combination of symbolic and physical violence clothed in abstraction and impersonality—the unity of the temperate and the terrifying in legal acts—that holds us before the law.[9]

Perhaps more so than anyone else, it was Robert Cover who called our attention to the disturbing disparity between the importance and ubiquity of law's violence and the vanishingly small attention paid it in legal theory and jurisprudential thought.[10] To be sure, there are treatises on punishment, on its forms and putative justifications. But the general link between law and violence and the ways that law manages to work its lethal will, to impose pain and death while remaining aloof and unstained by the deeds themselves, is still an unexplored and hardly noticed mystery in the life of the law.

By failing to explore the links between what passes as "mere interpretation" and law's violence—by failing to study the conditions for successful "interpretive violence"—legal theory and jurisprudence help maintain a cold separation between law's words and its deeds. To accede to this separation is, itself, to contribute to the invisibility of law's violence. It also encourages the false idea that the connections between text and the world (between reading and acting) are neutral, natural, and necessary when, in fact, these are contingent practices. Moreover, it is precisely these practices that require study if we are to grasp law's crowning achievement, namely, its reputation as the only alternative to general, barbaric violence when its own violence is a numbing commonplace of everyday life.

To borrow Cover's stunning phrase, law always plays on "a field

---

8. Interpretation is often divorced from violence, as if the latter were merely a matter of implementation or a defect of administration. See Robert Cover, "Violence and the Word," *Yale Law Journal* 95 (1986): 1601.

9. These questions are suggested by Jacques Derrida, "Devant la Loi," in *Kafka and the Contemporary Critical Performance*, ed. Alan Udoff (Bloomington: Indiana University Press, 1987).

10. See Cover, "Violence and the Word." See also Tom Dumm, "The Fear of Law," *Studies in Law, Politics and Society* 10 (1990): 29.

of pain and death."[11] But the pain and death it imposes, and the violence of its imposition, tend to be done in bits and pieces, extended over space and time, and parceled out among numerous agents whose connections with one another are austerely institutional or bureaucratic. The final deed is done to a stranger by a stranger, far removed from the events, interpretive acts, and judgments that triggered the process. Leviathan, it seems, is an insubstantial (if deadly) monster, alternately operating through disembodied choices, the manipulation of texts, and mere mindless, mechanical motions: the full-fledged, pain-imposing, responsible agent eludes our grasp. Indeed, thanks to the rhetorical ingenuity of those who interpret legal texts, the complex chains of bureaucratic connection, and legal theory's complicitous silence, the awful acts almost seem to have no cause. Even the pain and suffering come to have but a shadowy status, hidden from view, recorded in the barely audible testimony of those who endure them or buried in the recesses of unspeakable fears.[12]

Our principal concern, then, is to understand how legal theory can be so bloodless, so inattentive to law's violence.[13] The largely normative concerns of legal theory naturally gravitate to law's reason-giving activities, especially to the interpretations, judgments, and arguments of judges rather than to the grinding of gears and bodies that follow such deliberations. But to accept this separation between thought and action, between interpretive violence and physical force, is to turn one's back on what should be a central challenge to law and legal theory, namely, to characterize and respond to the gap between law's pervasive rhetorical appeal to reason and its extensive and allegedly rightful use of violence against persons. In our view, any theory of law must locate violence at the center of its concerns. It must examine law's devices for transforming and concealing its vio-

---

11. Cover, "Violence and the Word," 1601.

12. Elaine Scarry, *The Body in Pain: The Making and Unmaking of the World* (New York: Oxford University Press, 1985).

13. It is true, of course, that violence and law have sometimes been tied together in a definitional sense. See Alf Ross, *On Law and Justice* (Berkeley: University of California Press, 1959), 34; Hans Kelsen, *General Theory of Law and State*, trans. Anders Wedberg (New York: Russell and Russell, 1945); Noberto Bobbio, "Law and Force," *Monist* 48 (1965): 321. However, in these definitional efforts, the nature of legal violence, how it differs from other kinds of violence, and how it is exercised are rarely considered.

lence, for covering its tracks, and for turning lifeless words into bloody acts of violence.

It is difficult to imagine how law's violence could be more painfully present and, ironically, more absent, that is, invisible, than it was in *Francis v. Resweber*,[14] a case in which the United States Supreme Court allowed the State of Louisiana to attempt to execute a convicted murderer twice.[15] Perhaps no case better illustrates law's cunning capacity to authorize and conceal violence and pain by interposing a screen of impersonality and by focusing on process rather than persons. The dispositions revealed and devices deployed in the opinions in *Francis* appear repeatedly throughout what we will call law's "official story." That story is told most explicitly by various legal and political theorists whose writings are the principal subject of this essay. Our interest in that story takes as its point of departure the claim that law's violence is both ubiquitous and largely invisible. *Resweber* illustrates how this is possible.

As the Court recounted the facts, "Francis was prepared for execution and on May 3, 1946, . . . was placed in the official electric chair of the State of Louisiana. . . . The executioner threw the switch but, presumably because of some mechanical difficulty, death did not result."[16] Sometime later Francis sought to prevent a "second" execution by contending that it would constitute cruel and unusual punishment.[17] Justice Reed, writing for a majority of the Court, responded to this claim in what initially appears to be an unusual way. For him, questions about the alleged cruelty of Louisiana's plan had little to do with Francis, with whatever pain he may have suffered during the first "execution," or his anguished anticipations of the second.[18]

---

14. Francis v. Resweber, 329 U.S. 459 (1947).

15. For an interesting description of the case, see Arthur Miller and Jeffrey Bowman, *Death by Installments: The Ordeal of Willie Francis* (Westport, Conn.: Greenwood Press, 1988).

16. *Francis v. Resweber*, 460. A similar "failure" occurred recently in Florida though after several tries the condemned prisoner was actually executed. See "Electric Chair Tested on Vat of Water," *New York Times*, July 24, 1990.

17. Francis also alleged that a second execution attempt would violate the due process clause of the fourteenth Amendment (*Francis v. Resweber*, 462).

18. Indeed Willie Francis makes virtually no appearance in Reed's opinion. We learn little about him except that he was a "colored citizen of Louisiana" (ibid., 460). Neglect of the real-life experiences and feelings of the people whose fate is decided by law is characteristic of a wide range of legal decisions. See John Noonan, *Persons and Masks of the Law* (New York: Farrar, Straus and Giroux, 1976).

The Constitution, as Reed understood it, notwithstanding its prohibition of cruel and unusual punishment, clearly permits "the necessary suffering involved in any method employed to extinguish life humanely."[19] And what the Constitution permits, dutiful judges cannot, of course, deny. If Francis had to undergo a second, more deadly, dose of electricity, it was because the rules, not the judges, allow it. According to those rules, the fact of the first, unsuccessful execution would not "add an element of cruelty to a subsequent execution."[20] Here the bureaucratic pose, the judge as mere conduit of constitutional messages, is deliberately struck; the document speaks through the judge and the judge dutifully silences his own voice. Interpretation and the interpretive act are made invisible by the simple device of refusing to acknowledge any alternative readings; interpretation and the interpretive act are denied even as, in this willful omission, they are undeniably performed.

The constitutional question, as Reed saw it, turned on the behavior of those in charge of Francis's first "execution," those authorized to unleash law's violence. Their acts and intentions were said to be decisive in determining whether a second execution would be unconstitutionally cruel. From the facts as he understood them, Reed found those officials to have carried out their duties in a "careful and humane manner" with "no suggestion of malevolence"[21] and no "purpose to inflict unnecessary pain."[22] He described diligent, indeed even compassionate, executioners frustrated by what he labeled an "unforeseeable accident . . . for which no man is to blame,"[23] and concluded that the state itself would be unfairly punished were it

---

19. *Francis v. Resweber*, 464.

20. Ibid.

21. Ibid., 462.

22. Ibid.

23. Ibid. Indeed, in the only place where Reed tries to come to terms with what the first execution did to Francis he suggests, again relying on the image of the first execution attempt as an accident, that Francis could only have suffered "the identical amount of mental anguish and physical pain (as in) any other occurrence, such as . . . a fire in the cell block" (ibid., 464). While Reed described Francis as an "accident victim," the issue for Francis was the future as much as the past. For him, what was constitutionally significant was the connection between the violence inflicted on him during the first execution attempt and the violence that the state, with the Supreme Court's blessing, proposed to inflict on him in a second attempt.

deprived of a second chance to execute Francis.[24] A question about
the violence done to Willie Francis and the pain he suffered is thus
transmuted into an inquiry concerning the cause of the mishap (an
accident) and the accompanying intentions (nonmalevolent). This alchemy is concluded by the non sequitur that, since the state cannot
be deemed "blameworthy" in connection with the incident, a second
execution cannot constitute cruel and unusual punishment within the
meaning of the Eighth Amendment.

So remote was the Court's involvement with, and interest in,
Francis, in the pain he had already experienced and would again
experience, and in the violence it was unleashing against him, that
only late in Justice Burton's dissenting opinion was any reference
made to the effect of the first execution attempt on Francis himself.[25]
There we are told that his "lips puffed out and he groaned and
jumped so that the chair came off the floor."[26] Yet even here the
significance of Francis's pain is deferred and displaced since references to that pain, taken from affidavits by official witnesses to the
first execution, were included solely to point out a "conflict in testimony."[27] about whether any current had actually reached Francis
during the abortive execution attempt.

If anything, Justice Burton's dissent, somewhat paradoxically,
displays a revulsion to the judicial acknowledgment of, and involvement with, law's violence that exceeds even Reed's recoil. Indeed, it
is precisely because the majority opinion seems too nakedly to reveal,
though it does not explicitly acknowledge, the interpretive activities

---

24. It is clear (or clear enough) where Reed wanted to come out: unforeseeable
accidents cannot be regarded as "inherent" in any method of punishment (including
electrocution); on the other hand, every method (including electrocution) is susceptible
to such accidents. But this distinction, clear though it may be, sheds no light at all on
why "unforeseeable accidents" that cause extraneous pain do not constitute the kind
of cruel and unusual punishment that the Eighth Amendment forbids. As Justice
Burton's dissent points out, "the intent of the executioner cannot lessen the torture or
excuse the result" (ibid., 477). Moreover, Reed provides no reason for thinking that the
state must be found blameworthy before its punishments can be declared cruel and
unusual.

25. It is perhaps noteworthy that this reference is relegated to a footnote.

26. Ibid., 480 n. 2.

27. Ibid., 480. The conflict to which Burton refers involves whether any electric
current actually reached Francis's body during the first execution attempt and arose
when those in charge of the electrical equipment testified that "no electrical current
reached . . . (Francis) and that his flesh did not show electrical burns" (ibid., 481 n. 2).

of judges that Justice Burton cannot join his colleagues in their analysis of the acceptability of further violence against Francis. While he
selects what, on first glance, looks like a different route and reaches
a different conclusion on the question of whether a second execution
is constitutionally permissible, he leaves open the crucial factual
question of whether even his legal argument would, in the end, save
Willie Francis.[28]

According to Justice Burton, the majority opinion invites an embarrassing question regarding the *number* of failed executions the
Court would be willing to tolerate before declaring any further attempt to kill Willie Francis an instance of cruel and unusual punishment. The question appears to raise two distinct difficulties for the
majority's position, or so Burton implies. First, it makes clear that
some number of accidents, no matter how innocent, might indeed be
too many; if this is so, then the justices might in some case be obliged
to draw (rather than discover) the plainly blurry line at which point
the constitutional ban on cruel and unusual punishment would prohibit yet another attempted electrocution. Second, the question suggests that the majority opinion, at least by implication, accepts what
is for Burton the crucial fact—that Francis did receive a jolt of electricity and that, accepting that fact, it does not regard Francis's pain as
a legal nothing. That pain is at least the kind of thing that "adds up"
and becomes constitutionally intolerable if repeated too many times.

At the same time that Burton berated the majority opinion for
authorizing "death by installments,"[29] he cast about for a more bloodless stance, for a stance that would more fully clothe the question of
Willie Francis's fate with the trappings of law itself. He found one in
the specific language of Louisiana's death penalty statute, which
authorized death by means of an electric current and required "the
application and continuance of such current"[30] until death results.
With all the studied distance and abstraction of reasoning by hypo-
thetical, Burton noted that if any electricity flowed through Willie
Francis's body, it quite obviously lacked the intensity to kill him and

---

28. The importance of the interpretation of facts by appellate judges is highlighted
by Kim Lane Scheppele, "Facing Facts in Legal Interpretation," *Representations* 30
(1990): 42.
   29. *Francis v. Resweber*, 474.
   30. Ibid., 475.

had, therefore, to be turned off.[31] His "electrocution" thus involved a disruption (a *discontinuance*), in violation of the Louisiana statute.

In Burton's view of the case, whether Willie Francis should live or die would turn entirely on a simple factual matter: did any current reach Francis's body? Until this question is resolved, questions about his pain and the extent of his suffering simply do not arise. The bloodlessness of legal violence, law's knife-edge way with the gravest matters of life and death, is thereby reestablished.

Despite the fact that they reached different legal conclusions, the similarities between the Reed and Burton opinions are unmistakable and nicely illustrate the devices, sketched at the outset of our discussion, by which legal actors, especially judges, manage to efface law's violence, and in so doing, to distance themselves from it. In Reed's and Burton's efforts, legal rules (as well as other types of legal standards) play a crucial role. Thus, both seek to interpose a rule between themselves and Willie Francis. Both seek shelter in the illusion that they have no choice and that they discover the law rather than carve meanings from the body of law itself. On this account, the judge gives voice to the law while hiding both *its* body and *his* will.[32] Like Reed's, Burton's hands were tied by words, here by the language of a statute, there by the meaning of the Constitution. In both opinions, the reader is invited to regard the judge as a mere facilitator of what objective law requires, though in this case, as in so many others, the invitation is not easily accepted since the justices reached contradictory results. Of course, the attention lavished on rules does more than just make impersonal the doing of legal violence; it also diverts attention from the pain law inflicts, focusing instead on matters of meaning and interpretation.[33] The effect is to induce a vague but indelible impression that law is impersonal and temperate, rather than terrifying and painful.

The pervasive effort, not merely in *Resweber* but throughout the

---

31. This, according to Burton, is the crucial unanswered factual question on which he based his vote for a rehearing.

32. See Lawrence Douglas, "I Worry I'm Not, Therefore I Am," (paper presented at the annual meeting of the Law and Society Association, May, 1990), 3.

33. As Douglas notes, "Judges do not inscribe their interpretations in the manner of the magistrate in Kafka's Penal Colony, who carved his judgements onto the body of the accused in blood. Inscribed in a domain of violence, legal interpretation is an act of *effacing* violence. Yet the effacing of violence requires a violent interpretive act, which, in turn, must be effaced—another act of hermeneutic violence" (ibid., 2).

law, to deny interpretive violence is without doubt part of a more general effort to render the judicial act distant and bureaucratic in order to appear impartial and principled rather than personal and particularistic.[34] As Olivecrona notes,

> [a]ctual violence is . . . kept very much in the background. . . . Such a state of things is apt to create the belief that violence is alien to the law, or of secondary importance. That is, however, a fatal illusion. . . . [Law's] real character is largely obscured and this is done by means of metaphysical ideas and expressions. It is not bluntly said, e.g., that the function of the courts is to determine the use of force. Instead their function is said to be the "administration of justice" or the ascertaining of "rights" and "duties."[35]

Because the visible inscription of law on the bodies of persons is almost always jarring enough to induce some to reconsider the authorizing act, the effacement of the physical violence made possible by interpretive acts serves, in return, to efface the violence of interpretation itself. In general, then, the story law tells about itself focuses on its majesty rather than its monstrousness,[36] on its value-declaring, rights-enhancing, and community-building aspects,[37] not its "monopoly of legitimate violence."[38]

---

34. This effort is crucial to the premises of what is called the "rule of law" in liberal political thought. See Lon Fuller, *The Morality of Law* (New Haven: Yale University Press, 1964). See also Geoffrey Marshall, "Notes on the Rule of Equal Law," in *Equality*, ed. J. Roland Pennock and John Chapman (New York: Atherton, 1967); and Herbert Wechsler, "Toward Neutral Principles of Constitutional Law," *Harvard Law Review* 73 (1959): 1.

35. See Karl Olivecrona, *Law as Fact* (Copenhagen: Einer Munksgaard, 1939), 125, 127. For an exception see Justice Holmes's opinion in *American Banana Co. v. United Fruit Co.*, 213 U.S. 347, 356 (1908). Holmes said, "Law is a statement of circumstances in which the public force will be brought to bear upon man through the courts." However, as Minow argues, "[J]udges and top level bureaucrats do not have to see violence. Their jobs are structured so violence happens well down the chain of command, and they often have no point of reference for acknowledging the violence they hear others describe" ("Words and the Door," 14).

36. Michel Foucault argues that, in political and legal theory, "the King remains the central personage in the whole legal edifice of the West." See *Power/Knowledge*, trans. Colin Gordon, Leo Marshall, John Mepham, and Kate Soper (New York: Pantheon, 1980), 94.

37. See Robert Cover, "Nomos and Narrative," *Harvard Law Review* 97 (1983): 4.

38. The phrase "the monopoly of legitimate violence" is used by Max Weber. See H. H. Gerth and C. Wright Mills, eds. and trans., *From Max Weber: Essays in Sociology*

This (important) commonplace should not be allowed to conceal a second point about law's self-presentation, namely, that, even when it makes its violence rhetorically present, it is concerned to give reasons for its force. As Cover notes, "for those who impose the violence, the justification is important, real and carefully cultivated."[39] But the law seems not to notice that "[t]he perpetrator and victim of organized violence . . . undergo achingly disparate . . . experiences" and "for the victim, the justification for the violence recedes in reality and significance in proportion to the overwhelming reality of the pain and fear that is suffered."[40] When directed at its victims, attempts to rationalize law's violence thus fall upon deaf ears, deadened by the natural dissonance between reason and pain. Perhaps it is understandable, then, that those efforts tend to be fashioned for the benefit of those who are able and willing to hear them, namely, for ordinary citizens not immediately threatened by legal violence and for legal officials and theorists who have had a hand in constructing it. To sum up: to the compliant or the converted it is reason, not violence, that counts. So, for the most part, violence is not spoken of.

An exception is made for chilling reminders of the violence outside or before the law. In the presence of such reminders, law's violence makes its appearance as a necessary evil. In our own country, though, even this view of things is less prominent as a justification for law than an account that emphasizes the heady work of judges and their reason-giving activities over the brute force of Leviathan.[41] What the judge does, how the judge reads and understands legal texts, is at the center of contemporary legal thought.[42] In the extreme, law and adjudication seem hardly distinguishable.[43]

(New York: Oxford University Press, 1946), 78. See also Rudolph von Ihering, *Law as a Means to an End* (Boston: Boston Books, 1913), 230–46.

39. Cover, "Violence and the Word," 1629.

40. Ibid.

41. See Owen Fiss, "Objectivity and Interpretation," *Stanford Law Review* 34 (1982): 739.

42. See John Hart Ely, *Democracy and Distrust* (Cambridge, Mass.: Harvard University Press, 1980); and Ronald Dworkin, *Taking Rights Seriously* (Cambridge, Mass.: Harvard University Press, 1977). This preoccupation is also characteristic of much of the recent work of critical legal studies. For example, Duncan Kennedy, "Form and Substance in Private Law Adjudication," *Harvard Law Review* 89 (1976): 1685.

43. While there are many who do not privilege adjudication and who highlight other parts of law—its bureaucratic order, its regulatory apparatus, or even the voices of those whose lives it directs—and who would move attention from law's words to its

At the core of these understandings is a confidence, of relatively recent origin, in the capacity of language to confine and control human conduct, to regulate human will and desire by words rather than, always and directly, by the sword. Such confidence makes it possible to imagine that Leviathan might be tamed, that the monster might be harnessed and its powers put to work for ends of our own choosing. Leviathan, then, would tend to vanish, displaced, but not destroyed, by the rules ruling it. In such a world—our world—violence, too, would tend to become invisible and, more and more, attention would be concentrated upon the word.

Here, then, is a preliminary sketch of the interactions between law and legal theory that have shaped law's official story and shed light on how law both uses and conceals its use of violence. To be sure, not everyone accepts the story. Specifically, there is a critical perspective in contemporary jurisprudence that sharply challenges law's supposed reliance on the iron cages of reason and language. According to these critics, the story of law is inescapably the story of politics; it is a story of complicity in legitimating structures of hierarchy, inequality, and oppression.[44] Yet, ironically, exponents of this critical theory, like their mainstream enemies, end up privileging adjudication as the principal site of law.[45] They do so because they see law as a form of consciousness and legal doctrine as a useful vehicle by which to understand the consciousness they wish to change.[46]

Our worries about law's violence thus apply as well to these

---

deeds, their work has yet to displace or dislodge the focus on adjudication from its position in either the official or the critical story. See Kristin Bumiller, *The Civil Rights Society* (Baltimore: Johns Hopkins University Press, 1988). See also Sally Merry, "Concepts of Law and Justice among Working Class Americans: Ideology as Culture," *Legal Studies Forum* 9 (1985): 59; and Sarat, "' . . . The Law Is All Over.'"

44. See, for example, Duncan Kennedy, "Legal Education as Training for Hierarchy," in *The Politics of Law*, ed. David Kairys (New York: Pantheon, 1982).

45. This argument is developed by Frank Munger and Carrol Seron, "Critical Legal Studies versus Critical Legal Theory," *Law and Policy* 6 (1984): 257. See also Ed Sparer, "Fundamental Human Rights, Legal Entitlements, and Social Struggles: A Friendly Critique of the Critical Legal Studies Movement," *Stanford Law Review* 36 (1984): 509.

46. Robert Gordon, "New Developments in Legal Theory," in *The Politics of Law*, ed. David Kairys (New York: Pantheon, 1982). See also Karl Klare, "Labor Law as Ideology: Toward a New Historiography of Collective Bargaining Law," *Industrial Relations Law Journal* 4 (1981): 450.

contemporary critics of law's official story. While they have de-
nounced law as a system of power and power relations, they have
said little or nothing about law's physical violence and the connection
between the violence of interpretive acts and violence done to bodies.
They focus, instead, on law as an alienating force, as a reification and
mystifier of social relations.[47] From this perspective, law's violence
is almost exclusively cultural and symbolic rather than physical and
bodily. Thus, the critical story does little better than law's official
story in expressing law's violence and explaining its uses and concealment.

In taking preliminary steps toward the construction of a jurisprudence of violence, our concern is to do considerably more than encourage candor on the matter of legal violence. Rather, we are persuaded that law's story must be retold, acknowledging at the outset
the wrenching incompatibility between law's appeal to reason and its
reliance on force. To the extent that legal theory continues to privilege
adjudication (and, implicitly, language, reason, and rules) without
directly counterpoising law's violence, it facilitates the remarkably
effective practices developed by law to hide that violence from view.
If we are correct in thinking that legal theory contributes to the invisibility of law's violence, then we have every reason to reject a legal
theory, mainstream or critical, that fails to address directly the violence it will otherwise tend to license or vindicate.

Law's Own Story: From Commands to Interpretations

Law as Leviathan

Law's customary relation to violence is found in the infliction, or
threat, of pain or death. But its arsenal is not limited to this. Importantly, it also includes the images law creates and the stories it tells
of an even greater violence outside, or before, the law. One suspects
that the effectiveness of this second invocation of violence reduces,
at least at the margin, the need to use violence of the first kind. It
would be a mistake, however, to be too grateful for the effectiveness

47. See Peter Gabel, "Reification in Legal Reasoning," *Research in Law and Sociology*
3 (1980): 25. See also Peter Gabel and Duncan Kennedy, "Roll Over Beethoven," *Stanford Law Review* 36 (1984): 1.

of these forceful tales or narratives: rather, one should keep in mind that these tales tend to reduce the visibility of law's reliance on violence. Although they may also reduce the actual level of direct coercion that law is required to use, they do this by fueling our worst fears and nightmarish beliefs about ourselves and one another—they hold us before the law and induce compliance by making us captive to our own most cynical and despairing images of human nature.

In large measure, then, law authorizes itself and its bloodletting as a lesser or necessary evil and as a response to our inability to live a truly free life, a life without external discipline and constraint. To understand the law-constructing narratives that do this work, one naturally turns to Thomas Hobbes and his account of that supremely "lawless" world, the state of nature.[48] The Hobbesian picture of life builds upon an understanding of persons as driven by insatiable and unregulated will and desire. Moreover, these creatures are imagined to have no natural sympathies or affections for one another, or none that can be counted on where, as in a lawless world they always are, matters of self-preservation are even remotely involved.

So conceived, these beings confront the cruelest dilemma of the human condition, namely, whether to live freely but in perpetual insecurity or whether this freedom should be relinquished in the name of a greater security.[49] As Roberto Unger describes this dilemma,

> The apparent guarantee of your safety will be the final cause of your degradation. The self whose continuity your obedience insures is not your own ... The others save you from becoming nothing, but they do not allow you to become yourself ... The

---

48. Thomas Hobbes, *Leviathan*, ed. C. B. MacPherson (New York: Penguin Books, 1986). Hobbes described the state of nature as a condition of life in which men live "without a common Power to keep them in awe" (185). That condition is one, as every undergraduate knows, of violence or the perpetual fear of violence. Given rough equality of desire and power, men "endeavor to destroy or subdue one another," and are, as a result, " ... in a condition which is called Warre; such a warre, as is of every man against every man" (184–85). As Hobbes noted in one of the most famous passages in his work, life in the state of nature is "solitary, poor, nasty, brutish and short" (186).

49. Duncan Kennedy argued that this dilemma poses a fundamental challenge for liberal political theory. See Kennedy, "The Structure of Blackstone's Commentaries," *Buffalo Law Review* 28 (1979): 205, 211–13. See also Roberto Unger, *Knowledge and Politics* (New York: Free Press, 1975).

freedom to be unstable in your desires and pursue the goals you choose, after you have rendered tribute to Caesar, simply confronts you once again with the paradoxes of the morality of desire from which you were trying to escape.[50]

Yet for Hobbes the solution was unequivocal and unconditional. Power (and so freedom) must be transferred to a single entity (or person) if sufficient peace and security are to be realized.

Leviathan, in whom sufficient power is vested to keep "all in awe,"[51] is Hobbes's device for rescuing us from the will, desire, insecurity, and violence of the unregulated state of nature. The state or law (in Hobbes, the two are hardly distinguishable) is presented as a way of taming violence by producing, through social organization, an economy of violence.[52] It is Leviathan's (or law's) awesome force, not its objectivity, neutrality, and impersonality that, in this account, makes it socially valuable. Law's image is horrible and frightening and the more horrible and frightening the better.[53] Violence, or the promise of violence, saturates the world, lurking just below the surface; it overwhelms, drags down, and drowns all resistance.[54] Power dramatically displayed, not reason or morality, is the business of law. What brings us to law, and holds us, is fear, not just fear of law but fear of life without law.[55]

This story of law is not told only by those who, from the outside, write about law as political philosophers or legal theorists. It is also told by law itself in a wide variety of cases and situations, ranging from the commonplace to the most extraordinary and extreme. It is told to remind legal subjects of their own fallen nature and of the need for law to stand firm in its resistance to violence, even if that, itself, requires some measure of violence. Law's grip cannot be al-

---

50. Unger, *Knowledge and Politics*, 61.

51. Hobbes, *Leviathan*, 185.

52. This image is labeled "repressive law" by Philippe Nonet and Philip Selznick, *Law and Society in Transition: Toward Responsive Law* (New York: Harper Colophon Books, 1978), chap. 2. See also J. H. Hexter, "Thomas Hobbes and the Law," *Cornell Law Review* 65 (1980): 471; and Kelsen, *General Theory*, 21.

53. See Michel Foucault, *Discipline and Punish: The Birth of the Prison*, trans. Alan Sheridan (New York: Vintage Books, 1979). Foucault describes the deployment and decline of this image of law in chaps. 1 and 2.

54. See Olivecrona, *Law as Fact*, 127.

55. See Dumm, "Fear of Law"; and Olivecrona, *Law as Fact*, 143.

lowed to weaken or relent, especially where the cravings and drives of "human nature" are most powerful and threaten to do violence of their own. These are situations in which the law must bear down, redoubling its effort to constrain violence, if necessary, by doing violence.

In response to occasional efforts to avoid the law by limiting its jurisdiction, courts remind legal subjects that they can never, fully and finally, escape the danger of sliding back into the state of nature;[56] it beckons, taunts, and threatens always, like a kind of cruel in-law just on the other side of law's precarious achievement. As Justice Frankfurter once suggested in explaining the necessity of law, "no one, no matter how exalted his public office, or how righteous his private motive, can be a judge in his own case. This is what courts are for. . . . If one man can be allowed to determine for himself what is law, every man can. That means first chaos, then tyranny."[57] Here we are, in effect, admonished that the peace and security achieved by law's powers are themselves never singular, stable, or secure, and that we are always facing an abyss, embattled by our own lustful, barbarous nature.[58]

In the presence of such law-inducing narratives it is perhaps not surprising that the official story of law has been, at least until this century, almost exclusively a story of collective conquest of individual will and desire, of the gathering of forces to overcome our unruly nature and its violent appetites. While it is not the only story that might be told, and despite the gentler, Lockean subthemes of our constitutional tradition,[59] Hobbesian images and ideas were most predominant in the early phases of what we are calling law's official story.

---

56. See, for example, Walker v. City of Birmingham, 388 U.S. 307 (1967).

57. See United States v. United Mine Workers, 330 U.S. 258, 308–9, 312 (1947).

58. The famous case of Queen v. Dudley and Stephens, L.R. 14 Q.B.D. 273 (1884), reprinted in John Bonsignore, Ethan Katsh, Peter D'Errico, Ronald Pipkin, and Stephen Arons, *Before the Law* (Boston: Houghton Mifflin, 1974), 25, provides a useful example of such a legally constructed story. The threat of lawless violence is also deployed in United States v. Holmes, 26 Fed. Cas. 360 (C. E. D. pa. 1842), reprinted in Joseph Goldstein, Alan Dershowitz, and Richard Schwartz, *Criminal Law: Theory and Process* (New York: Free Press, 1974), 1023. *Holmes*, like *Dudley & Stephens*, is a case whose tragic circumstances begin with the sinking of a ship and the resulting murder trial of a sailor who attempted to save his own life, as well as the lives of others, by throwing passengers overboard from an overcrowded, leaking lifeboat.

59. In this tradition it is not the power or violence of law that is projected; instead

The success of this story over others, however, was not achieved without a battle; victory was gained in part by John Austin who waged war against a brand of natural law theory that sought to persuade us that even the beastly Leviathan was subject to a law not of human making.[60] Law might involve power over others, as the official story claimed, but it is not only a matter of power. It is, more elaborately, a matter of rules "laid down for the guidance of an intelligent being by an intelligent being having power over him."[61] Here, though law is linked to power, it is to operate by rule (in contrast to ephemeral, context-specific orders), by guidance (in contrast to ex post facto command), by reason (in contrast to sheer force and fear), and, possibly, by reference to rational ends (in contrast to Leviathan's unregulated whims).

Austin's contribution to the success of the Hobbesian story consisted largely of deft and thoroughgoing reconstruals of the natural law formulas, carefully retaining the language of "rule," "guidance," and "intelligent" direction, but emptying the words of their customary normative implications. Austin even agreed, as any good natural law lawyer would, that moral obligations take precedence over positive law. It would seem to follow that Leviathan, too, is bound by law and is not, as Hobbes would have it, the source of all law. How Austin reinterpreted the language of natural law and retained Leviathan while simultaneously acknowledging higher obligations is a project worth rehearsing.

Law, on Austin's account, *is* a matter of rules and reason, but only "in its literal meaning."[62] Moreover, "every law or rule (taken with the largest signification which can be given to the term properly) is a command."[63] But commands, it turns out, are nothing but par-

---

it is the ability of law to contain, check, modify, and regulate the power of the state that is highlighted. In this tradition, law secures us from the oppressive tendencies of the entity we create to protect ourselves from each other. See F. Hayek, *The Constitution of Liberty* (Chicago: Regnery, 1960).

60. John Austin, *The Province of Jurisprudence Determined*, reprinted as "Law as the Sovereign's Command," in *The Nature of Law: Readings in Legal Philosophy*, ed. M. P. Golding (New York: Random House, 1966), 77–98.

61. Ibid., 77–78.

62. Ibid., 77.

63. The idea that law is a command is, according to Austin, "the *key* to . . . jurisprudence" (ibid., 80). See also Wilfrid Rumble, *The Thought of John Austin: Jurisprudence*,

ticular "significations of desire" accompanied by the "power and purpose of the commanding party to inflict pain or evil in case the desire
be disregarded."[64] So, while law is a matter of rules, rules are but
commands that, in turn, are nothing but expressions or intimations
of a wish, tied to an intent and capacity to inflict an evil if "dis-
obeyed."[65] In this way, normative language is retained at the same
time its force is diminished.

Austin's second sleight-of-hand emerges in his handling of Leviathan's apparent subjugation to "higher obligations," specifically to
moral or divine law. Thus, according to Austin, moral law *does* take
precedence over human (i.e., Leviathan's) law, but this has nothing
to do with the superior merit or higher normative standing of moral
obligation in comparison to human law. Rather, what confers superiority on moral obligations is that the sanctions that accompany (or
threaten to accompany) their breach are far greater (e.g., eternal dam-
nation) than the sanctions that accompany breaches of human law.[66]
So, on this analysis, moral obligation trumps the requirements of
human law, but only in the sense of involving greater sanctions, not
in the sense of vitiating, or making nonobligatory, human laws that
happen to be morally iniquitous. Leviathan's subjects remain
"bound" to obey his commands—that is, liable to Leviathan's violent
reprisals—even where what is commanded is unspeakably immoral.
There is no escaping one's obligation merely because it conflicts with
another; at bottom, obligations are but forces and there is no absurdity, though sometimes much pain, in being subjected to forces that

---

Colonial Reform, and the British Constitution (London: Athlone Press, 1985). This is,
however, a hotly contested notion. For arguments to the contrary see Kelsen, *General
Theory*, 32; and Olivecrona, *Law as Fact*, 33.

64. Austin, *Province of Jurisprudence*, 80.
65. Ibid., 80.
66. Thus when moral obligations and human laws conflict, it is "always in our
interest to choose the smaller and more uncertain evil" and, as a result, to disobey the
positive law (ibid., 96). But even in such circumstances, Austin insisted on the validity
of state law; as he put it, "the existence of law . . . is one thing; its merit or demerit is
another" (ibid., 95). Austin believed that to deny the validity of a law, even a law that
violated moral principles, would lead to chaos, since it would justify people in claiming
that law's are morally iniquitous, and thus not valid, when they are merely inconven-
ient. Such an understanding would "proclaim generally that all laws which are perni-
cious or contrary to the will of God are void and not to be tolerated," and would, in
Austin's words, encourage "anarchy, hostile and perilous as much to wise and benign
rule as stupid and galling tyranny" (ibid., 98).

push and pull in opposite directions. To be sure, Leviathan's subjects face a terrible dilemma, namely, whether to obey an immediate earthly power or the distant sanctions of God. But they have obligations to obey both, even where that is literally impossible.

The trick here, as with "rule" and "command," is to empty the notions of "being bound" and "having an obligation" of their usual normative connotations. Thus, according to Austin, and wholly in keeping with Hobbes, law and legal obligation are entirely matters of force. To say that one is bound, under a duty, obliged, or has an obligation to do something is just another way of saying that one has been directed to do that thing and is liable to a certain evil if one fails to do it. But according to Austin, this is the meaning not only of law and legal obligation; rather, it is the meaning of obligation generally, including the obligations of divine law. The point is that *all* obligation is just a matter of power and pain because all commands are merely matters of power and pain. Obligation and law of all kinds, not just positive law, are just commands. Here perhaps Austin overpowers his master, since Hobbes at least seemed to attribute to divine law some efficacy and standing that did not depend on brute force alone.

It follows, then, that Austin's account of law is not a *selectively* cynical story. He did not, for example, construct an idiosyncratic account of legal obligation to assure it of a special autonomy and authority in relation to other normative systems. Instead, he made the still bolder move of denying that there is, anywhere, a form of obligation that is not finally a matter of awe. Positive law is nothing other than a system of orders backed by threats, but it could not be otherwise. Moreover, in this respect, positive law is indistinguishable from the moral or divine law since obligation, wherever it is found, is just a matter of force.[67]

The importance of this naturalizing of legal obligations, of analyzing them in terms of power and pain, is that authority or legitimacy is thus freed from any requirement of conformity with any extralegal standard. One is legally bound if one is the addressee of a

---

67. Thus, as we saw in Austin's discussion of the superiority of moral obligation to positive law, the gods, in their wisdom, may identify actions that ought to be undertaken or avoided, but our duties in this connection arise yet again only where such significations of desire are accompanied by the threat of sanction. Divine or moral law is obligatory only insofar as it is accompanied by a pain or an evil that we find intolerable. See W. E. Morison, "Some Myths about Positivism," *Yale Law Journal* 68 (1958): 212.

sovereign's command and is liable to an evil for disobedience, no matter how foul and morally iniquitous that command might be. Austin's account of law, while retaining the notion of "having an obligation" thus provides an alternative to the natural law theorists' central tenet that law must be morally good to be genuinely obligatory. According to Austin, positive law is obligating if and only if it is suitably supported by an apparatus of force and violence, of power and pain.

But law is not merely made autonomous, freed from the necessity of conforming to standards not of its own making. In addition, law's power and its propensity to inflict pain are reinstated as entirely permissible aspects of social life, since, after all, power and pain are the operative components of *all* forms of social control, legal or otherwise. Law, then, is not a renegade contrivance whose use of violence contrasts markedly and disturbingly with other kinds of social control.[68] While Hobbes sought to make law's violence acceptable to us by showing that, without it, even greater violence would ravage the earth, Austin might be said to have completed the Hobbesian agenda by showing that appeals to a higher law are finally appeals to force, just like positive law. Contrary to the promise of the natural law theorists, there is no alternative to force if society is to become a peaceable kingdom here on earth, fully fit for human habitation.

Morally iniquitous law is not really law, or so the natural law theorists had claimed. But, rejoined Austin in a now famous phrase, "(t)he existence of law is one thing; its merit or demerit is another."[69] And, he added, "to say that human laws which conflict with Divine law are not binding, that is to say, are not laws, is to talk stark nonsense."[70] By now his point is painfully clear; while he agrees that human law should conform to divine law, human law is obligatory

---

68. Austin's assimilation of legal with all other forms of obligation and his effort to persuade us that, at bottom, they are all constituted by force, is not apt to comfort those who are disposed to avoid confronting the violence of social life. It is, in fact, a reminder to them that things may be worse than they had imagined. But from the perspective of law's official story, Austin's jurisprudence is an apt successor, or complement, to Hobbes with its clearheaded presentation of the inescapability of law's violence. It is also a precursor of some elements of critical jurisprudence; see Wilfrid Rumble, "The Legal Positivism of John Austin and the Realist Movement in American Jurisprudence," *Cornell Law Review* 66 (1981): 986.

69. See Austin, *Province of Jurisprudence*, 95.

70. Ibid., 96.

(i.e., amply supported by threats of pain and coercion) whether it actually conforms or not.

In the end, then, little remains of Austin's robust, initial claim that law, in the first instance, "may be said to be a rule laid down for the guidance of an intelligent being by an intelligent being having power over him."[71] Law is thus distinguished from other natural forces, like volcanoes or earthquakes, by requiring "intelligent" origins, but the promise of linking law to rule-governed guidance aimed at rational ends is never realized; it dissolves in the cynical acids of Austin's naturalistic interpretation of all normative notions.

Austin's attempt to undermine the natural law tradition by retaining that tradition's language while abandoning its substantive commitments, especially its thesis that bad law is not really law, never won full acceptance, certainly not in this country, nor in Anglo-American jurisprudence generally. Thus Austin's effort to keep violence at the center of law while, at the same time, shrouding that violence behind the veil, the reassuring language of "rules," "guidance," and "intelligent" direction, cannot be cited as the root explanation of law's general success in effacing its own violence.

But Austin's positivism did not succumb to its archenemy, the natural law tradition. There are, of course, lively remnants of this tradition in our law and in writings about our law; recurring reference can be found to *noncoercive* "dictates" or "requirements" of morality, to enduring principles and normative judgments that putatively pertain to law and limit what can sensibly be said to count as law.[72] But the bits and pieces of this tradition do not knit together or cohere into anything resembling whole cloth, into a sustained or sustainable view of law in this country today. Ironically, the death knell of Austin's version of legal positivism was rung most compellingly by his self-proclaimed heirs, especially by H. L. A. Hart,[73] and, in turn, by Hart's chief critic, Ronald Dworkin.[74] Thus we must turn to the writings of these two theorists if we are to discern the contemporary trajectory of what we have called law's official story, and understand

---

71. Ibid., 77–78.

72. See Harry Jaffa, *The Crisis of the House Divided* (New York: Doubleday, 1959) and *Equality and Liberty* (New York: Oxford University Press, 1958). See also Hadley Arkes, *First Things* (Princeton: Princeton University Press, 1987).

73. See H. L. A. Hart, *The Concept of Law* (Oxford: Clarendon, 1961).

74. See Dworkin, *Taking Rights Seriously*, and *Law's Empire* (Cambridge, Mass.: Harvard University Press, 1986).

the capacity of law, so conceived, to conceal its connections with violence.

For both Hart and Dworkin, law is not centrally a matter of power, pain, and violence. Austin got this wrong. Rather, law, at its center, is a normative enterprise and is substantially caught up in an ongoing process of identifying, defining, and interpreting moral norms and commitments, especially those that are part and parcel of the society and legal regime in question. But the supposition that law is a normative enterprise, that it is actually permeated by judgments about what ought to be, not merely predictions about the prospect of pain, falls far short of explaining how such a story of law might manage to hide its own violence. To see things more clearly, this story, as well as the failings of Austin's theory, need to be sketched more fully.

Law as Rules

Hart's contribution to both elements of our undertaking—to seeing what appear to be serious difficulties in Austin's account and laying the foundation for a new vision of law—consists in showing that law can be understood as being normative without being made automatically (i.e., definitionally) subservient to morality. Here Austin was right: the existence of law is one thing, its merit or demerit, morally speaking, another. On the other hand, the natural law theorists were right that law is not merely a matter of force, and statements of obligation are not merely predictions of what will or is likely to happen, but of what ought or should happen. Hart saw clearly the strengths and weaknesses of both sides and made the most of both of them.

In particular, Hart makes much of the following: in Austin's view, it is impossible to differentiate between law and the actions of a gunman "who says to the bank clerk, 'Hand over the money or I will shoot.'"[75] Hart thinks it obvious that such a threat-backed order is not the conceptual equivalent of a duly promulgated lawmaking command of a political sovereign. Of the latter Hart said, "(t)hough it may be combined with threats of harms, a command is primarily an appeal not to fear but to respect for authority."[76] In contrast, the

---

75. Hart, *Concept of Law*, 19.
76. Ibid., 20.

gunman's demand induces only fear and no respect; if it succeeds, as well it might, this is because the gun obliges, not because the clerk has an obligation to the gunman to obey. The suggestion that law relies on respect for authority and on regard for obligation rather than fear as the principal way of inducing obedience marks the initial decoupling of law and violence and the beginning of a reconstruction, from within the positivist tradition, of law's story as a story about rules, their origins or grounds, and their interpretation.

Only by distinguishing between "having an obligation" and "being obliged" is it possible, Hart believes, to explain "familiar features of municipal law in a modern state."[77] If, as Hart and Austin agree, to be obliged entails falling within the ambit of a certain coercive power, then one who, for whatever reason, is impervious to that power cannot be obliged by it. On the other hand, we seem to think it makes perfectly good sense to suppose that one can have an obligation to someone without being obliged by that person, that is, without being subject to that person's coercive powers.[78] For example, one might incur a promissory obligation to another even though there is no prospect of being subjected to the promisee's coercion. But if this is so, "having an obligation," unlike "being obliged," cannot be centrally a matter of power and pain. They are, instead, centrally a matter of rules.

Ironically, it was with the proposition that law is essentially an affair of rules that Austin's account ostensibly began. But, according to Hart, Austin failed to take that starting point seriously, or, alterna-

---

77. Ibid., 77. Hart contrasts his own critique of Austin with earlier critics who try to show the inadequacy of that theory by invoking what Hart calls "borderline examples" like international or "primitive" law. In Hart's view, the understanding of law as orders backed by sanctions is, at best, only applicable to criminal statutes and is, as a result, unsuitable for the wide variety of civil and regulatory law. As he says, " . . . there are other varieties of law, notably those conferring legal powers to adjudicate or legislate or to create or vary legal relations which cannot, without absurdity, be construed as orders backed by threats." And, finally, not only does Austin's model fail to account for the breadth and variety of legal forms, but it also, according to Hart, "failed to account for the continuity of legislative authority characteristic of a modern legal system. . . ." For an argument suggesting closer links between Hart and Austin than Hart acknowledges, see Note, "Hart, Austin, and the Concept of a Legal System: The Primacy of Sanctions," Yale Law Journal 84 (1975): 584.

78. Hart, Concept of Law. See R. E. Hill, "Legal Validity and Legal Obligation," Yale Law Journal 80 (1970): 47; and Michael Payne, "Hart's Concept of a Legal System," William and Mary Law Review 18 (1976): 213.

tively, he misconstrued rules as consisting of nothing more than orders (or commands) backed by threats, treating them as a kind of
verbal projectile and stripping them of all normative content. It was
the absence of normativity in Austin's account of law that Hart found
most problematic and that needed to be restored, he thought, if many
commonplaces about law were to be preserved. The difficulty, however, was to infuse law with a normative quality but to do so without
subjecting it to normative standards not of its own making, that is,
to make law normative without embracing an extralegal, natural law
constraint.

Hart's solution was to draw attention to the normativity of social
rules. In contending for their normative dimension, he characterized
rules as social practices, as relatively stable patterns of conduct in a
community that regards or accepts them as exhibiting not just what
is done but what *should* or ought to be done. To borrow Hart's example, it is *merely* a social habit that many people regularly go to the
theater on Saturday night. It is, however, *more* than a habit (even if
a decaying one), *more* than a mere regularity, that people arriving at
the queue go to the back of the line rather than cut in front. But what
more is it?

According to Hart, it is the acceptance of this practice as a standard of right conduct, of what one ought to do, that distinguishes it
from a mere regularity. And this acceptance of the practice *as a standard* is revealed in characteristic ways, especially by the fact that
deviations are regarded as lapses or faults and as warranting, and
often receiving, criticism and pressure for conformity.[79] Those who
dare to break in on a queue are apt to find themselves roundly re-
buffed and uniformly hooted to the back of the line.

When certain social practices are regarded as constituting a standard of conduct, they are also regarded as providing members of a
community a *reason* for acting or abstaining without reference to
force. Participants in the practice will typically express themselves in
the language of "ought," "right," and "should," though (to avoid the
mistake of natural law theorists) it is important to notice that they
need not thereby imply that the practices have any moral force at
all.[80] Still, to the extent that they believe they ought or should act as

79. Hart, *Concept of Law*, 54.
80. Ibid. See Note, "H. L. A. Hart on Legal and Moral Obligation," *Michigan Law
Review* 73 (1974): 443.

the practices indicate, they must ipso facto believe they have some reason to act that way. The reason (or motive) they have has no necessary connection with force or the threat of force. Law's connection with violence is thus displaced as legal theory celebrates normativity.

This injection of normativity into law does not conclude Hart's story. He recognizes that there may be things one ought to do (e.g., attend to one's health) that are not obligatory. Hart proposes to accommodate this distinction by suggesting that social rules give rise to an obligation only where the demand for conformity that accompanies them is particularly insistent and where the social pressure brought to bear on those who deviate is great.[81] Here, it must be admitted, force of sorts seems to reappear. But as against Austin's jurisprudence, in which force and obligation are all but synonymous, force is important for Hart in only a secondary or derivative way. It is a means for the realization of law, an ancillary motive to obey law's edicts, available for those who might otherwise falter. It is not, as in Austin, an essential feature of law.

In Hart's account, the normative or "ought to" dimension of legal obligation, brought into being by its connection with social rules, is already in place, doing most of the work that, in Austin's account, would have to be done by force alone.[82] It appears, then, that Hart has managed to navigate between the Scylla of law-as-morality and the Charybdis of law-as-force. He has, it seems, accomplished the miraculous: law is, centrally, an affair of rules (i.e., autonomous normative standards) and is only obliquely a matter of power, pain, and violence. Law-as-monster, the bloodletting beast, has finally been tamed.

---

81. Hart, *Concept of Law*, 86.

82. This distinction is suggested by Olivecrona, *Law as Fact*, 134; and Bobbio, "Law and Force," 327–28. In fact, as Bobbio points out,

The content of the rules of chess is the game of chess, just as the content of grammar is speaking; of rhetoric, persuasion; of aesthetics, poetry; of logic, thought; of fashion, dressing. But is there a type of behavior which . . . is the proper content of legal rule? Is there a legal behavior, of which law is the rule in the same way there is a linguistic behavior of which grammar can be said to be the rule? . . . If the law is a body of rules which regulate coercion, or the exercise of force, this means that coercion or force is the specific object of legal rules, in the same way as language is the specific object of grammar. . . . The rules which regulate . . . [force] are a class of rules which distinguish them from other classes of rules in terms of their object. The class of rules is "law."

But Leviathan's submission has still further complications, even in Hart's argument. Commands or orders, the carriers of law in Austin's scheme, are typically aimed at others, not at oneself. The idea of issuing orders or commands to oneself seems comical, requiring a story of multiple selves if it is to be taken seriously at all. In contrast, there is nothing odd about being subject to and bound by a rule that one has had a hand, even an exclusive hand, in promulgating.[83] Rules, then, can be self-binding or, more accurately, binding for those who make them, not merely for others.[84] And this opens up the possibility, unthinkable to Hobbes and Austin, that the maker of law might itself be subject to law. Since for Hobbes and Austin the fount of law was the mythical monster that commanded others but did not submit to others' commands, law's source could not be constrained by law. But if law is a matter of rules and rules can as easily apply to their authors as to others, it follows that legal officialdom can itself be subject to law.[85] Leviathan, the mighty beast that roamed the Hobbesian imagination as the legally illimitable source of law, is not just tamed but is dismembered as well.

If Hart's constructive account can be sustained, he has made it possible to see how law and legal obligation might be distinguished from Leviathan's reign of terror. And though, even in Hart's account, legal obligation finally makes appeal to force and coercion, law's connection to violence is softened, mediated always by the initially cerebral, cognitive regard for rules. The realm of law is finally rid of the lawless beast that, in Hobbes's and Austin's theory, always included the unpalatable risk that Leviathan might one day imbrue the

---

83. Thus, a legislator is bound by the traffic laws he or she has helped enact and a governor must observe the extraordinary curfew that he or she has imposed.

84. Moreover, it is now easy (and important) to see how, in Hart's theory, legal officials and not just other persons might themselves be subject to legal restrictions or obligations. Thus, Hart contends that at the center of law is a master (social and legal) rule that is itself the product of the behavior and critical reflective attitudes of the system's officials. It is this (usually complex) set of normative practices that establishes the criteria for identifying all of the other rules of the legal system and that gives the system its unity or closure. Moreover, by virtue of the very same (namely, their own) convergent habits and commitments, legal officials themselves incur an obligation to observe the law's master rule. In this vaguely bootstrap fashion, legal officials become bound by the law's most basic norm.

85. This account of law is called "autonomous law" by Nonet and Selznick, *Law and Society*, 54. See also Roberto Unger, *Law in Modern Society* (New York: Free Press, 1975).

earth with the blood of precisely those who had sought its protection. While, in Hart, law's power has not been ruled out, it has been made subject to the governance of rules. The residue of Leviathan's might is absorbed into a system of normative standards that can greatly reduce the danger of its being deployed randomly. Again, Hart's story advances our project. Without denying law's violence, he makes it more acceptable. He shows that even violence can be made to submit to the regulative force of rules.[86]

If law, including law's violence, is a matter of rules, then law, including law's violence, will tend to be perceived, in its most visible moments, as a largely sedentary enterprise, an affair of the mind rather than the body.[87] For the most part, though, law's violence will not be very visible. Law encoded as a system of rules makes possible an elaborate separation of visible power from the activities of the officials who authorize its deployment. So, for example, judges are called upon to identify and interpret the rules; others determine the facts and apply the rules to the facts they find; still others execute the legal will and take the practical steps to implement judgments and decisions made elsewhere. In these ways, law's violence is made to occur far from the place where deliberation, reason-giving, and judgment take place, far from the place where the activities of law are carefully recorded, easily inspected, and susceptible to critical assessment.[88] The law's rules may require that blood be spilled, but those who interpret the rules are spared that unseemly sight. In fact, those who interpret the rules and direct their application in given cases do

86. Furthermore, in Hart's theory, the existence of role-creating social rules makes unnecessary the concentration of power in a single person or body; it can, instead, be *dispersed* in accordance with power-conferring rules. It can, in addition, be *constrained* by those authorizing rules, and limit the will and desire of persons who happen to occupy official positions. While it is true that taming will and desire by means of rules does not fully and finally eliminate the prospect of violence, it greatly assists, at least in principle, in establishing conditions of traceability and accountability.

87. See *Francis v. Resweber.* To the extent that law is thought of, as Hart would recommend, in terms of regulative rules and practices, it will inescapably by conceived of as an essentially interpretive enterprise, as the business of officials (and citizens) attempting to identify the pertinent standards, to understand them, and to apply them to their own and other cases or situations. And, to the extent that the activities of law can be viewed in this way, their connection with violence will seem both remote and unproblematic.

88. See Cover, "Violence and the Word." In the end it is this distance of violence from the site of adjudication that renders contemporary jurisprudential theories, whether official or critical, unable to make law's violence visible.

not see or confront those rules' final, corporeal meaning.[89] To themselves as well as to others, the interpreters' connection with violence seems too distant and insubstantial to produce an inhibiting sense of guilt or the taint of personal responsibility.

More pointedly, legal officials, insofar as they follow rules, have both a right and an obligation to take the steps the rules prescribe.[90] Legal decision making becomes, at least in theory, lockstep rule following, bureaucratic and conforming On this account, the violence of the interpretive act is effaced. As in *Francis v. Resweber*,[91] the question one asks about the actions taken is first and foremost whether they conform to rules. When they do, such acts become authoritative; they become the acts of law itself rather than the acts of a particular legal official. A rule-governed conception of law appears to have the capacity to confer authority on its officials in one fell swoop, providing their activities a blanket of prima facie justification for every act they perform under color of law, that is, with the blessing of some salient rule.[92] To be sure, challenges can be levied against acts that are claimed to be authorized, but barring some specific difficulty, legal violence tends to be legitimated in a wholesale manner and responsibility is transferred from human agents to a structure of formal, faceless rules.

But this tidy and inclusive picture of the relationship between law's violence and its rules is unsettled by the inescapable fact that neither social rules nor the statutes and other standards created by law from scratch are ever entirely clear and immune from indeterminacy and conflicting interpretations. While Hart insists that most terms (and so, most rules) have a core of settled meaning that makes their application in standard case clear and unproblematic, he grants that most terms also have a penumbra, a fuzzy region where, in special cases, it is impossible to say with certainty whether the term does or does not apply.[93] Here, Hart admits, on the periphery, but

---

89. See Minow, "Words and the Door."

90. See Ernest Weinrib, "Legal Formalism: On the Immanent Rationality of Law," *Yale Law Journal* 97 (1988): 949. Nonet and Selznick argue that this understanding is a "potent resource for legitimating power" and "as a result the power of the judiciary, because it seems limited, is easier to justify." See *Law and Society*, 61.

91. See *Francis v. Resweber*.

92. For a contrasting argument, see Philip Soper, "Legal Theory and the Claim of Authority," *Philosophy and Public Affairs* 18 (1989): 209.

93. Hart, *Concept of Law*, 119.

only here, something in the nature of judicial discretion is required.[94] As if to console us in the face of this "occasional" indeterminacy, Hart opines that "[u]ncertainty at the borderline is the price to be paid for general classifying terms in any form of communication of matters of fact."[95]

This concession signals greater difficulties for Hart's account of law and for his effort to tame unruly will, desire, and the human proclivity to do violence than he appears to have appreciated. Just as it is not always clear what a rule requires or forbids, it is not always clear just when a rule ceases to be clear. There is, then, a second-order fuzziness that infests Hart's rule-based story of law; cases that some will see as marking the existence of a gap requiring extralegal appeals, others will see as still falling within a rule's clear ambit. But if such a discrepancy persists even after all the facts are in, then a vagueness about a rule's vagueness is implied.[96] No doubt tertiary and still higher orders of indeterminacy are sometimes to be found, but this prospect need not be pursued to see that the open-endedness

---

94. Thus, he contended, it is clear that the rule "No vehicles in the park" excludes trucks, tanks, and bicycles, but like all general terms, the meaning of *vehicle* is vague; there are cases in which its meaning "runs out," and does not decisively rule on unprovided for cases. Are skateboards or rollerskates vehicles? And what about prams or perambulators? Might the statute countenance a small fighter plane mounted on a pedestal to honor pilots lost at war? Here, Hart suggests, the meaning of *vehicle* is of no help, and the official has no choice but to exercise a certain amount of discretion, to fill in the gap, to complete the rule for purposes of this borderline case.

95. Hart, *Concept of Law*, 125. Because the borderline case is, by definition, exceptional, Hart's acknowledgment of such uncertainty gives little ground to the rule skeptic who thinks that law is not a matter of rules at all, that rules are but "pretty playthings" invoked largely to rationalize a decision after it has been reached on other grounds. An interesting version of rule skepticism is presented by Jerome Frank, *Courts on Trial: Myth and Reality in American Justice* (Princeton: Princeton University Press, 1949). The skeptic, Hart suggests, is really just a disappointed absolutist who, having discovered "that rules are not all they would be in a formalist's heaven," mistakenly concludes that rules do "nothing to circumscribe the area of open-texture." Hart rejects this all-or-nothing view; that rules have "exceptions that cannot be exhaustively stated" does not mean that they have no capacity to bind at all (ibid., 135). Hart contended that a "preoccupation with the penumbra" was itself an important source of "confusion in the American legal tradition." See Hart, "Positivism and the Separation of Law and Morals," *Harvard Law Review* 71 (1958): 593, 615.

96. This vagueness about law's vagueness is, we think, evident in the recent and current debate about the accuracy of what is called the "indeterminacy" thesis in critical legal studies. See Mark Tushnet, "Following the Rules Laid Down: A Critique of Interpretivism and Neutral Principles," *Harvard Law Review* 96 (1983): 433; and Fiss, "Objectivity and Interpretation."

of law-as-rules may be quite widespread, initial appearances to the contrary notwithstanding.[97]

At the borderline, where the meaning of rules is unclear, discretion, that is, judgment unfettered by any existing legal rule, is required.[98] Here an official has no choice but to reach beyond law for extralegal standards or considerations that legal materials, *ex hypothesi*, are unable to provide.[99] This means, however, that, contrary to Hart's analysis of legal obligation, citizens' rights and duties are not always determined by reference to antecedently existing rules; alternatively, it means that sometimes law's power is brought to bear against citizens though, in fact, they have no legal obligation in the case at hand. In either case, it means judges are sometimes directly implicated in the deadly consequences of their choices, unshielded by the protective garb of rules.

Where the rules "run out," there is, in Hart's account of law, no place for the legal official to hide, no way to deflect or deny purely personal responsibility for the decision made.[100] It is apparent, however, that judicial discretion reintroduces into the heart of law the problem of personal will and desire. If judges are free to legislate at the margins of law without the guidance of rules, then law itself, that enormous concentration of power that is tolerable, if at all, only in light of the assurances that ironclad rules seemed to provide, may once again, in imitation of Leviathan, emerge as the self-defeating *source* of unregulated pain and paralyzing insecurity.

Of course, uncertainty in law is most visible when officials render conflicting judgments or when they openly confess or contend that the rules conflict or have a gap or are simply silent on the matter at hand. But this kind of difficulty is easily masked by a boldfaced

97. See William Joseph Singer, "The Player and the Cards: Nihilism and Legal Theory," *Yale Law Journal* 94 (1984): 997.

98. See Kenneth Culp Davis, *Discretionary Justice: A Preliminary Inquiry* (Baton Rouge: Louisiana State University Press, 1969). See also Aharon Barak, *Judicial Discretion* (New Haven: Yale University Press, 1989).

99. Hart *Concept of Law*, 132, 141. See also E. H. Taylor, "H. L. A. Hart's Concept of Law in the Perspective of American Legal Realism," *Modern Law Review* 35 (1972): 606.

100. From the perspective of law's own story, the issue of such judicial discretion takes on great importance. It takes on added importance when efforts are made to produce a democratic legality and to lodge lawmaking authority in popularly elected legislative institutions. See Alexander Bickel, *The Last Dangerous Branch: The Supreme Court at the Bar of Politics* (Indianapolis, Ind.: Bobbs-Merrill, 1962).

refusal to acknowledge the latitude that a system of rules makes available.[101] Correlatively, it is relatively easy to conceal the interpretive violence that is invariably done in cases not genuinely governed by a rule. A resourceful judge can always find *some* rule that, at least dimly, pertains and around which it will be possible to construct a story sufficiently plausible to withstand charges of wholly personal decision making. But this, in turn, will suffice to preserve the pretenses of the law-as-rules model. Given this ready defense, rule-centered jurisprudence may have the unhappy consequence of creating spaces for violence that are unavailable even to an Austinian sovereign since, for this beast, the ruse of rigid rules does not exist.[102]

In the treacherous enterprise of attempting to justify law's violence by invoking images of an even greater violence outside of law, we have reached a critical juncture. The specter of human nature turned cruelly against itself, ceaselessly employed in a struggle for more and more power and poised at every turn to do deadly battle, is an intolerable vision of human existence. The bare possibility of such a world, let alone its actualization, cannot help but tempt "rational beings" to embrace *whatever* is necessary to avoid this condition. If that is the unfettered but more organized and predictable violence of Leviathan, so be it. To be sure, violence is violence no matter what its source, but there is reason to think that a world governed by a single power great enough to keep all in awe would be less violent than one in which power is unregulated and is distributed equally among equals.[103] And in a world of unabashed violence, less is better than more.

But Leviathan is dead. So is its legal surrogate, the Austinian sovereign. In their places we have been invited to embrace a far less fearsome image of law, one that retains references to violence only as a distant and vaguely disagreeable backdrop to the governance of rules. But those who might embrace this vision of law have as much

---

101. Compare Zell v. American Seating Co., 138 F.2d 641 (1943); and Trident Center v. Connecticut General Life, 847 F.2d 564 (9th Cir. 1988).

102. Noonan, *Persons and Masks*.

103. Though in the latter world everyone's power would be minuscule compared to the power of a Leviathan, each would have the ultimate power, the power to inflict death; not even Leviathan's power exceeds this. But among Hobbesian beings, if nearly everyone stands roughly on a par with everyone else, and is capable of killing and being killed by everyone, there is, as Hobbes warned, the real prospect of a perpetual bloodbath.

to worry about as their fellow citizens who might violate its provisions. The former must also make certain that the system of rules is not a mask for official lawlessness, making possible and concealing a massive arena of personal power, of unbridled will and desire, that falsely represents itself as impersonal and disinterested decision making.

Unless the danger of unruly rules, of rules that require and authorize strong discretion, can be blocked, acceptance of law as a system of rules may unwittingly reintroduce Leviathan into our midst, but with this horrifying difference: welcomed gratefully within our gates like a twentieth-century Trojan horse and given the reins to rule, the monster will conduct its deadly affairs, completely undetected by us. If law as a system of rules is to represent a real alternative to Leviathan by making its violence visible and moderate, we need firm assurance that rules, not personal will and desire, are really determining law's actions. Rules rife with the kind of indeterminacy that Hart's account appears prepared to tolerate cannot provide that assurance; more likely, those rules will merely mask the very latitude that conjures up, as it did above, images of Leviathan's surreptitious return.

Dworkin's "Defense": Discretion Denied

It was as a friendly critic that Hart proposed to rehearse and revise Austin's account of law, to replace the apparatus of orders, commands, sanctions, and sovereigns with the operation of rules and, in so doing, preserve Austin's insistence on law's autonomy (especially its nonsubservience to morality), while making room, as Austin did not, for law's normativity. Though not everyone agrees,[104] some writers have suggested that rather than revise Austin, Hart buried him. Hart, too, has his "friends," among them, perhaps most prominently, is Ronald Dworkin.

Faced with Hart's acknowledgment that legal rules are gap-ridden and fuzzy-edged, Dworkin incisively drew out the unhappy implications. Hart, correcting Austin's command theory, contended

---

104. See, for example, Brian McCalla Miller, "The Social Rule Theory of Law" (Ph.D. diss., University of Michigan, 1982). For a more muted version of the same general attitude, see J. R. Lucas, "The Phenomena of Law," in *Law, Morality, and Society*, ed. P. M. S. Hacker and J. Raz (London: Oxford University Press, 1977).

that statements of legal obligation imply the existence of a corresponding legal rule that applies to the relevant parties and specifies what they are or are not to do. It follows, Dworkin observed, that where, in Hart's scheme of things, there is no rule or where the only relevant rule is indeterminate with respect to the matter at hand, legal results are generated entirely ex post facto, by operation of the judge's declarations. But to acknowledge this is to grant that, in these cases, legal power is lawlessly brought to bear on life, limb, or property in a way that Hart's account of law cannot justify and, despite the pretenses and trappings of legality, that cannot be distinguished from violence of the most ordinary, sordid kind, of the kind Hobbes feared would devour us in the state of nature.

Surveying Dworkin's dissection of Hart's account of law, one might feel, as Plato says Leontius did upon encountering the corpses of executed criminals lying along the roadside, he "wanted to go and look at them but at the same time was disgusted and tried to run away."[105] Like Leontius, Dworkin did not run away; he did not abandon the bloodied remains of Hart's account of law or simply brand it as an attempt that failed on its own terms. Nor did he accept Hart's account as a satisfactory demonstration that law is a matter of rules, but only up to a point, after which law's unregulated violence resumes its deadly business.

Rather, Dworkin set about resurrecting the body he had mortally wounded, trying to breathe new life into Hart's project by making available to law the materials it needs to combat the affliction of indeterminacy, a disease to which all systems of gap-ridden, fuzzy rules are naturally susceptible. His strategy was to show that every *mature* legal system, the likes of ours in the United States, has the resources to beat back the disease and kill the threat of indeterminacy. These resources consist of additional legal standards, namely, policies and principles, not just rules, as Hart had too narrowly supposed.

A rule, Dworkin suggests, has a specific and datable origin, for example, an executive order, a statute, or a constitutional amendment. Of equal importance, a rule has a canonical formulation that purports to exhaust its content completely.[106] This is not to suggest

---

105. *The Republic of Plato*, trans. Francis MacDonald Cornford (Oxford: Oxford University Press, 1968), 4: 439e, p. 137.
106. Dworkin, *Taking Rights Seriously*, 25.

that rules are never vague. On this point Dworkin and Hart agree entirely. But even a vague rule, for example, a statutory regulation that disallows "unreasonable rates," purports to draw an all-or-nothing boundary so that, if a rate is finally judged unreasonable, it is conclusively forbidden.

By contrast, "No man may profit from his own wrongdoing"[107] is not a rule, but a principle, though no amount of staring at the examples alone will reveal the difference. One must be familiar with the law, with the way principles have made their way into the legal system and with the way they function in that system. The prohibition against profiting from one's own wrong gained standing in our law gradually, by accretion; it was not decreed, enacted, or pronounced. Nor does it function in the all-or-nothing way that rules do; that a certain act is an instance of wrongful profiting may not conclusively settle the legal situation to which it applies. Rather, the principle is a relevant consideration, something that must be taken into account but which, in a given case, may lose out to a stronger, competing principle or to a rule.[108] In contrast, a rule that is "defeated" by another rule is not really a rule of the system at all.

In any mature legal system, Dworkin contends that (as an em-

---

107. Ibid., 26.

108. Ibid., 290. "When lawyers," Dworkin suggested, "reason or dispute about legal rights and obligations, particularly in . . . hard cases . . . , they make use of standards that do not function as rules, but operate differently as principles, policies and other sorts of standards" (ibid., 22). By policies, Dworkin has in mind a "kind of standard that sets out a goal to be reached, generally an improvement in some economic, political or social feature of the community (e.g., rough equality of material well-being)," and by principle he means standards that are to be observed not because doing so will advance some chosen end, but because they are requirements "of justice, or fairness or some other dimension of morality." In his view, those standards abound in our law—in court decisions, statutes, constitutions, and so on. Unlike rules, however, their application is not limited to circumstances carefully detailed in advance; what they require or forbid can never be determinately spelled out.

The effort to find non-rule-based elements in the legal system is, of course, not limited to Dworkin. Other contemporary commentators have been similarly preoccupied with trying to identify such elements. See, for example, Bruce Ackerman, *Reconstructing American Law* (Cambridge, Mass.: Harvard University Press, 1984). See also Fiss, "Objectivity and Interpretation." Such standards are, nonetheless, necessarily part of law itself and, as such, they create binding legal obligations. Here, however, the person obligated is the judge. Dworkin uses the idea of principles and policies to fill in the openness and indeterminacy Hart found at the margins of law. For a critical assessment of his effort to do so, see Stephen Munzer, "Right Answers, Pre-Existing Rights, and Fairness," *Georgia Law Review* 11 (1977): 1055.

pirical matter) legal principles abound. Indeed, they are so numerous and so wide ranging in their content that it is impossible to take seriously the supposition that a case might exist that entirely escapes their reach. Conversely, if every case falls under the purview of one or more principles, then every case is subject to regulative standards. Even cases that reveal gaps in existing legal rules or that fall plainly in the penumbra of a rule's indeterminacy will still be within the governance of one or more legal principles. It is, then, never the case, Dworkin concludes, that legal officials are actually free of all legal material and therefore free (and perhaps implicitly authorized) to decide legal matters by reference to extralegal materials, including their own private preferences and desires.

To be sure, it cannot be maintained that it is impossible for private will and desire to enter the law in the form of judicial misconduct, but activism of the kind that Hart's account of law seemed to permit, that is, strong discretion, is never necessary and never permissible in a mature legal system.[109] Not only is there every reason to suppose that every case is covered by at least some legal principle, Dworkin also contends that there are reasons to believe that every case has a single "right" answer.[110] But one need not take this further step with Dworkin to see the boldness of his response to Hart's difficulties. Unless we can be assured of the existence of relevant legal materials in every imaginable case, we shall be forced to countenance the possibility, contrary to Hart's deepest convictions about law, that some legal obligations are inevitably the result of extralegal considerations.[111] While in schizophrenic moments, Hart appears

---

109. As a result, he denied that judges ever exercise the kind of discretion Hart acknowledged or that judges ever go outside law in making their decisions. Dworkin distinguishes the kind of discretion Hart was willing to recognize, what he calls "strong discretion", from another kind that he labels "weak discretion." Dworkin argues that, in contrast to Hart's understanding of discretion, weak discretion means only "that an official must use judgment in applying the standards set him by authority" (*Taking Rights Seriously*, 32). See E. Bodenheimer, "Hart, Dworkin, and the Problem of Judicial Law-Making Discretion," *George Law Review* 11 (1977): 455.

110. See "Is There Really No Right Answer in Hard Cases?" in Ronald Dworkin, *A Matter of Principle* (Cambridge, Mass.: Harvard University Press, 1985), 119–45.

111. Dworkin, *Taking Rights Seriously*, 15. The need to give a satisfactory account of legal obligation arises for Dworkin because, as he put it, "Day in and day out we send people to jail, or take money away from them, or make them do things they do not want to, under coercion of force, and we justify all of this by speaking of such persons as having broken the law or having failed to meet their legal obligations. . . ."

prepared to accept this contradictory outcome,[112] Dworkin holds te-
naciously to Hart's initial intuition that legal obligation, properly so-
called, is always a dictate of (or under the substantial constraint of)
some salient legal standard.

Ironically, in a way that resembles Hart's defense of Austin,
Dworkin manages to save Hart's scheme only by undermining the
latter's hope to erect a sharp boundary between legal and nonlegal
material, between law and not law. Law and legal decision making
require theory construction and arguments of an elaborate and unavoidably untidy character.[113] Legal meaning cannot, contrary to
Hart, either be read off the surface of self-validating legal materials
or, alternatively, confidently cast aside as having no bearing at all
when the language of rules becomes vague.[114] In almost every case,
judges must consider a considerable array of legal materials, including rules, principles, and other kinds of standards, all of them inter-
acting and having differing and varying weights, and requiring, finally, a normative argument to generate a specific outcome.[115] In

Here Dworkin seems to take seriously the question of law's violence; yet, in fact, he
raises the specter of law's violence not to advance inquiry into the nature of that
violence but to raise the stakes in an argument about interpretive practices in legal
institutions and the justification for legal decisions. As he notes, it is the "concepts of
law and legal obligation" that provide society's "warrant to punish" (ibid., 16). See
Philip Soper, "Dworkin's Domain," *Harvard Law Review* 100 (1987): 1166.

112. Hart, *Concept of Law*, 128.

113. Dworkin has, over the last several years, offered several somewhat different
descriptions of this theory-building activity. Compare *Taking Rights Seriously* and *Law's
Empire*. Each, however, involves the judge as an interpreter of the community's values
as reflected in its legal tradition. As Mark Tushnet points out, this "enterprise is caught
between an apologetic thrust, because it must refer to the values of the community,
and a critical thrust, because the community's values are somehow supposed to explain
why legislation adopted by the community is inconsistent with the community's truest
values." See Mark Tushnet, *Red, White and Blue: A Critical Analysis of Constitutional Law*
(Cambridge, Mass.: Harvard University Press, 1988), 137.

114. See Ronald Dworkin, "Law as Interpretation," *Texas Law Review* 60 (1982):
527. For a contrasting view, see Stanley Fish, "Working on the Chain Gang: Interpretation in Law and Literature," *Texas Law Review* 60 (1982): 551, and "Dennis Martinez and
the Uses of Theory," *Yale Law Journal* 96 (1987): 1773.

115. The practices of law—its modes of argument, its history, its political frame—
cannot be lashed together into a stable string of terms that can produce specific results
in particular cases. The problem, as Dworkin saw it, is not just that the general terms
used to express the requirements of rules are peripherally vague. Rather, legal rules
reside in a sea of shifting standards whose bearing on rules and on other legal material
can be discovered only by engaging in relatively thick theorizing about the entire body
of law under whose "rule" a particular case happens to fall (Dworkin, *Taking Rights*

such a conception of law, judges and adjudication are assigned an enormous importance.[116] One begins to understand, then, why Dworkin believes that the law never "runs dry" in the way Hart supposed.[117] And one also begins to understand why Dworkin abandoned the image of law as limpid language fully fixing a determinate order and replaced it with the idea of law as a coherent set of interpretive practices.[118]

In Dworkin's work, the "interpretive turn" is taken in full view.[119] Law is neither centrally a matter of will and the power to back it up with force, nor is it a matter of chiseled rules. Law viewed as the sovereign's violent domination over his subjects is also rejected. At the same time, law's distinctive monopoly on "legitimate" violence tends to be forgotten or well hidden from view[120] even as its

---

Seriously, chap. 4). Thus, even "clear" cases are not clear in the sense that Hart imagined; their meaning and implications are not revealed pellucidly and on their face. Where they seem clear, it is because many judges happen to endorse the same, or sizable portions of the same, theories of law. Moreover, the completeness of law exists at the level of interpreted elaborations of those theories not as a deductive consequence of specific legal formulas. Some suggest that this argument actually creates another alternative to positivism and natural law theories. See John Mackie, "The Third Theory of Law," *Philosophy and Public Affairs* 7 (1977): 111.

116. See Marshall Cohen, ed., *Ronald Dworkin and Contemporary Jurisprudence* (Totowa, N.J.: Rowman and Allanheld, 1983). See also Kent Greenawalt, "Discretion and Judicial Decision: The Elusive Quest for Fetters that Bind Judges," *Columbia Law Review* 75 (1975): 359, and "Policy, Rights, and Judicial Decision," *Georgia Law Review* 11 (1977): 991; Noel Reynolds, "Dworkin as Quixote," *University of Pennsylvania Law Review* 123 (1975): 574; David Lyons, "Review: Principles, Positivism, and Legal Theory," *Yale Law Journal* 87 (1977): 415; Joseph Raz, "Legal Principles and the Limits of Law," *Yale Law Journal* 81 (1972): 823; Symposium, "*Law's Empire*," *Law and Philosophy* 6 (1987): 281.

117. See Dworkin, *Law's Empire*. Also Soper, "Dworkin's Domain."

118. Here, then, is the conceptual space Dworkin has carved out: Hart is right that law is a matter of determinate rights and obligations. On the other hand, Hart is mistaken that law is always, and only, a matter of rules whose clear, settled meaning is itself generally sufficient to dictate determinate results. Rather, in Dworkin's theory, law is almost always a matter of conflicting standards that do not enjoy the canonical concreteness of rules. These standards enter the judicial mind not as words that cast a prefabricated or preformed shape on legal thought, but as an array of conjectures, conventions, and considerations that rightly influence arguments and outcomes, but that alone never dictate a specific answer to a legal question.

119. Dworkin suggests that interpretation is an effort "to impose meaning on . . . [an] institution . . . and then to restructure it in light of that meaning" (*Law's Empire*, 47). See also Fiss, "Objectivity and Interpretation," and James Boyd White, *Heracles' Bow* (Madison: University of Wisconsin Press, 1985).

120. See Olivecrona, *Law as Fact*, 127.

connection to carefully formulated constraints and canonical standards is substantially diminished.[121] In its place, the Hobbes/Austin version of law—as regulating our lives, with violence if need be—is recast to resemble the activity of those who are telling the story, viz., legal philosophy.[122] And who, more than the philosopher, is so removed from law's violence, from the violence their writings and normative arguments help efface? In Dworkin, law and philosophy tend to merge; unsurprisingly, questions about violence tend to disappear.[123]

---

121. The final and crucial irony is that, according to Dworkin, reduced reliance on rules and language and increased interpretive demands do not occasion judicial discretion (see Dworkin, *Taking Rights Seriously*, 32–33). So long as interpretation occurs in the presence of the welter of standards available in law it is never free of legal constraint and never outside the law. See Note, "Dworkin's Rights Thesis," *Michigan Law Review* 74 (1976): 1167. The very conditions that make interpretation necessary make discretion unnecessary and impossible. Will and desire, as well as power and pain, disappear and are replaced with the mental activities of those who declare law's meaning.

Here we follow Cover in his critique of the interpretive turn. As he suggests, "The violent side of law and its connection to interpretation and rhetoric is systematically underplayed in the work of both Dworkin and White. . . . White reiterates in his book his central claim that 'law . . . is best regarded not as a machine for social control, but as what I call a system of constitutive rhetoric: a set of resources for claiming, resisting and declaring significance.' I do not deny that law is all those things that White claims, but I insist that it is those things in the context of the organized social practice of violence" (see "Violence and the Word," 1602 n. 2).

122. For Dworkin, as for Hart, the job of legal theory is to provide an understanding of why people obey, and why they ought to obey, the law. In this way, the alliance between law and legal theory is cemented and the official perspective is brought to the center of legal scholarship. The phrase *official perspective* is taken from Edmond Cahn, "Law in the Consumer Perspective," *University of Pennsylvania Law Review* 112 (1963): 1, 4.

123. Dworkin's jurisprudence increases the distance between law's producers and its consumers. If even explicitly formulated rules do not have clear or obvious meanings, and even clear cases are really unclear, a person untrained in the intricacies of jurisprudence and moral philosophy can never be sure about the requirements of law until the appropriate authorities have spoken. Thus, perhaps it is appropriate that Dworkin labels his ideal judge Hercules.

Paradoxically, however, the sources of justification for law's violence multiply even as they become less visible and comprehensible. For law's consumers this adds insult to injury as their pain recedes further and further from the center of law. Far from humanizing law, the move from Austin to Dworkin insulates officials who are so consumed with figuring out the meaning of law's rules, principles, and policies that they cannot look up as the bodies of law's victims are confined, condemned, or, like Willie Francis, given a double dose of death.

The Space of Law

What we have referred to as law's official story began in Hobbesian images of life without law, in a world of scarcity and insecurity. With the emergence, or creation, of law and of a unifying violence sufficient to overcome the warring wills of free individuals, a calmer, if not freer life is, at least according to Hobbes and Austin, made possible. Subsequent theorists (Hart and Dworkin) tell a similar story of law's calming influence, though they maintain that such influence arises from law's close connection to the social practices of its community rather than from the threat of violence. Their theories encourage ordinary citizens to submit to law by reassuring us that officials, too, are subject to its restraints. Here they seek to escape the Hobbesian paradox of Leviathan as itself a source of fear and danger.[124]

The theories of Hart and Dworkin are of utmost importance for those concerned to understand the transformation of law from a violent, commanding, awe-inspiring presence to something grounded in practices, rules, principles, and preoccupied with resolving interpretive dilemmas. If law derives from, or is rooted in, aspects of a community's social practices and contains within itself disciplining moral principles, then law's violence will appear to be domesticated from the outset. Here legal authority is derived from familiar, home-grown practices. Here legal authority is weighted down with rules

---

It may be, in fact, that Dworkin's account provides judges and legal officials with an excuse for severity in the application of law. If law is everywhere fixed and determined, if law is a seamless web that cannot anywhere be disturbed without disturbing it entirely, then there is little room for individual adjustment, lenience, or sympathy. If, as Dworkin insists, officials exercise judgment but have no choice, it follows that they are neither free to soften law's violence nor are they responsible for it.

Such a system when it does not manage (or bother) to conceal the fact that it deals in violence and pain, will tend to subdue those facts by claiming them as the natural or necessary results of legal standards, standards which themselves are sufficiently capacious to contain judicial discretion and minimize interpretive violence at the periphery as well as the center of adjudication.

124. It might be argued that neither Hart nor Dworkin provide satisfactory answers to the Hobbesian dilemma since both presuppose the existence of social practices of a kind that Hobbesian creatures could hardly be expected to have. The persons imagined in Hart's theory, unlike those imagined by Hobbes, appear to be embedded in complex social relations, to share an array of critical standards, and are responsive to one another's evaluative assessments. Nevertheless, because Hobbes's psychological assumptions are rather extreme, the theories of Hart and Dworkin appear at least superficially plausible concerning the pressing problem of how power might be regulated without positing still more power somewhere else in the social system.

and principles. Here the specter of violence seems remote. Violence is all but vanquished, or so a reading of law's official story would have us believe.

But is this story really believable? Even if one supposes that human beings are not so narrowly self-interested that they are unable to participate constructively, to honor a system of social practices, or to recognize implicit moral principles, legal officials are a special case. They wield powers that are plainly dangerous. In fact, their power becomes more dangerous as it becomes less visible, Moreover, even if we partially reject Hobbes's psychology, law remains a palpable risk for even moderately self-interested, self-preserving individuals, particularly as there can be no firm absolute assurance that officials will not turn their back on the rules and deploy the awful power of Leviathan as their will or whimsy dictates. And why shouldn't they? They, after all, do not differ substantially from us, and we know how easily we are tempted to deviate or to ignore practices, rules, and principles in the name of will, convenience, or whimsy.[125] Perhaps the official story explains how law as a system of rules is *possible*, but to convince us that it is *actual* (and reliably so), finally to persuade us of law's journey from violence to interpretation, something more must be added to the account.

The general contours of this necessary supplement seem clear enough: given man's allegedly immutable character, there is no choice but to modify the conditions under which that character operates, to make a distinctive space of law.[126] If legal institutions are not to become the sites for the recreation of the Hobbesian drama of will and desire, if the bloodletting which is, of necessity, associated with those institutions is not to reappear in an arbitrary and uncontrolled fashion, they must provide, or be provided with, the institutional accommodations and institutional culture which will make possible reasoned and disinterested deliberation and the complex interpretive work that Dworkin describes.[127] Law must be made extraordinary and removed from the realm of normal human transactions through an array of devices and contrasts that set law off from power and its

---

125. See *The Federalist* (New York: Modern Library, 1956), 337: "If men were angels, no government would be necessary. If angels were to govern men, neither external nor internal controls on government would be necessary."

126. We borrow this phrase from Dumm, "Fear of Law."

127. See Bickel, *Least Dangerous Branch*.

gratifications and from any robust contact with daily life. The aim, then, is to alter the conditions so much that nothing remains on which will and desire might operate or that might unleash an unruled, untamed outburst of official violence.

The devices to do so are numerous and, in our own constitutional tradition, have been subject to elaborate commentary. The most important include an independent judiciary, life tenure for judges, and a constitution amendable through a complex process of overlapping extraordinary majorities. All these devices are based on the belief that law must be separated from politics and politics removed from the legal process. In *The Federalist No.* 10 (Madison), for example, we are introduced to a view of politics that bears striking resemblance to the Hobbesian state of nature. In this account, politics is a realm in which reason never escapes passion and in which the pursuit of self-interest is fueled by self-love,[128] yet the space of law is something dramatically different. Note Hamilton's description of the judiciary in *The Federalist No.* 78 as having

> no influence over either the sword or the purse; no direction either of the strength or of the wealth of the society; and can take no active resolution whatever. It may truly be said to have neither *force* nor *will*, but merely judgment; and must ultimately depend upon the aid of the executive arm for the efficacy of its judgment.[129]

In this description, law's space is defined precisely by what it lacks rather than by attributes it possesses.[130] Its deficiencies appear to be

---

128. In this account, politics combines the rational and the irrational in such a way that the pursuit of interest can never be fully separated from the "impulse of passion" (*The Federalist*, 54). Reason is inexorably connected to "self-love," opinion to "passions" (ibid., 55). Because men are naturally "much more disposed to vex and oppress each other than to co-operate for the common good" (ibid., 56), the political realm, as the Federalists saw it, is fragmented, factionalized and fractious. Moreover, the Federalists believed that the characteristics of politics, especially its unruliness, are "sown in the nature of man."

129. Ibid., 504.

130. Or perhaps it is simply that Hamilton meant us to see law as female, lacking "influence" and "direction," unable to be active and ultimately dependent, taking the arm of the male. Readings of the gender of law are now common, but usually go in the opposite direction—law as male. See Martha Minow, "Justice Engendered," *Harvard Law Review* 101 (1987): 10 and n. 7. See also Robin West, "Jurisprudence and Gender," *University of Chicago Law Review* 55 (1988): 1, and "Disciplines, Subjectivity, and Law."

its virtues; those deficiencies assure us of its harmlessness and its incapacity to do violence.[131] Who or what is able to carve out such a space? Who or what is able to vanquish force and will except some other, although unnamed, force and will? At the creation, law must be the child of a violent resistance,[132] a resistance which having vanquished its enemies leaves that space, or cedes that space, to "judgment." Mere judgment, "merely judgment," such phrasing leaves us to wonder exactly what makes judgment such a diminutive. Instead of worrying about law's violent nature, about its Leviathan-like commands and sanctions, we are led to worry about its weakness, about its capacity to make its mere judgments stick, about its capacity to execute those judgments and, through them, to execute.[133] A cruel trick indeed; the horrible, horrifying Leviathan is dismembered, cut up, and rendered lame if not impotent.

But how, more fully, are constraints on judicial power to be assured? Toward the end of *The Federalist No. 78* Hamilton suggests, anticipating Hart, that " . . . it is indispensable that they should be

131. While politics is presented as the realm of armament or commerce, of active battle and the pursuit of wealth, the space of law appears as a terrain in which force and will, those remnants of the state of nature brought into civil society, have no place, a terrain from which they have, like biblical sinners, been exiled. See *The Federalist*, 504.

132. See Derrida, "Force of Law," 991.

133. It is, of course, the legacy of Hamilton's description of the space of law, and the worries it generates, that are played out in *Francis v. Resweber*. Given that description, one can understand how Justice Reed might see the issue of a "second" execution as a proverbial test of manhood. The manhood at stake was precisely Willie Francis's manhood, his capacity to withstand pain and, in so doing, prove himself able to exert his will against the will of the collective. Francis, the "colored" citizen, could it be that he would be able to endure and defy? Merely to utter the possibility, let alone to award the contest to Willie, would unleash the violence lurking outside the law or admit that the whole thing, the very imagining of such a possibility, was a cruel hoax or a fraud.

Thus, Reed first transforms Francis's case into a primal test of wills, a revolutionary refusal to die at the state's appointed time, and then he domesticates both by suggesting that Francis survived by "accident." Yet no such rhetorical trick can silence the threat that persists just below the surface. As a result, Reed praises the state for its intentions and its purity of motive, like a coquette flattering her protector, like an empty space that must "ultimately depend upon the aid of the executive arm for the efficacy of its judgments."

Willie Francis must be given back to his executioners; Willie Francis must die lest they be rendered powerless by a legal act and return the favor by leaving law to make and enforce its mere judgments. To have sided with Francis would have severed the connections of loyalty and mutuality that bind law and state and make it possible for law's space to be simultaneously a space of judgment and a space of power.

bound down by strict rules and precedents, which serve to define and point out their duty in every particular case that comes before them."[134] This hermeneutic vision of the space of law won early endorsement in our constitutional history, perhaps most famously in Justice Marshall's opinion in *Marbury v. Madison*.[135] There, Marshall announced that the job of the judge is to adhere to "the plain import of the words (of law)" and to be guided by "their obvious meaning."[136] In Marshall's view, the power of language insured that "law need not be just a matter of power."[137] Power is thus expelled from

134. *The Federalist*, 510. Yet even he worried that "few men in the society" would be able to play law's game and operate successfully in the space of law. In this space such men are allowed to serve so long as they are on "good behavior" (ibid., 511). Thus, in the end, it is law's dutifulness that earns our praise and our protection.

135. 1 Cranch 137, 2 L. Ed. 60 (1803) reprinted in Gerald Gunther, *Constitutional Law*, 11th ed. (Mineola, N.Y.: Foundation Press, 1985), 2.

136. Repeatedly Marshall invoked the idea that the Constitution is a written instrument, as if in its being written there was an assurance of stability and comprehensibility, an assurance that judges could and would speak the voice of the law rather than their own voice, an assurance that they would be bound by the language of the written law, compelled by marks on a page. See Charles Fried, "Sonnet LXV and the 'Black Ink' of the Framers' Intention," *Harvard Law Review* 100 (1987): 751. For particularly interesting examples of this faith in the power of language, see the "plain meaning rule in statutory interpretation"; Richard Posner, "Statutory Interpretation: In the Classroom and In the Courtroom," *University of Chicago Law Review* 50 (1983): 800; and Kenneth Abraham, "Statutory Interpretation and Literary Theory: Some Common Concerns of an Unlikely Pair," *Rutgers Law Review* 32 (1979), 676. Another example is provided by the parol evidence rule. See Stanley Fish, "The Law Wishes to Have a Formal Existence."

137. Fried, "Sonnet LXV," 759. Marshall accepted, too, the necessity of the judiciary remaining absolutely removed from "political questions." As he put it,

The province of the court is solely to decide on the rights of individuals, not to enquire how the executive, or executive officers, perform duties in which they have a discretion. Questions in their nature political, or which are by the constitution and laws, submitted to the executive, can never be made in this court. (Ibid., 5)

It is, however, ironic that Marshall was able to rely on such a seemingly clear disclaimer of judicial power to justify a stunning assertion of that power. At the same time, he reverentially describes the limited power of courts he discovers in the Constitution, what is nowhere explicitly written, namely the right to declare acts of Congress unconstitutional.

In addition, he presented himself as bound to the plain meaning of the Constitution and required, almost against his will, to invalidate an act of Congress expanding the jurisdiction of the Court. Of course, in so doing, he appropriated for the judiciary a far larger jurisdiction, a right to review all acts of Congress against a standard of constitutional measurement. Self-abnegation turns out to be self-aggrandizement. Because "it is emphatically the province and duty of the judicial department to say what

the space of law, and, as a result, law can operate "through reason and understanding rather than physical constraint."[138] Law's willfulness and law's violence are yet again made invisible.

Because it has neither force nor will, law itself must be solicitous of those that possess them;[139] law is bonded to the state as a necessary act of self-preservation. In return for the state's protection, law must guard state power. Law can play this role because to it is given the word. Here we see the miraculous ways in which law, precisely through its diffidence, is able to turn words into deeds and judgments into acts of violence while, at the same time, denying its complicity in those acts. Thus, deference properly conceived and properly presented turns into power. As Cover reminds us,

> The judicial word is a mandate for the deeds of others.... The context of a judicial utterance is institutionalized behavior in which others, occupying preexisting roles, can be expected to act, to implement or otherwise to respond in a specified way to the judge's interpretation.... When judges interpret, they trigger agentic behavior within ... an institution or social organization.... Legal interpretation must be capable of transforming itself into action.... In order to maintain these critical links to effective violent behavior, legal interpretation must reflexively consider its own social organization.[140]

In defining the space of law it is important that the judicial power appear wholly reactive and that courts diffidently await the eclectic

---

the law is," (10) law can be emphatic about both its province and its duty, defining and yet limiting its own jurisdiction. Here the work of law is solely interpretive and the business of commands, sanctions, and the deeds of violence is left to others.

138. Ibid., 760.

139. It is true, perhaps, that the process of interpretation must at some point come to an end, and Marshall would have it do so in the decisions of courts. For a contrary view, see John Brigham, *The Cult of the Court* (Philadelphia: Temple University Press, 1988). See also Ronald Nagel, *Constitutional Cultures: The Mentality and Consequences of Judicial Review* (Berkeley: University of California Press, 1989). But having the last word does not, given Hamilton's description of the courts, mean getting one's way. To have effect, judicial words must be turned into the deeds of others. So one answer to the problem of finality—and to the worry that law may amount to nothing more than what the courts say it is—is to remember the weakness of courts and their dependence on others.

140. Cover, "Violence and the Word," 1611.

petitions of disgruntled parties or sporadic appeals from other branches of government. What Bickel called "the passive virtues,"[141] for example, the doctrines of standing, ripeness, and political questions, facilitate the translation of deeds into action even as they seem to require judges to abstain, defer, and avoid, whenever possible, making final decisions. Such a constellation of injunctions and expectations contributes powerfully to the creation of a space of law that appears at once removed and insulated, deliberate and reasoned. To the extent that this becomes a dominant picture, a space for interpretive work is created not through an alteration or transformation in the Hobbesian psychology of the judge, but through the deft manipulation of institution, culture, and tradition. And this manipulation, in turn, contributes massively to the concealment of law's own responsibility for pain and death as well as the extent of its violent involvements.

Beyond the Space of Law: Critical Jurisprudence

There is, of course, another side to the story, a side less protective of the space of law. This side of the story seeks to break down and open up that space and to expose the emptiness of Hamilton's understanding by politicizing our understanding of law. It shows the way will and power operate within the space of law, thereby exposing the limits of a disciplinary understanding of language and the emptiness of any confident proclamation of the adequacy of legal principles. The "critical story" calls into question law's legitimating narratives,[142] and, in so doing, makes it harder to accept its lethal deeds.

But does this critical turn in jurisprudence and legal theory do any better than the official story at making law's violence visible and in restoring the question of violence to a central place in legal theory?

---

141. Bickel, *Least Dangerous Branch.*

142. Gary Peller suggests that at least some elements of the critical story never had such disruptive potential. See Peller, "The Metaphysics of American Law," *California Law Review* 73 (1985): 1151. Peller argues that the "assertion that 'law is politics' has ceased to threaten the legal world. This has happened not because the law side of the equation has been determinately reconstructed, but because the politics side has been impoverished" (1153). For contrary views, see Lon Fuller, "American Legal Realism," *University of Pennsylvania Law Review* 82 (1934): 429; Roscoe Pound, "The Future of Law," *Yale Law Journal* 47 (1937): 1, and "The Call for a Realist Jurisprudence," *Harvard Law Review* 44 (1931): 697.

The answer, we think, is both yes and no. Critics have exposed the violence of the interpretive practices of judges and, in so doing, identified their partiality and biases. However, critics have, for the most part, operated within the terrain defined by traditional jurisprudence and, as a result, have limited themselves to arguing about the nature of rules, principles, and the interpretive activities of judges. The contest is joined over the meaning of law's words, not its deeds; law's texts, not its awesome force; its symbolic violence, not the connection between that violence and the physical violence that law deploys. While a radically different understanding is presented, physical violence remains hidden from view. We are provided with another bloodless story of law.

The contemporary history of that story begins with legal realism. This early twentieth-century intellectual movement, while by no means singular or unified,[143] attacked the conception of law as an independent, objective, apolitical system for applying preexisting rights to particular cases.[144] Realists tried to show that law was indeed ideological, biased, irrational, and itself fully embedded in a representational system that actually constructed what it purported to represent.[145] They did so by exposing the indeterminacy of legal

---

143. It is important to recognize that realism was a historical phenomenon more than an analytic legal theory or organized political movement. Grant Gilmore, "Legal Realism: Its Causes and Cure," *Yale Law Journal* 70 (1961): 1037, characterized its historical significance as the "academic formulation of a crisis through which our legal system passed during the first half of this century." See also William Twining, *Karl Llewellyn and the Realist Movement* (Norman, Okla.: University of Oklahoma Press, 1973), 78.

144. Felix Cohen, "Transcendental Nonsense and the Functionalist Approach," *Columbia Law Review* 34 (1935): 809. See also Karl Llewellyn, "Some Realism about Realism," *Harvard Law Review* 44 (1931): 1222, and "A Realistic Jurisprudence—The Next Step," *Columbia Law Review* 30 (1930): 431. In the era of freedom of contract that preceded realism and that reached its highpoint with Lochner v. New York, 98 U.S. 45 (1908), it was assumed that

> law was not political because it was not ideological—it contained no bias toward any particular societal group. Legal decisions flowed rationally. . . . The right to contract, as the courts continually emphasized, protected the free will of both employers and employees. . . . [Judges] were convinced that they were in touch with the true meaning of the social relations with which they dealt. . . . (Peller, "Metaphysics of American Law," 1213)

145. Peller, "Metaphysics of American Law," 1239–40. Peller suggests that realism demonstrated that

> there could be no rational, as opposed to ideological, content to legal reasoning. . . . Legal reasoning required that . . . events be grouped into general categories of similarity and difference. But all such categories, according to realist argu-

doctrine as well as the rhetorical devices used by judges to mask that indeterminacy.

Judicial decisions could not, according to the realists, be explained by reference to what were somewhat derisively labeled "paper rules."[146] Judges are never compelled by rules because, in any and every case, there are a variety of plausibly relevant possibilities made available by them. Realists thus opposed the efforts of legal theorists who tried "to give an instantaneous snapshot of an existing and completed system of rights and duties,"[147] and they argued that

> [l]egal concepts . . . are supernatural entities which do not have a verifiable existence except to the eyes of faith. Rules of law, which refer to these concepts, are not descriptions of empirical social facts . . . nor yet statements of moral ideals, but are rather theorems in an independent system. It follows that a legal argument can never be refuted by a moral principle nor by any empirical fact. Jurisprudence, as an autonomous system of legal concepts, rules and arguments . . . is a special branch of the science of transcendental nonsense.[148]

The problem, as the realists saw it, was not that rules lacked authority; it was, instead, that there were always competing sources of authority and no clear guidance about how to choose among them.[149] As a result, realists suggested that assumptions about deductive or analogical reasoning that provided the basis for much of law's official story could not, in practice, be sustained.[150] In Cohen's

---

ments, were simply rhetorical; they were not determined by any objective reality. Since the rhetorical categories themselves had no positive content, the application of the categories to particular events necessarily involved political and ideological choices. . . . The deconstructive strand of realism thus made the serious political charge that all legal rationalizations offered for the existence of a particular state of affairs were ideological myths. . . .

146. Llewellyn, "A Realistic Jurisprudence."

147. Cohen, *Transcendental Nonsense*, 844.

148. Ibid., 821.

149. Ibid., 1252. See also John Dewey, "Logical Method and the Law," *Cornell Law Quarterly* 10 (1924): 17.

150. See Dewey, "Logical Method." As they understood the nature of legal decision making,

the vertical move from the general rule to the particular case and the horizontal move from one case to another required mediation through a representational account, legal rules and principles are, at best, empty abstractions with no real-world referents outside of legal discourse,[151] and law's official story works through an elaborate set of fictions that convince us that rules and principles have a real existence.[152] As a consequence of this understanding we also tend to accept the Hamiltonian image of the separation of legal judgment from force and will.[153] In contrast to this traditional view, Cohen, like other realists, asserted that all legal decision making is political in the narrow sense that decisions are not dictated by preexisting rules[154] and in the broader sense that

---

structure within which the particular was like the general or one case was like another. This introduced political and . . . social choices regarding the delineation and extension of representational categories which would define the boundaries of similarity and difference. In the place of determinacy and necessity signified by a realm of law separate from politics, this approach emphasized contingency and open-ended possibilities as it exposed the exercises of social power behind what appeared to be the neutral work of reason. (Peller, "Metaphysics of American Law," 1224)

Take, for example, Felix Cohen's discussion of the supposedly binding force of precedent. See Cohen, "The Ethical Bases of Legal Criticism," *Yale Law Journal* 41 (1931): 201. Cohen claimed that the doctrine of stare decisis imposed, at least in theory, a kind of horizontal constraint for judges; yet, in practice, Cohen claimed that no legal decision could ever be "logically inconsistent with any other decision" and that "it will always be logically possible to frame a single rule requiring both decisions." Moreover, as he saw it, to assert that a precedent is binding, one must have already made a judgment about the similarity or difference between two cases. That judgment cannot itself be dictated by any rules. And where cases are found to be different, one must still decide whether such differences are legally significant. That judgment was, in Cohen's view, "not a problem of logic but of ethics." For a recent exposition of this point, see Andrew Altman, "Legal Realism, Critical Legal Studies and Dworkin," *Philosophy and Public Affairs* 15 (1986): 205, 209.

151. Cohen, "Transcendental Nonsense," 811.

152. Cohen called this "thingification" (ibid., 811).

153. "When the vivid fictions and metaphors of traditional jurisprudence are thought of as reasons for decisions, rather than poetic or mnemonic devices for formulating decisions reached on other grounds, then the author, as well as the reader, of the opinion or argument is apt to forget the social forces which mold the law and the social ideals by which the law is to be judged" (ibid., 812).

154. Here we see the kind of skepticism in the face of which Hart would later acknowledge indeterminacy at the margins of law. Hart, *Concept of Law*, seems to take up the realist challenge quite directly in several places. See Taylor, "Hart's Concept of Law." Thus, for example, Hart acknowledges that "there is no single method of determining the rule for which a given authoritative precedent is authority," yet he suggests that "in the vast majority of decided cases there is little doubt. The headnote is usually correct enough" (Hart, *Concept of Law*, 131). Later on the same page he again notes that while "there is no authoritative or uniquely correct formulation of any rule to be

law is itself an ideological system whose rhetoric and theory are used to advance particular interests and claims.[155]

The inner life of law, according to the realists, is thus not substantially different from life outside the space of law. The most critical of the realists suggested that judicial decisions are, in the end, no more than rationalizations for the desires of judges or the social interests they represent.[156] Here they stressed the continuity rather than discontinuity of law and politics; here they suggested that our narratives of life before, or outside, the law provide useful guides for understanding how law itself worked. If there is will and desire outside the law, there is will and desire in the space of law as well. As a result, judges could not claim that they were simply and inexorably speaking the law; they could not deny their own agency and their own responsibility. They could not claim to be exempt from political accountability because of the distinctive qualities of the space of law. The work of the realists thus was inconsistent with any notion of a rule of law distinct from politics, and it exposed "the exercises of social power behind what appeared to be the neutral work of rea-

---

extracted from cases . . . there is often very general agreement, when the bearing of a precedent on a later case is in issue, that a given formulation is adequate."

Yet the realist critique aimed to demonstrate that indeterminacy could not be confined to the margins, that it was a pervasive fact of legal life. As Cohen argued,

. . . [c]onfusion arises when we think of a judicial decision as implying a rule from which, given the facts of the case, the decision may be derived. . . . [E]lementary logic teaches us that every legal decision and every finite set of decisions can be subsumed under an infinite number of general rules, just as an infinite number of different curves may be traced through any point or finite collection of points. Every decision is a choice between different rules which logically fit all past decisions but logically dictate conflicting results in the instant case. (Cohen, "Transcendental Nonsense," 844)

For another example of the latitude provided by legal materials, see Karl Llewellyn's discussion of statutory interpretation in *The Common Law Tradition: Deciding Appeals* (Boston: Little, Brown, 1960), 521–35.

155. See Robert Hale, "Coercion and Distribution in a Supposedly Non-Coercive State," *Political Science Quarterly* 38 (1923): 470.

156. Jerome Frank, *Law and the Modern Mind* (New York: Tudor Press, 1930), 109, argued that decisions in most cases are "worked out backward from conclusions tentatively formulated" in advance. Or as Yntema put it, "Of the many things which have been said as to the mystery of the judicial process, the most salient is that decision is reached after an emotive experience in which principles and logic play a secondary part." See Hessel Yntema, "The Hornbook Method and the Conflict of Laws," *Yale Law Journal* 37 (1928): 468, 480.

son."[157] As Yntema put it, "The ideal of a government of law and not of men is a dream."[158]

Realists thought that by raising questions about the law/politics distinction they could shake the very foundations of the legal order. Some tried to do so without a clear program; others had a reformer's zeal to change the direction of legal policy.[159] But realism itself did not take up the question of law's violence and of the pain inflicted in the name of the law. While realists were very much interested in tracking the law in action, they did not seriously attend to the intimate connection between law's capacity to act and its capacity to deploy violence. For those interested in reform and policy changes, emphasizing the bloodthirstiness of law would have been counterproductive; for those primarily interested in critique, the issue of violence was either taken for granted or was simply beside the question.

As a result, realism left a mixed legacy. To some extent, the power of realist insights radically transformed prevailing understandings of law. Yet it is equally true that realism was a kind of "house radicalism." It was disruptive, to be sure, yet ultimately it insured continuity in the kinds of issues that would be central to jurisprudence. It provided the grounds upon which revisionist accounts could be developed, accounts that would, themselves, further elide violence, blood, and pain.[160] Moreover, some contemporary heirs of the realist legacy have argued explicitly that the question of violence,

---

157. Peller, "Metaphysics of American Law," 1223. As Cohen, "Ethical Bases," 217, put it, "[W]e . . . shift the focus of our vision from a stage where social and professional prejudices wear the terrible armor of Pure Reason to an arena where human hopes and expectations wrestle naked for supremacy."

158. Yntema, "Hornbook Method," 476.

159. See Laura Kalman, *Legal Realism at Yale, 1927–1960* (Chapel Hill: University of North Carolina Press, 1986).

160. For a similar view, see John Brigham and Christine Harrington, "Realism and Its Consequences: An Inquiry into Contemporary Sociological Research," *International Journal of the Sociology of Law* 17 (1989): 41. Indeed, we have already seen how the official story responded to the realist account, how Hart, for example, incorporated elements of realism while attempting to defend law from the full weight of the realist critique, and how Dworkin responded by conceding the inadequacy of a rule-based model of law. Dworkin, it seems, did more than make concessions in the face of that critique; he took realism seriously and used it to his advantage. He understood that, given the choice between acknowledging the indeterminacy of rules and abandoning the space of law on the one hand, and preserving that space by redefining law to incorporate nonrule-based standards on the other, mainstream legal thought would, by and large, enthusiastically embrace the latter path.

blood, and pain should not be the major forces for legal theory. As Gordon explained, " . . . the power exerted by a legal regime consists less in the force that it can bring to bear against violators of its rules than in its capacity to persuade people that the world described in its images and categories is the only attainable world in which a sane person would want to live."[161]

These critics contend that the oppressive power of law is, in fact, found in its ability to convey an image of rationality and order, of neutrality, objectivity, and consistency when it is, in truth, contradictory and partisan. For them, that power is thus discursive, rhetorical, and ideological.[162] Law works by constituting consciousness and by helping to constitute social relations. Force, physical violence, and the pain that they produce are, to be sure, an important medium of law's power, but, in the critical account, they fade into the background. The question becomes not why there is so much violence and pain or how law might be transformed through the recognition of its lethal character, but, rather, why people put up with a life in which human dignity is denied in the details of everyday life. Law is thought to colonize souls so that it can leave bodies intact. The horror of modern life, as the critics understand it, is not that the tanks roll or that the executioner's job is done. It is, instead, found in the fact that there is so much consent and so little outright coercion.[163] Thus, as Trubek argues,

> [f]or those who engage in the critique of legal thought, ideas in some strong sense can be said to "constitute" society. That is, social order depends in a nontrivial way on society's shared "world views." Those world views are basic notions about hu-

The range of revisionist accounts goes far beyond Hart and Dworkin and incorporates the so-called legal process school, law and economics, some elements of law and literature, and the law and society movement. However, each of these accounts reenacted, in some way, the kind of partial incorporation and domestication of realism that is displayed in Hart and Dworkin. See Mark Tushnet, "Post-Realist Legal Scholarship," *Wisconsin Law Review* (1980): 1383.

161. Robert Gordon, "Critical Legal Histories," *Stanford Law Review* 36 (1984): 109.

162. Many critical legal studies pieces are specifically presented as analyses of ideology. See, for examples, Alan Freeman, "Legitimizing Racial Discrimination through Antidiscrimination Law: A Critical Review of Supreme Court Doctrine," *Minnesota Law Review* 62 (1978): 1049; Klare, "Labor Law as Ideology"; Gabel, "Reification in Legal Reasoning."

163. Gordon, "New Developments in Legal Theory."

man and social relations that give meaning to the lives of society's members. Ideas about the law—what it is, what it does and why it exists—are part of the world view of any complex society. . . . Critical legal scholars read ideologies. . . . They believe that by demonstrating the falseness or incoherence of our dominant legal concepts, critique can lead to change through an imaginative reconstruction of our social reality.[164]

To say that law is discursive, rhetorical, and ideological is, however, to say more than that law constitutes consciousness. It is to suggest that law is, itself, the site of ideological struggle, and that ideological struggle is, itself, the way to transform law. Thus, contemporary critics have tried to update the realists' indeterminacy critique[165] and to expand it beyond the realm of rules, to a deeper, more abstract level.[166] They have carried on their ideological struggle with the hope that systematic demonstration of the contradictions and

---

164. David Trubek, "'Where the Action Is': Critical Legal Studies and Empiricism," *Stanford Law Review* 34 (1984): 575, 590, 610. Mark Kelman, *A Guide to Critical Legal Studies* (Cambridge, Mass.: Harvard University Press, 1987), 300–301 n. 17, claims that

> Ideology fits in two distinct ways in a world picture where the free political subject must be resuscitated. First . . . the question "Why no revolution" may recur as a question of the lack of will to revolt. . . . Second, insofar as . . . [critics] see themselves as political organizers as well as society's students, active debate over ideology becomes politically transformative; undermining the hegemony of ruling ideals becomes a necessary project. . . . [T]he preoccupation . . . with the metaethical question, the problem of discerning moral truth . . . in part arises from the sense that the appropriate political stance is far more open to issue.

165. Here, strong claims are made about the indeterminacy of language and about the inability of words to play the disciplinary role assigned to them in the "official story." See Singer, "Player and the Cards." These claims are, however, now played out in a careful examination of principles, philosophical ideals, and theories of society. Contemporary critics suggest that political struggles outside the space of law are replicated and reproduced in the legal product of those struggles, and deny that judges can, through some special alchemy, rise above or transcend them. What they can do, critics allege, is mask their embeddedness in, and involvement with, political struggles through talk about rules, principles, and precedents. In all this talk, critics allege, law's official story would have us believe that "the many conflicts of interest and vision that lawmaking involves, fought out by countless minds and wills working at cross purposes, . . . [become] the vehicle of an immanent moral rationality whose message could be articulated by a single cohesive theory" (Roberto Unger, "The Critical Legal Studies Movement," *Harvard Law Review* 96 [1983]: 563, 571).

166. This analysis of postrealist critical jurisprudence is suggested by Altman, "Legal Realism."

indeterminacy of all postrealist reconstructions of law,[167] the presence of which is ignored, denied, or repressed, would loosen law's hold on the soul and the imagination.[168]

As one example, Duncan Kennedy identified what he calls "fundamental contradictions"[169] in the ethical and political presuppositions of law and suggested that one cannot rescue law from the indeterminacy thesis, as many postrealist legal theorists have tried to do, simply by expanding its domain beyond rules to incorporate principles, policies, procedures, or standards of efficiency. He contended that nonrule-based standards are themselves profoundly at war with one another. "At this deeper level," Kennedy wrote, "we are divided among ourselves and also within ourselves, between irreconcilable visions of humanity and society and between radically different aspirations for our common future."[170]

Individualism and altruism, the recognized need for, and yet profound fear of, others, freedom and security, each makes its presence felt in law;[171] moreover, each exerts a substantial and plausible,

---

167. See Mark Tushnet, "Truth, Justice and the American Way," *Texas Law Review* 57 (1979): 1307, and "Critical Legal Studies and Constitutional Law: An Essay in Deconstruction," *Stanford Law Review* 36 (1984): 623; see also Duncan Kennedy, "Cost-Benefit Analysis of Entitlement Problems: A Critique," *Stanford Law Review* 33 (1981): 357; Morton Horowitz, "Law and Economics: Science or Politics," *Hofstra Law Review* 8 (1980): 905; Mark Kelman, "Misunderstanding Social Life: A Critique of the Core Premises of Law and Economics," *Journal of Legal Education* 33 (1983): 274.

168. So pervasive is the emphasis on the analysis of contradictions in critical legal studies work that Mark Kelman recently suggested that it forms the basis for "a standard four-part critical method" (Kelman, *Guide to Critical Legal Studies*, 3). According to Kelman,

> Critics attempted to identify a contradiction in liberal legal thought, a set of paired rhetorical arguments that both resolve cases in opposite, incompatible ways and correspond to distinct visions of human fulfillment. . . . Second, the Critics tried to demonstrate that . . . contradiction is utterly pervasive in legal controversy, even in cases where practice is so settled that we nearly invariably forget that the repressed contradictory impulse could govern the decision at issue. . . . Third, Critics have attempted to show that mainstream thought invariably treats one term in each set of contradictory impulses as privileged. . . . Fourth, the Critics note that, closely examined, the "privileged" impulses describe the program of a remarkably right-wing, quasilibertarian order. (ibid., 3–4)

169. See Kennedy, "Form and Substance." Kennedy has subsequently repudiated the fundamental contradiction; see Gabel and Kennedy, "Roll Over Beethoven."

170. Kennedy, "Form and Substance," 1685.

171. The precise identification of contradictions varies in critical legal studies work. Kelman summarizes the contradictions so far identified as follows:

albeit inconsistent, pull on the judge as he or she faces the task of decision. Yet Kennedy contends, contra Dworkin,[172] that there is no rule or principle that itself clearly resolves these inconsistent pulls and determines which principle or policy to favor in a particular case:[173] "We are unable to distinguish particular fact situations in which one side is more plausible than the other. The difficulty, the mystery, is that there are no available metaprinciples. . . ."[174]

This story succeeds, if it succeeds at all, when it exposes the political contingency of law's official story and of its self-constructing narratives and when it makes visible the violence of law's interpretive practices. It demonstrates that what has been presented as necessary and indispensable to the realization of common purposes is merely the effect of a particular form of social power, "the victory of a particular way of representing the world that then presents itself as beyond mere interpretation, as truth itself."[175] For critics,

> ethically principled reconstruction . . . of doctrine is ruled out by the law's internal contradictions, such contradictions being

(1) the contradiction between a commitment to mechanically applicable rules as the appropriate form for resolving disputes . . . and a commitment to situation sensitive, ad hoc standards. . . . (2) the contradiction between a commitment to the traditional liberal notion that values or desires are arbitrary, subjective, individual and individuating while facts or reason are objective and universal and a commitment to the ideal that we can "know" social and ethical truths objectively. . . . (3) the contradiction between a commitment to an intentionalistic discourse . . . and a determinist discourse. . . . (*Guide to Critical Legal Studies*, 3)

172. Dworkin tried to resolve the problem posed by the identification of contradictions and inconsistencies in legal principles by arguing that they have differing weight, that some principles logically take precedence over others. His theory that judges should resolve cases by applying the soundest theory of law implies, if it cannot demonstrate, that there is some metatheoretical way to measure the appropriate weights of the differing principles that may be in play in any case. See *Taking Rights Seriously*, 26.

173. Critics claim that we can never know, certainly and finally, what a text, whether literary or legal, political or philosophical, really means such that a single, determinate, or correct reading is compelled. The language through which rules and principles are codified and communicated will never sit still long enough for any interpreter to gain control over it and master the multiplicity of its meanings. For recent proponents of critical legal studies, it is, in fact, the multiplicity of meanings, this profusion of the possible, that plagues the effort of law and legal theory to pin things down and tell a convincing story of the rationality of law or the separation of law and politics.

174. Kennedy, "Form and Substance," 1724.

175. Peller, "Reason and the Mob: The Politics of Representation," *Tikkun* 2 (1987): 28.

symptomatic of the law's conception in ideological compromise and struggle. . . . This means that there is simply no soundest theory of settled law, and so Dworkinian efforts to rescue legal determinacy by appealing to such a notion fail.[176]

In the critical story, political adjudication of the kind Dworkin acknowledges is but a thin veil for the more robust politicization of law that he would find problematic. The outside is, if you will, already inside law; the conventions and practices of adjudication cannot repel the political without repelling law itself, and, as a result, they cannot insure a safe haven for neutral, objective, deliberate, and principled decision.[177] If this is the case, then violence, violent deeds inscribed in law's name upon the bodies of citizens, the very violence

---

176. See Altman, "Legal Realism," 223. Here too, however, Dworkin may have a resilient reply. Like other mainstream theorists seeking to defend the legitimacy of law, Dworkin must surely be concerned with allegations that law is political, that judges, not rules or principles, are ultimately responsible and accountable. Yet Dworkin himself concedes that adjudication is political because, in what he calls "hard cases," not everyone will agree with any particular judicial effort to identify principles most compatible with the soundest theory of law. See *Taking Rights Seriously*, 127. But note that this concession is the equivalent of his acknowledgment of weak discretion. Surely judicial interpretations can be, and are, controversial, yet they are, in Dworkin's view, legitimate to the extent that they are constrained by legal principles and are compatible with the dictates of the soundest theory of law.

The soundest theory of law can only perform its role in guiding adjudication and, in so doing, preserve the space of law if it exercises significant constraint on the will and desire of judges. Critics deny that it does or it can. Recalling the insights of legal realism, now described in the language of ideology, they suggest that "because the authoritative legal materials, in replicating the ideological conflicts of the political arena, contain a sufficient number of doctrines, rules and arguments representing any politically significant ideology a judge who conscientiously consults the materials would find his favored ideology . . . and conclude that it was the soundest theory of law" (Altman, "Legal Realism," 230–31). Here, judges operating in what at first appears to be Dworkin-like fashion proceed ideologically and, with ingenuity, get to call their ideological constructions law. As a result, strong discretion is disguised and makes its appearance as weak discretion.

177. To be sure, judges and mainstream legal theorists can and do give plausible accounts of legal texts; yet critics claim that they can always demonstrate that those accounts are partial, incomplete, and inadequate. If this is the case, then the image of the judge as bound, trapped, compelled by rules and principles, as devoid of will and desire or able convincingly to articulate the soundest theory of law, is again exploded and replaced with an image of the judge as moral agent and political actor, choosing and imposing, rather than discovering, the meaning of law.

Occasionally, but all too rarely, judges themselves make visible the plasticity of legal language and, in so doing, call into question law's official story. Thus, the Califor-

in which the critics themselves evidence little interest, is, at least in one way, not radically different from the violence it displaces, since it ultimately serves particular interests and originates in the expression of particular wills. Thus, justification for law's violence cannot be found in claims about its distinctiveness and about the separation of the space of law from politics and necessity.[178]

The critical story in jurisprudence, because it politicizes law, may help to make law accountable, and it may open up new possibilities for constructing and using law and for arranging, and rearranging, social power.[179] Or having called into question law's major legitimating claims it may prepare the way for a return to a legal world in which necessity is again more important than legitimacy. At its most extreme, however, it displays little interest in understanding what a world of necessity would look like, and in coming to terms with law's capacity for a furious, and fearsome, revenge. Even more explicitly than its mainstream jurisprudential counterpart, it turns away from law's bureaucratic bloodiness and looks elsewhere in the hope of exposing the secret of law's dominating power. "The law," we are told, "does not enforce anything . . . because the law is nothing but ideas and the images they signify."[180] By focusing on the hegemonic

---

nia Supreme Court forcefully repudiated the official story in a recent case arising from an alleged breach of contract. The court suggested that contractual obligations flow only from the intentions of the contracting parties, rather than the words of the contract. It explained that it is not feasible to determine intention from words by saying that "if words had absolute and constant referents, it might be possible to discover contractual intentions in the words themselves. . . . Words, however, do not have absolute and constant referents. . . . [J]udicial belief in the possibility of perfect . . . expression . . . is a remnant of a primitive faith in the inherent potency and inherent meaning of words." See Pacific Gas & Electric Co. v. G. W. Thomas Draying and Rigging Co., 66 Ca.2d 33, 38 (1968). Or, see Judge Frank who, in a contract case involving the parol evidence rule, said, "Candor compels the admission that were we enthusiastic devotees of that rule, we might so construe the record as to bring this case within the rule's scope." See Zell v. American Seating Co., 644.

178. Claims about indeterminacy and the effort to show continuity between law and politics are designed to undermine the legitimacy of the existing legal order. See Duncan Kennedy, "The Political Significance of the Structure of the Law School Curriculum," Seton Hall Law Review 14 (1983): 14.

179. Roberto Unger, Politics: A Work in Constructive Social Theory, 3 vols. (New York: Cambridge University Press, 1987).

180. Peter Gabel and Jay Feinman, "Contract Law as Ideology," in Kairys, The Politics of Law, 181. Compare to Derrida, "Force of Law": " . . . [L]aw is always an authorized force. . . . [A]pplicability, 'enforceability' . . . is the force essentially implied in the very concept of justice as law. . . ." (925).

power of legal ideas and devoting itself to the critique of those ideas, critical theorists have found, we think, effective ways to do battle with Hart and Dworkin; they have not, however, helped us to see or to cope with the bloodlust and bloodletting that is so much a part of our legal order. To do so we must look elsewhere.

Conclusion: Toward a Jurisprudence of Violence

There is a deep schism between a jurisprudence of rules and principles, whether traditional or critical, and the practice of legal violence, a schism rarely noted and nowhere bridged. The former is always concerned with law's rhetorical justifications and with the question of whether assent and obedience are warranted, the latter with pain, bloodletting, and the role the pervasiveness of violence plays in the constitution of the legal subject. The former is preoccupied with authority and legitimacy, the latter with techniques for managing or maiming human bodies. In this essay, we have told how law's official story, grounded initially in terrifying Hobbesian images of life outside the law, has been successively transformed into a story about rules and principles in which references to physical violence, particularly to law's own violence, are both rare and far removed from the persons and bodies that inflict and suffer pain. We have, that is, retraced the steps by which legal theory has become a story about judges, interpretation, and adjudication.

While the words of judges authorize violence, they seem not to carry it out.[181] Yet judges do violence in both a symbolic and instrumental sense, even as they seek to hide both. The violence of legal interpretation is disembodied. Or, rather, the violence that judges do is done to subjects who are disembodied by law's procedures and its fictions, subjects stripped of any history and of connection to the human community.[182] The process of (re)embodying subjects and

181. This is a point recognized early on by Hart, *Concept of Law*. Foucault and others remind us of the emergence of a more dispersed disciplinary power. See *Power/Knowledge*. Law in a complex society could hardly be expected to operate through the immediacy and directness of commanding sovereigns.

182. See Noonan, *Persons and Masks*. Natalie Zemon Davis, *Fiction in the Archives: Pardon Tales and Their Tellers in Sixteenth-Century France* (Stanford: Stanford University Press, 1987), tells about the many ingenious ways through which those subject to law try to resist this process.

applying physical violence is left to others. When the symbolic violence stops, such physical violence begins;[183] when specified incantations are performed behind law's bureaucratic facade, blood can then be spilled.

So long as legal theory is preoccupied with understanding what judges do and how they do it, so long as law is equated with adjudication, we will see law only as judges see it. So long as critical legal theory seeks only to expose the will and desire that inevitably are part of the interpretive task and rests content with deconstructing law's ideologies, we will be blind to the ways in which ideological oppression ultimately depends on law's monopoly of violence. While critics eagerly, and by now almost effortlessly, demonstrate law's indeterminacy, the machine quietly rolls on. Death is authorized and death is done.[184] People are arrested and find themselves in jail. Property is taken and personal liberty abridged. This is, we think, the central insight of Cover's critique of the interpretive turn in legal scholarship.[185] This is, we think, why we give in so easily to the colonization of our souls and imaginations. Somehow it seems easier to give in to this insidious but not deadly power, or perhaps just to turn away, than to face law's pervasive violence.

We do not suppose, however, that anyone is completely lulled into thinking that law is nonviolent. On the contrary, as we noted elsewhere, law's occasional use of violence is generally insisted on as a regrettable but necessary device to motivate the recalcitrant and reassure the acquiescent. On this perception of things, the affairs of law are amply accommodated and made theoretically intelligible by reference to the operations of a system of rules; only peripherally and marginally is there need to supplement this account with mention of the force used to counteract the outlaw.

---

183. Cover, "Violence and the Word."

184. "If the origin of law is a violent positioning, the latter manifests itself in the purest fashion when violence is absolute, that is to say when it touches on the right to life and to death" (Derrida, "Force of Law," 1005).

185. Yet the critical impulse with its demand that law own up to its deep politicization is in itself by no means insignificant. We cannot know whether deauthorizing law will minimize law's violence or simply precipitate greater brutishness in the service of maintaining order. However, it may, and we hope it does, provoke a different conversation, a conversation that bridges the gap between law's use of violence and its presentation as the only alternative to violence. It is this antimony that qualifies violence as a principal concern for legal theory.

But if all of this is so, is law's violence, despite its practical and pragmatic importance, of any real theoretical interest? Is there, indeed, a genuine need for what we have called a jurisprudence of violence? To no one's surprise, we think there is. But there is need to say more about it. Here we briefly sketch the contours of such an enterprise, but make no attempt to advance a theory of our own.[186]

We begin with the seemingly unproblematic claim that law's violence, though largely invisible in the interpretive work of judges, is, nonetheless, experienced and felt—most often as a brooding specter—both by legal subjects (that is, by ordinary citizens) and by various officers of the law (e.g., district attorneys, police, wardens, and executioners). To mention these several roles is already to allude to persons who, if they are mentioned at all, figure only vaguely and obliquely in traditional jurisprudence, a perspective that is dominated, as we have seen, by judges and the concerns of judges. In contrast, a jurisprudence of violence would, we believe, focus on the disparate experiences of ordinary citizens and various legal officials, especially on understanding how pervasively the law's violence constructs their self-perception, influences their motives and dispositions, and determines what they are disposed or ill disposed to do. Here we can only allude to aspects of these two sets of experiences, experiences that are passed over in virtual silence by contemporary legal theory but which, because of their relation to law's use of force, would seem to require what we have called a jurisprudence of violence.

To glimpse the inability of a jurisprudence of rules and principles to capture the experience of legal subjects appropriately, it is important to tease out some of the subliminal messages of this jurisprudence. The claim that law is a system of rules and principles suggests, and is meant to suggest, that law is, or should be, also an affair of reason, that it is permeated by reason, by *reason* rather than will, by *reason* rather than violence (for the most part, anyway). The principal linkages between rules and reason are clear enough; rules are meant to regulate or guide conduct by having meaning, an understandable meaning, indeed, by being understood *as* meaning this or that. The discovery of this meaning is generally regarded as an achievement of intellect or reason.

---

186. Much of what we say here draws, as does the entire essay, on Cover's seminal essay, "Violence and the Word."

But the link between rules and reason does not end here. Rules cannot determine or shape conduct unless they are understood as providing those they address a sufficient reason to do or abstain from doing as they direct. The idea of a system of rules includes, then, the idea that rules themselves generally afford legal subjects good reasons to observe them. Rules are conceived of as devices to direct and motivate conduct. They fail if they are not discovered, or, where discovered, if they cannot be understood, or if one rule conflicts with another rule making full compliance impossible, or if they do not provide sufficient reasons to be observed—hence the emphasis on the word, on meaning, and on interpretation.[187]

Law conceived of as a system of rules and principles thus embraces a vision of legal subjects as rational agents who, by and large, if they understand what is expected of them, are generally responsive to normative suasion.[188] The task of law and legal theory, then, is to make those rules and principles clear as regards both their content and their justification. To the extent that these goals are realized, noncompliance can be attributed to deficiencies in the legal subject, say, a culpable lack of understanding or a wayward disregard of the rules. In either case, the disobedient subject becomes fair game for law's use of violence, to assure conformity even where direction-by-rule has failed.

Here, then, is a facially plausible account of legal theory's preoccupation with rules and principles as well as its substantial indifference to law's violence; so long as legal rules and, for Dworkin, legal principles are in place, then the use of force—assuming that it, too, is governed by rules and principles—is wholly appropriate and of secondary theoretical importance. But this composite picture of human agency and of the operation of legal rules and principles on law's ordinary citizens *wars* with law's reliance on, and use of, violence. Inescapable force, pain, and violence tend to short-circuit the pathways of rational agency that are plainly implied in the jurisprudence of rules just described and that figure prominently in most attempts to provide prima facie justification for the authority of law so conceived. Force does not invite the engagement or cooperation of our

---

187. See Lon Fuller, *Morality of Law*, chap. 2.
188. Robert Gerstein, "The Practice of Fidelity to Law," in *Compliance and the Law*, ed. Samuel Krislov, Keith Boyum, Jerry Clark, Roger Shaefer, and Susan White (Beverly Hills, Calif.: Sage Publications, 1972).

capacities as rational agents to determine our behavior. It gets our attention whether we are attending or not; it moves us whether we understand or not; it does not wait for reason's assent.

The subjects of force are, in the moment of violence, acted on as mere objects. Their capacity for self-direction is bypassed and they are brought into, or reduced to, a passive, thinglike state. The point here is not to contend that law's use of violence violates Kantian strictures regarding the treatment of persons as persons; rather, the point is to draw attention to the radical difference between, indeed the incommensurability of, these two ways of acting on persons.[189] Even where their natural predilections might take them in other directions, persons who nonetheless act from their own understanding can identify their conduct as their own or as a product of the social rules of a community in which they are members; in contrast, persons moved by force or pain are distanced from themselves and their community. They are held hostage to their own bodies, experiencing them as conduits of a kind of terrorism against their capacities as rational agents or social beings.[190]

Force is disdainful of reason; it pushes it aside; it takes over completely. Reason and force have no way to share control of human agency. Where the two meet in battle only one can win, and given the levels of force, pain, and violence at law's disposal, law, wherever it wants, is assured of victory. It appears, then, that law's violence does not sit well—indeed, it wars with—the conception of human agency that is built into, and held out to us by, a jurisprudence of rules.

More is at stake, however, in this concern for the constitutive effects of law's violence than an instrumental conception of law, a

---

189. Kant, after all, was a retributivist on matters of punishment. See Immanuel Kant, "The Metaphysical Elements of Justice," part 1 of *The Metaphysics of Morals,* trans. John Ladd (Indianapolis, Ind.: Bobbs-Merrill, 1985). See also Herbert Morris, "Persons and Punishment," in *Human Rights,* ed. Abraham Melden (Belmont, Calif.: Wordsworth, 1970), for a defense of the propositions that persons, rather than being "treated" or "cured," have a right to be punished.

190. See Scarry, *Body in Pain.* The use of violence makes frightfully clear law's unwillingness to impose its will, and to bypass our own will, completely. It is, in fact, fully prepared to use our own bodies against us, all the while representing itself as the instrument and protector of rational agency. Law's known willingness to do this gives at least some credence to our suggestion that general observance of the rules of law may owe more to this terrifying proclivity than to the suasive powers of law's reason-guiding standards.

conception long associated with, among other things, concerns for the deterrent effect of legal punishment.[191] To speak about law's violence is to speak about its pervasive cultural residue, the way it insinuates itself into consciousness and conditions responses. Every instance of lethal force by law enforcement, every sentence imposed, every execution holds out images of our own fate at the hands of law and coldly reminds us of the way social life is forged and maintained.

It will be objected that the argument hinted at here conflates the extraordinary and the extreme (i.e., the imposition of law's will by force to gain subjects' obedience) with the ordinary and common-place (i.e., the placid, pain-free conformity with law's direction); it will be objected that we move too quickly from law's monopoly of legitimate violence to the wholesale erosion of human agency in the face of that monopoly. In response to this challenge we are reminded of Cover's image of the convicted criminal who walks " . . . to pro-longed confinement, usually without significant disturbance to the civil appearance of the event."[192] But, Cover observes, it would be "grotesque to assume that the civil facade is 'voluntary.'"[193] The more plausible interpretation is that the man is aware of the "overwhelm-ing array of violence ranged against him, and of the hopelessness of resistance or outcry." In sum, "most prisoners walk into prison be-cause they know they will be dragged or beaten into prison if they do not walk."[194]

Cover's comments are germane to law generally. What is the experience of legal subjects in the face of law? To what extent do they respond to it in the way that the model of rules and principles sug-gests (i.e., through their capacities and dispositions as rational agents)?[195] Alternatively, to what extent do legal subjects tend to experience law in the way Cover says prisoners do, as mere automata

---

191. See J. Andeneas, *Punishment and Deterrence* (Ann Arbor: University of Michi-gan Press, 1984). See also Jack Gibbs, "Punishment and Deterrence: Theory, Research, and Penal Policy," in *Law and the Social Sciences*, ed. Leon Lipson and Stanton Wheeler (New York: Sage, 1986), 319–68.

192. Cover, "Violence and the Word," 1607.

193. Ibid.

194. Ibid.

195. The growing literature on procedural justice emphasizes the importance of such capacities in governing responses to law. See Tom Tyler, *Why People Obey the Law* (New Haven: Yale University Press, 1990). See also E. Allan Lind and Tom Tyler, *The Social Psychology of Procedural Justice* (New York: Plenum Press, 1988).

who walk, who execute the motions required of them, but only because they have looked past or seen through the rules to the violence that awaits them were they to try to do otherwise. Here, one can begin to see that no attempt to conjoin a jurisprudence of rules and principles with a story about violence can succeed merely by portraying that violence as marginal, or peripheral, or as a background phenomenon.

The crucial point, apparently unnoticed in the jurisprudence of rules and principles, is that law's violence can play the role that the "official story" requires of it if only if that violence *is generally available*. But if it *is* generally available, then there is every reason to be attentive to its effects on legal subjects, to the role it plays in shaping their lives and constituting them as subjects, whether or not the violence is actually deployed, whether or not it is actually brought to bear on their bodies.[196] Specifically, if that role is large, then, from the perspective of ordinary citizens, the jurisprudence of rules and principles would seem to be a charade, played out to colonize our souls, to spare us untold actual violence by encouraging acceptance of the illusion that as rational agents we could have chosen otherwise.[197]

---

196. Perhaps we should clarify the grounds of our suggestion that law's promise of violence, allegedly required to threaten the disobedient and to assure the subservient, seriously threatens the entire conception of law as a system of rules. As ordinary citizens, law's official story solemnly assures us that law's violence will be brought to bear against those, and only those, who would dare resist its requirements. We know, then, that law is implicated in the business of inflicting pain. Moreover, for that pain to do the work assigned it, it must be great enough to overwhelm those who would resist, to outweigh or subdue or simply destroy the renegade reasons a person might dare to have. The law's aim in all of this is not to extract a "price" for nonconformity. It is not playing a game; it means to exact obedience.

Perhaps the point is made most clearly by observing that a perfectly designed legal system of the kind that is defended in a jurisprudence of rules would make such a compelling "show" of pain that its actual deployment would be unnecessary. But to imagine such a system of law is not to imagine a world perfectly governed by rules and reason; it might well be a world that is governed entirely by an exquisitely acute and paralyzing anticipation of law's promise to do violence. But to be governed by this is to be governed by fear, by an image of one's self, one's will, being wholly overcome, ravaged, by pain. And such a fear, or pain (as Robert Cover, in "Nomos and Narrative," and, most recently, Elaine Scarry, in *The Body in Pain,* have contended) destroys everything, even the most cherished goals, even the strongest reasons. But where this is so, law's claimed affinities to reason are undeniably broken.

197. In such a world, even one in which officials scrupulously observe the rules of the system, Leviathan has returned. For, in fact, law's violence, even if infrequently deployed, is by no means peripheral or marginal. Frequency of deployment is a poor measure of law's capacity to overpower the will and make compliance nonoptional. On the contrary, the most effective reign of terror would be one in which the anticipa-

We maintain, then, that one aspect of a jurisprudence of violence would be the development of appropriate ways to talk about, to represent, and understand ordinary citizens' experience of law, including, but almost certainly not limited to, the effect of law's physical violence (or the threat of it) on these persons' experience of law and their reasons for acting as they do. The question is whether legal theory can retain its vaunted distinction between reason and force and assign to law the legitimating virtues of the former at the same time that it tacitly embraces, or simply ignores, law's reason-destroying violence. As we have been suggesting, there is reason to think that official violence is incompatible with any compelling jurisprudence of rules and principles.[198] There is reason to think, that is, that the logic of violence overwhelms the operation of rules and principles and trivializes the latter in the actual experience of ordinary legal subjects. A jurisprudence so divorced from human experience can have little claim to our allegiance, either as theorists or as ordinary citizens.

So much for the need for a jurisprudence of violence to explore and adequately represent the effects of law's threat and use of force on the constitution and dispositions of legal subjects. Of probably equal importance (though here we discuss the subject only very briefly) is the need for a jurisprudence of violence to study the effects of legal force, not just on those who fear or suffer it, but on those who inflict it, namely, legal officials. Here again Cover has anticipated us. He has reminded us, for example, that law's violence must not only overcome the wills of legal subjects, it must also override the inhibitions nearly all of us have against inflicting pain on others. To understand law's violence requires, then, study of the devices and cues law uses "to bypass or suppress the psychosocial mechanisms

---

tion of violence is so ferocious that violation is all but unthinkable. In sum, *because* we are rational agents and therefore have, as the official story requires, the capacity to understand and anticipate, one may not reasonably infer from law's infrequent violence that the violence (or the anticipation of it) does not rule the day. As Hobbes, *Leviathan*, 186, deftly observed, a condition of war consists not in battle only "but in a tract of time wherein the will to contend by battle is sufficiently known." Just so, a regime of violence need not be one that uses force in each and every case; it is enough that it is generally understood to be able and willing to do so.

198. It does not follow, of course, that legal violence is never justified; the fact remains, as Cover remarks, "we should not pretend that we talk our prisoners into jail." To the extent that a jurisprudence of rules suggests that law is entirely a matter of rules and reasons, only minimally grounded in violence, it is tantamount to the notion that prisoners freely walk to jail.

that usually inhibit people's actions causing pain and death."[199] If the inhibition against violence were perfect, then law and law's violence would be largely unnecessary; and if the inhibition were "not capable of being overcome through social signals, law would not be possible."[200] What these signals are and the conditions of their effective employment must deeply shape the consciousness and practices of legal officialdom.

Law's violence requires elaborate social organization in other ways as well. Specifically, it requires the cooperation of numerous people (e.g., police and wardens and executioners); the judge who is unmindful of this will find that his or her decisions have little practical effect. And this suggests that the interpretive activities of judges cannot be the hermetically sealed enterprise of the kind imagined in a jurisprudence of rules and principles. Dworkin's Hercules must raise his head from law's written texts and accommodate the pragmatic demands of a cooperative social enterprise. As Cover contends, legal interpretation is "bonded," that is, "bonded at once to practical application (to the deeds it implies) and to the ecology of jurisdictional roles (the conditions of effective domination)."[201] Here, in the psychologies of officials and in practical demands confronting official action, we find additional reasons to be skeptical about the adequacy of a jurisprudence of rules and principles as well as additional reasons to think that a jurisprudence of violence is necessary.

From the perspective of legal subjects and legal officials, we have tried to clarify the principal concerns of a jurisprudence of violence. We have not, however, made an attempt to advance such a theory ourselves. Moreover, nothing we have argued purports to establish the impossibility of joining together, in a single theory, a suitably rich understanding of law's violence with a jurisprudence of rules and principles. We have contended only that contemporary jurisprudence, whether traditional or critical, has yet to face up to this pressing challenge.

---

199. Cover, "Violence and the Word," 1614. See also Stanley Milgram, *Obedience to Authority* (New York: Harper and Row, 1974); and Herbert Kelman and Lee Hamilton, *Crimes of Obedience: Toward a Social Psychology of Authority and Responsibility* (New Haven: Yale University Press, 1989).

200. Cover, "Violence and the Word," 1613.

201. Ibid., 1617.

Contributors

Martha Minow is Professor of Law at Harvard Law School.

Boaventura de Sousa Santos is Professor of Sociology in the School of Economics at the University of Coimbra (Portugal).

Robin West is Professor of Law at the University of Maryland School of Law.

Stanley Fish is the Arts and Sciences Distinguished Professor of English and Professor of Law at Duke University.

Austin Sarat is the William Nelson Cromwell Professor of Jurisprudence and Political Science at Amherst College.

Thomas R. Kearns is William H. Hastie Professor of Philosophy at Amherst College.

Index

Abolition, 55, 56

Abortion, 17, 27, 33–34; and rights discourse, 59, 60; and the Constitution, 119, 122

Adjudication, 160, 219–20, 235n.88, 245; case-by-case, 30; Fish on, 205; and interpretive violence, 247n.123; and politics, 263; and law's violence, 265, 266

Adorno, T. W., 92, 95

Aesthetics, 85, 100, 102, 113

Affirmative action, 27, 37, 66

African-Americans, 33, 55, 56–57, 64–65, 71. *See also* Race

Agency, rational, 268, 269, 270, 272n.197

Agnosticism, 101, 102

AIDS, 7, 96, 116

Alienation, 35, 221

Altruism, 261–62

American Banana Co. v. United Fruit Co., 218n.35

Anthropology, 16, 41, 43, 44, 113

"Antifoundationalist theory hope," 198–99

Anti-Semitism, 71

Antitrust cases, 27

Anxiety, "of contamination," 88–89

Apel, Karl-Otto, 93

Arbitration, 21

Archimedes, 149

Arendt, Hannah, 71, 88n.15

Art, 18, 44, 100, 112; and the paradigm of modernity, 92, 93, 95

Attorney General, U.S., 16–17

Aura, 112, 113

Austin, John, 11, 225–34, 239, 244, 246, 247; and natural law theory, 225, 228–29; on positive law, 228

Austria, 71–73

Authoritarianism, 8, 91, 93, 123–27; and the "legalistic mind," 125; and interdisciplinary movements, 129

Authority, 17, 34, 52, 66, 137; divine, and right to life activists, 35, 51; feudal and royal, 36; Habermas on, 38; and the rule of law, 39; challenges to, 54, 58; and the participation of individuals, 67; skepticism towards, 72–73; moral, of law, 125; and a rule-governed conception of law, 236; Hart and Dworkin on, 247–48, 256n.154; justification of, 268

Autonomy, 10–11, 159–61, 203; notions of, and abortion, 34, 35; individual, as a political choice, 46; and rights discourse, 59; and minorities, 60–61; and the paradigm of modernity, 82, 84, 87, 89; as a necessary aspect of the good life, 122; and morality, 132; and interpretation, 159–61, 179, 181, 182

Avant-garde movements, 89–90

Bachelard, Gaston, 89

Bacon, Francis, 92

Bateson, Gregory, 96

Bentham, Jeremy, 131

Bias, 41, 129n.7, 254

277

Bible, 172, 209, 250n.131
Bickel, Alexander, 253
Bilateral exchanges, direct, 182
Bill of Rights, 56. *See also* Constitution
Blacks. *See* African-Americans
Bloom, Allan, 31n.12, 32n.13
Bloom, Harold, 79
Bobbio, Norberto, 233n.82
Body, 53, 235
Bohm, David, 95–96
Boulding, Kenneth, 79
Bumiller, Kristin, 115
Bureaucracy, 38, 46, 86, 210, 211; and the paradigm of modernity, 86, 87, 91, 93, 110; and legal decision making, 236; and law's violence, 266
Bürger, Peter, 90
Burke, Edmund, 28
Burton, Steven J., 197, 207, 215–17
Busing, 119

California Fed. Sav. & Loan Ass'n v. Guerra, 24n.7
Capitalism, 7; and the paradigm of modernity, 81–94, 104–5, 107, 108–9, 112; and modern state law, 112, 116
Caplan, Lincoln, 26–27
Capra, Fritjof, 95–96
Chauvinism, 47, 71
Chernobyl, 7, 96, 116
Chew, Geoffrey, 95
Chicanos, 64–65
Children, 6, 15, 21, 56, 59; and the rule of law, 36; exclusion of, 54–59; disabled, 75; and busing, 119
Christianity, 54, 70n.84, 209
Cicero, 197
Citizenplace, 106, 108
Citizens, 238, 263, 267, 268, 271–72
Civil law, 231n.77
Civil War, 23
Class, 24, 61, 64, 65, 91; new, composed of fetuses, 33; universal, 86; bourgeoisie, 86, 87–88; and para-

digm of modernity, 86, 87–88, 91, 93, 109; politics, 87–88, 97, 105–6; reification of, 109
Coercion, 234, 259–60
Cohen, Felix, 255–57, 256n.150
Collateral agreements, 171, 173
Collectivism, 45, 46, 105, 107
Columbia Nitrogen Corporation v. Royster Company, 169–71, 172
Commands, 225–28, 230–31, 234, 240–41, 252n.138
Communication, 53, 75, 100, 101–2, 142, 149
Communism, 20, 88, 104
Communitarianism, 46–48, 129, 137–57
Community, 34, 39, 40, 244n.113; and individuals, 17, 32, 45–48, 49, 67; and the paradigm of modernity, 81–91 passim, 97, 109, 112; principle of, 81, 84, 90, 91, 97, 112; and the good, 122, 145; and civic republicanism, 138–40; and the space of law, 247; and law's violence, 265; rules of, and legal subjects, 269
Compassion, 12, 214
Comte, August, 86, 112
Concentration, 85, 86, 87, 89–90
Conformity, 139, 232, 233, 236, 270, 271n.196
Congress, U.S., 16, 22, 68n.79, 251n.136, 251n.137
Conscience, 17, 35
Consciousness, 19, 97, 220, 260, 273; and material structures, 51; and social patterns, 53
Consensus, 101–2; rational, 19, 21, 28, 68; West on, 136, 137, 145
Consequences, discussion of, 31
Consequentialism, 30
Conservatism, 8, 28, 136, 137; and abortion, 34, 35; and republicanism, 46; and interdisciplinary movements, 129, 130, 146–47, 151
Consistency, 184, 259

Constitution, 33, 56, 126, 249, 251n.136; and Supreme Court nominees, 16–17; amendments to, 22, 215, 241; and pornography, 48; Arendt on, 88n.15; and abortion, 119, 122; as moral and legal criterion, against which particular laws are judged, 124; and the protection of fundamental interests, 155; and cruel and unusual punishment, 214, 215, 217; history of, and a hermeneutic vision of the space of law, 251

Context, 39, 40, 54, 66; emphasis on, 68; localism of, 100; social, hyperproductivity of, 113–14, 115

Contradictions, 260, 261, 262–63

Copernicus, N., 51

Corbin, Arthur, 174–75, 176

Corporations, 40, 111, 113

Corporatism, 91

Corps intermédiaires, 109

Cost-benefit analysis, 31, 20, 71

County of Allegheny v. American Civil Liberties Union, 70n.84

Cover, Robert, 39, 211–12, 219, 252, 266, 270, 272–73

Criminal law, 17, 59, 241, 270

Critical legal studies movement, 30–32, 59; Kearns and Sarat on, 259–64

Critical stories, 253–65 passim

Critical theory, 31, 36, 42

Dalton, Clare, 193–97, 207

Death, 4, 12, 16, 253, 266; and law's violence, 11, 12, 212, 221; "of reason," 119. See also Death penalty

Death penalty, 213–17

Decision making, 195, 236, 253, 261–62; and the ideal of neutrality, 37; and rules, 239; and theory construction, 244–45; and politics, 256n.150

Declaration of Independence, 56

Deconstruction, 31, 57, 266

Dekker Steel Co. v. Exchange National Bank of Chicago, 168n.25, 172

Deleuze, Gilles, 92

Democracy, 24, 44, 108, 109, 114–15; and human authority, 51; and the paradigm of modernity, 87, 107, 108, 109; and power forms, 108; and territorial law, 111

Derrida, Jacques, 53n.52, 161, 210n.6, 264n.180, 266n.184

Descartes, René, 92, 102

Desire, 53, 101–3, 118, 224; Hobbes on, 222, 223, 248–49; "significations of," 226; and Hart's account of law, 237; unregulated, 240; private, and judicial misconduct, 243; and interpretation, 246n.121, 266; of judges, and rationalizations, 257; and the space of law, 257

Dewey, John, 49, 55n.66, 98, 108, 255n.150

Dicey, A. V., 84

Difference, concept of, 57, 58, 64, 65, 72

Dignity, 124, 259

Disabled persons, 15, 36, 54–59, 74

Discipline, 38, 222, 260n.165, 265n.181

Discretion, 3, 237, 238, 243n.109, 246n.121, 247

Discrimination, 27, 37, 61, 115

Dispute resolution, 21

District attorneys, 267

Divine law, 226, 227, 228–29

Divine order, 42

Domestic law, 111

Domination, 53, 58, 60, 101, 108

Douglas, Lawrence, 217n.33

Durkheim, Emile, 106, 109

Duty, 227, 238, 251n.138, 255

Dworkin, Ronald, 39; Sarat and Kearns on, 11, 229–30, 240–48, 258n.160, 262–63, 265, 273

Ecology, 91, 93, 97, 104, 109

Economics, 1, 7–9, 30–31, 91,

Economics (*continued*)
259n.161; and liberty, 45; and cost-benefit analysis, 71; and individual self-perception, 73; and mainstreaming, 75; and the paradigm of modernity, 87, 109; and interdisciplinary movements, 127–50 passim
Education, 40, 55, 56, 57, 74–75; and the paradigm of modernity, 87, 99; and integration, 119; vs. ignorance, 132. *See also* Law schools
Edwards v. Aguillard, 70n.84
Egalitarianism, 34, 53, 57, 138, 141, 157
Eigen, M., 95
Einstein, Albert, 43, 51, 95
Emancipation, 7–8, 81–94 passim, 101–11 passim
Engels, Friedrich, 55
England, 71, 117
Enlightenment, 4–5, 17, 54; assumptions, about reason, 4, 8, 12, 51, 119–20, 125, 137, 151–52; Western philosophy since, and the foundations of truth and knowledge, 41; and Renaissance humanism, 51; ideal, West on, 119–20, 124–25, 126, 135, 139; and legal authoritarianism, 124–25, 126
Epistemology, 4, 7, 20, 75, 150–51; positivist, 89; and modern science, 95–96; foundationalist, 98; and ideal utilitarianism, 133, 134. *See also* Knowledge
Equality, 54, 59; and the paradigm of modernity, 82, 84, 85, 87, 89, 97; and community health, 141
Essentialism, 45n.43, 73n.86, 106
Ethics, 96, 138, 150. *See also* Morality
Ethnocentrism, 41
European Community, 113
Evil, 71–72, 222, 226, 227, 228
Exchanges, direct bilateral, 182
Exclusion, 54–59, 61, 63, 67; and the rule of law, 37; and the paradigm of modernity, 85, 86, 87, 89–90

Executions, 259, 267, 270, 273
Experimentalism, 43–44

Family, 23, 36, 38, 55; and religious beliefs, 68; subjectivity of, 106; native law of, 111
Farnsworth, E. Allan, 182
Fascism, 43, 90
Federalism, 249–51
Federal laws, 22
Feminism, 2–3, 5–7, 8–10, 12, 45n.43; and the pornography industry, 17; and abortion, 36; and sex differences, 45n.43; and education, 56–57; and criticism of rights, 59–60; and partial truths, 63
Fetuses, 17, 33, 34, 60
Feyerabend, Paul, 98
Fiction, 53–54, 85
Fish, Stanley, 8, 9–11, 159–208
Fiss, Owen, 139
Force, 11–12, 267, 272–73; law as, 233; Hart on, 233, 234; Hamilton on, 249; and law as the child of violent resistance, 250; absence of, in the law, 252; and law's power, 259; subjects of, as objects, 269; and legal judgment, 256
Formalism, 10–11, 85, 88, 159–208, 237n.95
Foucault, Michel, 38, 101, 107–8, 218n.36, 265n.181
France, 109
Francis, Willie, 213–18, 235n.87, 236, 246n.123, 250n.133
Francis v. Resweber, 213–18, 235n.87, 236, 246n.123, 250n.133
Frank, Jerome, 237
Frankfurter, Felix, 224
Freedom, 120, 124, 157, 188; academic, 31; and abortion, 36; and religious minorities, 55; and domination, 58; and the paradigm of modernity, 82, 84, 85, 87, 89, 107; and the method of reason, 120; from forgetting, 205; relinquishing

of, in the name of a greater security, 222–23; and the space of law, 247; and judicial decision making, 261–62
Freud, Sigmund, 51, 52, 55
Fried, Charles, 26–27
Fundamentalism, 17, 35, 70n.84

Gadamer, Hans-Georg, 38, 98
Geduldig v. Aiello, 22n.5
Gellner, Ernest, 79, 102
Gemeinschaft, 95
Gender, 65, 97, 249n.130; and segregation, in the workplace, 24–26; images of, and power, 26; as socially constructed, 45n.43; and labels of inferiority and defectiveness, 55
General Electric Co. v. Gilbert, 22n.5
Generality, 67, 120, 121
Generalization, 48, 52
Genesis, 172
Genocide, 72
Geometry, non-Euclidean, 43
German Revolution of 1918, 89
Gesellschaft, 95
Gilmore, Grant, 185
Global blockage, 91–94
God, 51, 52, 57, 101, 227
Gödel, Kurt, 95
Goldman v. Weinburger, 68n.79
Goodrich, Peter, 202–5, 207
Gordon, Robert, 259
Gouldner, Alvin, 85, 86n.12
Government, 17, 27, 248n.125, 257; regulation, and abortion, 33–34, 35; assistance, through welfare and employment rights, 36; economic planning, 45; and the space of law, 252, 253. *See also* State
Gramsci, Antonio, 89

Häbermas, Jurgen, 38, 53, 90, 94, 101, 201
Haken, H., 95

Hamilton, Alexander, 249, 253, 156, 252n.139
Happiness, 9, 132–39, 141, 144, 151–52
Hart, H. L. A., 11, 229–47, 250, 258n.160, 265
Harvard Law School, 27
Hassan, Ihab, 98
Hegel, G. W. F., 86, 90, 92
Hegemony, 83, 86, 264–65; and the paradigm of modernity, 88, 89, 90, 92, 112, 116; West on, 139
Heidegger, Martin, 79
Heisenberg, Werner, 51, 95
Heller, Agnes, 102, 106
Henderson, Stanley, 182, 185, 187
Hermeneutics, 21, 38–39, 48, 128–29
Heterogeneity, 6, 68–69, 70–71, 73
Heterosexuality, 60, 61, 64–65
Hierarchy, 46, 47, 51, 55; and multiplicity, 72; and "bad" communities, 138, 139; and the law's violence, 220
Hilferding, Rudolf, 82
Historical determination, 106
History, 16, 68, 180, 206–7; and reason, 34, 42; and knowledge, 40, 41, 43; and truth, 44; partial, 50–68; and marginal people, 57, 62; and identity, 63; and the paradigm of modernity, 80–118
Hobbes, Thomas, 11, 12, 81; Sarat and Kearns on, 209, 222–25, 227, 234, 247–49, 253, 265, 272; and Leviathan, 209, 234, 247, 272n.197; account of the state of nature, 222–23, 241, 249; and "law's official story," 224–25; on unregulated power, 239n.103; psychology of, 247n.124, 248, 253
Hobbie v. Unemployment Appeals Commission, 69n.81
Hobsbawm, Eric, 117
Holism, 106
Holmes, Oliver Wendell, 218n.35
Holocaust, 52, 72

House of Commons, 103
Household place, 106, 108
Human law, 226, 228–29
Human nature, 121–22, 123, 134, 135; and law's violence, 222, 223, 224, 239; the Federalists' view of, 249n.128
Humanism, 17, 68, 162
Humanities law, 8–9, 127–50 passim
Huyssen, Andreas, 88, 94, 99

Idealism, 85–86, 135, 156–57
"Ideal speech situation," 38
Ideology, 254n.145, 257, 263n.176; and legal advocacy, 28–29; relativism as an, 42; and the paradigm of modernity, 84, 86, 91; and the working class, 91; and legal reformism, 116; and rhetoric, 178, 203; and power, 259; and the transformation of law, 260–61; of law, deconstruction of, 266
Identity, 6, 45, 53, 57, 63; racial, 64; as a false god, 65; and the paradigm of modernity, 82, 84, 87, 89; and the human presence, 109. *See also* Individualism; Self
Impartiality, 36, 37, 39, 50, 59, 67
In Re Soper's Estate, 175–77
Inconsistency, 187, 194
Incrementalism, 28
Indeterminacy, 6, 10, 35, 266; of legal language, 58; of rights, 61; and partiality, 67; thesis, 237n.96; of rules, 241, 242, 243, 258n.160; Hart on, 256n.154; of all postrealist reconstructions of law, 261
Individualism, 133, 139, 140, 146, 157, 261–62; liberal, 17; autonomous, 20; and abortion, 35–36; competitive, 36; and self-interest, 46; and exclusion, 54; methodological, 106. *See also* Community, and individuals
Industrialism, 54
Industrialization, 90–91

Instrumental conception of law, 269–70
International law, 111
Internment camps, 61
Interpretation(s), 245–46, 247n.123, 248; and the rule of law, 38; and knowledge, 40, 44, 45; and democratization, 108–9; evaluation of, West on, 119; Fish on, 159–61, 179, 181, 182; conflicting, 236–37; violence of, 236, 262; in Dworkin, 246n.121, 263n.176; and the space of law, 252, 253; and law's violence, 254, 265, 267; and ideological oppression, 266; and the link between rules and reason, 268; Cover on, 273
Intersubjectivity, 41, 145–46, 150–57
Irony, 54, 98

James, William, 98, 99
Jantsch, E., 95
Jencks, Charles, 109
Judges, 33–34, 119, 121, 273; and the rule of law, 39; and partiality, 70; and marginal peoples, 73; and law's violence, 210, 265–66; and rules, 235, 239, 241; array of legal materials considered by, 244–45; and the language of the written law, 251n.136; misconduct of, and private will and desire, 243; life tenure for, 249; and decision making, 253; and the violence of interpretation, 254; and legal realism, 255, 257; and the doctrine of stare decisis, 256n.150; and excuses for severity, 257n.123. *See also* Discretion; *specific individuals; specific cases*
Juries, 21
Justice, 22, 33, 119, 120; and the rule of law, 37; and specificity and particularity, 39; "partial," 76–77; and the paradigm of modernity, 82, 84, 87, 89; informalization of, 110;

"neutral truths" of, 121; and formalism, 161, 171, 193
Justification, prima facie, 236, 268

Kafka, Franz, 217n.33
Kant, Immanuel, 120, 269
Kearns, Thomas, 11–14, 209–73
Kelman, Mark, 261nn.168, 171
Kelsen, Hans, 88, 161–62
Kennedy, Duncan, 261–62
Knowledge, 6, 19, 20, 50, 52; and rationality, 9, 50, 89, 148; and power, 19, 45, 50, 58; and paradigm shifts, 21; foundation of, 40–45; and subjectivity, 41, 132, 136, 153–54; as partial, 62; assertions of, and exclusion, 65; and the paradigm of modernity, 89, 99–101, 89, 113, 118; legal, professional and nonprofessional, distinction between, 113; and reason, 119, 150; ideal of, and interdisciplinary movements, 140–41, 149, 152–53, 155; problem of, and legal economists, 132; happiness as an object of, 134, 135–36; intercommunitarian, 139, 140; moral, 156. See also Epistemology
Kortum v. Alkire, 210n.3
Koyré, A., 97
Kozinski, Alex, 162–66, 171, 180
Kuhn, Thomas, 20, 197

Labor groups, 36, 56, 91, 96, 117
Laclau, Ernesto, 105, 106–7
Laissez-faire, 45, 46, 84
Language, 6, 41, 45, 52, 54, 56; and power, 58; of rights, 59; and identity, 63; and the criticism of power relations, 73; sign, 75, 76; and the paradigm of modernity, 101; and formalism, 159–208; capacity of, to confine and control human conduct, 220; and law's violence, 220, 221; and natural law theory, 232;

"limpid," law as, 245; reliance on, in Dworkin, 246n.121; power of, Marshall on, 251; disciplinary understanding of, limits of, 253; of the written law, and assurances of stability and comprehensibility, 251n.126; plasticity of, 263n.177. See also Rhetoric
Law enforcement, 270
Law schools, 18, 20, 67, 124, 125; curriculum of, 26, 29–32, 48; interdisciplinary movements in, 123, 127–50
Lebenswelt, 85
Legal realism, 2–4, 20, 42, 131, 132, 133, 254–61
Legislatures, 24, 155, 244n.113; and abortion, 35; and lobbyists, 67; of the European Community, 113
Legitimation crisis, 54
Leontius, 241
Leviathan, 209, 212, 219, 220, 221–30, 248, 250, 271n.197
Levinson, Stanley, 139, 238, 239–40
Liberalism, 1, 46, 150
Libertarianism, 46, 136, 147
Liberty, 40, 45, 54, 59, 266
Literalism, 176, 177, 225–26
Lobbying, 24, 67
Localism, 6–7, 68–69, 100
Local perspective, 200
Local practices, 4, 20, 67
Lochner v. New York, 254n.144
Locke, John, 81, 224
Logic, 43, 59, 202, 257n.156
Loyola Law School, 18
Luddite movement, 116, 117
Luhmann, Niklas, 115
Lynch v. Donnelly, 70n.84

McGowin, J. Greeley, 188–92
Madison, James, 249
Mainwill v. Oyler, 160n.1
Marbury v. Madison, 251
Marginality, 53, 54–66, 72
Markets, 84, 87, 97, 155

Marshall, Thurgood, 24, 192–93, 251, 252n.139
Marx, Karl, 51, 52, 55, 86
Marxism, 31, 53, 104, 105–10. *See also* Marx, Karl
Masterson v. Sine, 171–72, 173
Maternity leave benefits, 5–6, 22, 23, 24, 66
Matsuda, Mari, 61
Maturna, H. R., 95
Maximal law, 112, 113
Meaning, 19, 35, 38–39, 46, 48; and the structure of language, 52; and texts, 54; multiple, 67; symbolic, 71; cultural, of the avant-garde movements, 90; and the paradigm of modernity, 92, 102, 111; plain and clear, Fish on, 159–78; multiplicity of, 262n.173; and the linkage between rules and reason, 267, 268
Mediation, 21, 84, 107, 255n.150
Medical profession, 17, 21, 26, 33; and abortion, 35; and labels of inferiority and defectiveness, 55
Mental illness, 55, 56
Merton, Robert, 89
Metaphor, 18, 19, 256n.153
Metaphysics, 46, 108, 218
Microethics, 85, 93, 96
Microevolutions, 114–18
Mill, James, 131, 132
Mind, 42, 125; and the body, 53, 235
Minerva, 90
Minimalism, 8, 112–14, 135
Minow, Martha, 5–7, 15–77, 210n.2, 218n.35
Miscegenation laws, 139
Mitchell v. Lath, 174n.39
Modernism, 83, 86, 88–89, 94–95, 98. *See also* Modernity, paradigm of
Modernity, paradigm of, 7–8, 80–118; rise and decline of, in advanced capitalist societies, 81–94; topoi for, 94–105; and politics and law, 105–118

Modernization, 83, 94, 102
Moral: truth, 8, 121, 122–23, 140; and practical rationality, 85, 92, 96; obligation, 160, 177, 179, 182–83, 185, 187, 190–91; law, 226, 227, 228–29. *See also* Ethics; Morality
Morality, 8, 10, 20, 132, 155, 223; and relativism, 42, 67, 72; and totalitarianism, 43; Nietzsche on, 51; and reform, 56; and rights, 61; "anxiety of contamination" by, 88; West on, 119, 120, 121, 122, 152, 157; and legal authoritarianism, 123, 124–26; and interdisciplinary movements, 127, 129, 130, 132, 133; and the community, 154; and sympathy, 156; and the autonomy of law, 159–61, 240; principles of, 179, 207; of self-interest, 182; noncoercive "dictates" of, 229; and law, Hart and Dworkin on, 230, 233; and language, 232; law as, 233; and legal realism, 255. *See also* Ethics; Moral
Morin, Edgar, 98
Mothers, welfare, 210
Mouffe, C., 105, 106–7
Mozert v. Hawkins County Pub. Schools, 69n.80
Municipal law, 231
Mysticism, 12, 41

Napoleonic Code of 1804, 85
Native Americans, 33, 55, 69n.83
Naturalism, scientific, 41–42
Natural law, 1, 179, 228–29; John Austin on, 225; and normativity, 232; theories, alternatives to, 245n.115
Nature, 34, 35, 222–23, 241, 249
Nazism, 52
Neo-Luddism, 114–18
Neopragmatism, 8, 125
Neutrality, 27, 28, 58, 223; of law, claims of, 2, 3; and the rule of law, 36, 37, 39, 67; and the relationship between knowledge and power,

50; rules of, imposition of, 59; and rights discourse, 59; image of, and the oppressive power of law, 259

New Deal, 56

New Rhetoric, 101

Nietzsche, Friedrich, 51, 101

Nihilism, 3, 4, 44

Nonabsolutism, 43–44

Noncompliance, 268

Non-Euclidianism, 43

Nonviolence, 266

Normativity, 232–34, 235, 240

Nuclear annihilation, 91, 93, 104

Obedience, 204, 222, 231, 270

"Objectistics," 100, 113

Objectivity, 2, 3, 42, 50, 223; and the rule of law, 36, 37, 39, 40; standards of, and communities, 138, 139, 140, 142, 151; image of, and the oppressive power of law, 259

Obligation, 39, 231; moral, 160, 177, 226–27; "ought to" dimension of, 233–34; Hart on, 234, 238, 241, 243–44; Dworkin on, 243–44; contractual, and the intentions of contracting parties, 264n.177

Offe, Claus, 82, 93

Official story, law's, 11–12, 224, 225, 229–30, 260n.165; as a story about rules, 231, 248; and judicial discretion, 238n.100; as believable, 248; and the space of law, 253; and legal realism, 255–56; political contingency of, 262–64; and the plasticity of legal language, 263n.177; and the availability of law's violence, 271

Old Testament, 172, 209

Oldenberg, Claes, 18

Oliva, Bonito, 100

Olivecrona, Karl, 218

Ong, Walter, 100

Operation Rescue, 33

Oppression, 38, 58, 67, 72, 76; of minorities, 61; and claims to knowledge, 66; West on, 146; and the law's violence, 220; ideological, 266

Ovid, 179

Pacific Gas & Electric Co. v. G. W. Thomas Drayage & Rigging Co., 165–66, 172

Pain, 21, 228, 231; and law's violence, 11, 12, 212–38 *passim,* 265, 271n.196; and sympathy, 153, 155; responsibility of, 253; and legal realism, 258; and law's power, 259; persons moved by, and the community, 269

Paradigm(s), 20–21, 26, 59; of modernity, 7–8, 80–118; of inquiry, 41

Partiality, 10, 62, 66–69, 254; and moral relativism, 72; recognition of, and minorities, 75; and partial justice, 76–77; Santos on, 99

Particularity, 39

Partisanship, 27, 178, 259

Paternalism, 47, 155

Patriarchy, 108

Peace movement, 97, 104, 109

Peller, Gary, 253n.142, 254n.145

People v. La Voire, 210n.4

People v. McGrandy, 210n.4

Perelman, Chaim, 98

Persuasion, 19, 20, 174, 175, 197

Pippin (musical), 74

Plato, 241

Pluralism, 5, 6, 7, 110, 201; values of, 43; of legal words, 67; and theory and practice, 68–69, 70–71; and respect for difference, 72

Police, 36, 267, 273

Policies, 241, 242n.108; discussion of, in law schools, 31; preoccupation with, 246n.123; law as grounded in, 247; reform, and legal realism, 258; and the indeterminacy thesis, 261

Politics, 3, 12, 55, 56, 253; and the goal of seeking the truth, 20; and

Politics (*continued*)
partisanship, 27, 178, 259; and
law, unavoidable linkage of, 28–
29; discussion of, in law schools,
32; participation in, and rights, 33;
and reason, 34–35; and absolut-
ism, 42; of self-interest, 46–47; and
postmodernism, 58; and marginal
people, 62; and partiality, 66; and
minorities, 75–76; class, 87–88, 97,
105–6; "anxiety of contamination"
by, 88; and the desirable and the
possible, 103; and interest and capacity, 103–5; and law, in the
postmodern transition, 105–18;
and freedom, 107; and power, 108;
and the space of law, 249–50,
251n.137; and legal realism,
254n.143; and decision making,
256n.151; and law, distinction between, 257–58; and adjudication,
263; and law's official story, 262–
64; and law's violence, 264
Pornography, 17, 48
Positive law, 227, 228
Positivism, 35, 179, 231; and the rule
of law, 38n.22; and the "anxiety of
contamination," 89; Austin's, 229;
alternatives to, 245n.115
Posner, Richard, 134, 135
Postmodernism, 6–8, 53, 62, 134;
and reason, 52, 66, 119, 120–21,
125–30 *passim*; and marginal people, 57–58; critique of, 66; and the
paradigm of modernity, 79–118;
characteristics of, catalogs of, 98
Postrealism, 260n.166, 261
Poststructuralism, 2–3, 5, 6, 8–10, 12
Poverty, 45
Power, 2, 7, 9, 230, 233; and knowledge, 19, 45, 50, 58; and rationality, 19, 20, 57, 66, 256n.150; and
images of gender, 26; and the Solicitor General, 27; and ideology,
28–29; discussion of, in law
schools, 31; of groups of scientists,

41; governmental, 45; of self-interest, 46; of the community, and the
individual, 47; "will to," 51; patterns of, and communication, 53;
and postmodernism, 57, 58; and
language, 58; and rules of formal
equality, 59; and powerlessness,
63; criticism of, language used for,
73; critique of, and skepticism, 76;
four major forms of, 108, 112; and
politics, 108, 111, 112; and the concept of the good, 122; legal, morality of, 124–25; preferences and
choices as the products of, 137; law
as the discourse of, 202; law as a
system of, 221, 225–26; and peace
and security, realization of, 223;
and commands, 227; and positive
law, 228; and social control, 228;
and obligation, 231; and rules, 235,
238; unregulated, and violence,
239–40; Dworkin on, 245; regulation of, problem of, 247n.124; judicial, 250–53; and the space of law,
251–52; state, and the law, 252;
and legal realism, 257; oppressive,
259; and law's official story, 262;
law's dominating, secret of, 264–
65; and law's violence, 266
Pragmatism, 1, 7, 125–26; and the
rule of law, 39, 55n.66; and knowledge, notions of, 42; and the paradigm of modernity, 98, 101; and
utilitarianism, 131; and doctrinal
inconsistency, 194
Precedent, 30, 31, 125, 251
Pregnancy, 5–6, 22, 23, 24, 59, 60
Prigogine, I., 95
Principles, 188, 192–93, 241,
242n.108; of community, 81, 84,
90, 91, 97, 112; West on, 124; Fish
on, 159; and decision making, 244;
preoccupation with, 246n.123; and
legal authority, 247–48; moral,
179, 248, 255; adequacy of, 253; nature of, arguments about, 254; as

abstractions, 256; and the indeterminacy thesis, 261; and judicial interpretations, Dworkin on, 263n.176; jurisprudence of, and a jurisprudence of rules, 265, 272, 273; and law as an affair of reason, 267, 268, 270–71

Prison, 270

Privacy, 33–34, 46, 47, 188; illusion of, 48n.49; and women's rights, 59, 60

Private discrimination, 27

Pro choice activists, 33–34

Production law, 111

Professional standards, 27–28

Progress, 4, 112, 117, 120

Progressives, 28, 33, 34, 55

Property, 266

Prostitutes, 36n.20

Psychology, 20, 41, 46, 247n.124, 248, 273

Public school textbooks, 17

Pull v. Barnes, 188n.65

Punishment, 29, 210, 213–17, 269–70. *See also* Death penalty

Purcell, Edward A., Jr., 42

Queen v. Dudley and Stephens, 224n.58

Race, 24, 36, 64, 65, 97; and the rule of law, 36, 37; and exclusion, 54–59; and labels of inferiority and defectiveness, 55

Racism, 47, 56

Rape, 59–60

Rationalism, 7, 12, 32–36, 156; debate over, and abortion issues, 34; and the rule of law, 39–40; Habermas on, 53

Rationality, 1, 3, 7, 35, 117–18, 260n.165, 262n.173; Enlightenment assumptions about, 4, 8, 12, 51, 119–20, 125, 137, 151–52; Minow on, 5–6, 18–21; and knowledge, 9, 50, 89, 148; and law's violence, 11–12, 220, 221, 223, 239, 272; instrumental, 18–19; and

power, 19, 20, 57, 66, 256n.150; and rational consensus, 19, 21, 28, 68; paradigm of, and law and economics analysis, 30; Habermas on, 38, 53; and the rule of law, 39–40, 48; logics of, as in Weber, 81, 85, 88–89, 91–93, 95; global, modern ideal of, 94–105; "crisis" of, 148; and choice, in *Webb v. McGowin*, 190; and politics, 249n.128; and self-love, 249n.128; and legal realism, 254n.145; image of, and the oppressive power of law, 259. *See also* Reason

Reagan, Ronald, 20, 27

Reason, 25, 26, 119–23, 225; and analogy, 30, 255; and truth, 41, 51, 121–22; authority of, 52; universal concept of, 57; critique of, paradigm shift represented by, 59; sovereignty of, as a false god, 65; and morality, 119, 120, 122–23; and postmodernism, 66, 119, 120–21, 125, 126, 127, 128, 130; and formalism, 161; and the space of law, 252; and social power, 256n.150; and rules and principles, 267–69; and human agency, 268, 269. *See also* Rationality

Reed, Stanley, 213–17, 250n.133

Reform, 33, 92, 116–17, 258; and women's rights, 24–25, 26; and the Solicitor General, 28; and marginal people, 55–59; and pregnancy, 60

Reformation, 17, 51, 54

Reformism, 112, 114, 115, 116–17

Regulatory law, 231n.77

Reification, 105, 109, 221

Relativism, 42, 43–44, 67, 72

Relativity, theory of, 43

Religion, 6, 17, 24, 40, 54–59, 66; and the rule of, 37; and the will to power, 51; and secular institutions, 68–70; and chauvinism, 71; and the paradigm of modernity, 93

Representation, 99–100

Republicanism, 46–47; West on, 138–
40, 144–45, 148, 150–51, 155
Resistance, 54, 56–59, 73
Restatement Second, Contracts Second
(American Law Institute), 184–86,
187, 195
Revisionism, 258, 259n.161
Revolution, 54, 260n.164; and the
paradigm of modernity, 81, 89, 92,
112; scientific, 97; reform vs. debate, 116–17
Rhetoric, 7, 10–11, 246n.121, 257,
259–60; truths of, 44; of rights, 56,
59–62, 61; medieval, 98; and the
paradigm of modernity, 99, 117–
18; and the nature of law, 194–98,
199–200, 202, 206, 207. *See also*
Language
Right to life movement, 33, 35
Rights, 6, 33–36, 50, 218; of disabled
persons, 17; of women, 22–26, 27,
33, 35, 59–68 *passim*; protection of,
beyond a utilitarian calculus, 30;
dispute about, and law school curricula, 48; rhetoric of, 56; debate
over, and the "insider and outsider stories," 58; and the critical
legal studies movement, 59; feminist criticism of, 59–60; language
of, 59–60; "critique of the critique
of," 60–62; indeterminacy of, 61;
theories, deontological, 71; and
modern understanding of law,
111; Hart on, 238; and legal realism, 255
Roe v. Wade, 33
Romanticism, 85–86
Rorty, Richard, 98
Rousseau, Jean-Jacques, 81, 92
Rule, parol evidence, 10, 264n.177;
Fish on, 165, 166–67, 168–74, 180,
181; jurisprudence of, and a jurisprudence of principles, 265, 272,
273
Rule of law, 6, 36–40, 49; as a hermeneutic process, 48; idea of, and re-

form activities, 56; criticism of, and
the "insider and outsider stories,"
67
Rule(s), 3, 28–29, 31, 124; and formalism, 165–81 passim, 193, 202;
and law's violence, 221; law as a
matter of, 225, 226, 227; Hart and
Austin on, 229, 230–47; normative
dimension of, 232; as self-binding,
234; "master," 234n.84; and skepticism, 237n.95; definition of, 241–
42; Dworkin on, 240–47; and judicial power, 251; nature of, arguments about, 254; "paper," 255; as
abstractions, 256; and indeterminacy, 258n.160, 261; and law's violence, 266; and reason, link between, 267, 268, 270–71. *See also*
Rule, parol evidence; Rule of law

Saint-Simon, Henri, 79
Samford, William H., 192
Santos, Boaventura de Sousa, 6–7, 8,
79–118
Sarat, Austin, 1–14, 119, 209–73;
West on, 120, 122–23, 125–27, 137
Scarry, Elaine, 271n.196
Scheiber, Harry, 196
Schools, 37, 38, 74–75. *See also* Law
schools
Science, 4, 8, 12, 20–21, 31, 41;
Purcell on, 42; and marginal peo-
ple, 57; and fundamentalism,
70n.84; cognitive-instrumental ra-
tionality of, 91–92, 95; and the
paradigm of modernity, 91–93, 95,
97, 101, 103, 110
Scottish Enlightenment, 84, 153n.24
Self, 41, 46, 49; interest, 46, 182, 248;
sovereignty of, 47, 48; and iden-
tity, 53; and language, 54; and
other, 99–100; collectivism of, 105,
107
Senate, U.S., 16
Sentences, criminal, 270
Sex discrimination, 22, 23, 25–26, 59

Sexism, 56
Sexuality, 60
Sexual sodomy, 119
Slavery, 55, 61, 132
Sloterdijk, Peter, 48n.49
Smith, Adam, 81, 84
Social control, 56, 228, 246n.121
Socialism, 34, 46, 85, 88, 108, 116. *See also* Marxism
Socialization, 86, 203–4
Socrates, 132
Solicitor General, U.S., 26–27
Solidarity, 82, 84, 87, 89
Sophists, 20
Souls, 259, 266, 271
Space, of law, 247, 249–50, 251n.137, 252, 253, 257
Stalin, Joseph, 89–90
Standard(s), 27–28, 38, 57; of rational determinacy, 186, 195; of right conduct, 232; and judicial discretion, 247n.123; nonrule-based, 258n.160, 261; of efficiency, and the indeterminacy thesis, 261
Stare decisis, doctrine of, 256n.150
State, 7, 22, 36, 39, 45–48; sovereignty of, as a false god, 65; and the paradigm of modernity, 84, 87, 90, 93, 97, 107, 109, 111, 112; principle of, 84, 87, 90, 97, 112; and the transnationalization of the economy, 91; reification of, 107; and the individual, and the *corps intermédiaires*, 109; and systemic law, 111; law, modern, 112, 114–18; self-preservation of, and the law, 252. *See also* Government
State v. Gough, 210n.4
Statism, 97
Statutes, 22, 67, 119, 121, 172, 241
Statutory rulings, 22
Storytelling, 6
Structuralism, 53
Subject, 105, 265, 268; and law's violence, 265–66, 267; and force, 269, 271, 272–73. *See also* Subjectivity

Subjectivity, 9, 34, 40, 53; and knowledge, 41, 132, 136, 153–54; full achievement of, utopian vision of, 85; of the family, 106; and the postmodern transition, 106–7, 112; and legal fetishism, 117; West on, 119–57. *See also* Subject
Suffering, 212, 219
Suffrage, 87
Supreme Court, 27, 160, 264n.177; nominees to, 17; and the Pregnancy Discrimination Act, 22; and pregnancy and maternity leaves, 22, 24; and the Solicitor General, 26–27; and local trial courts, 67; rejection of a Christmas public display, 70; and diversity and autonomy, principles of, 121–22. *See also specific cases*
Surrogacy contracts, 121, 124
Sympathy, 150–57, 188
Systemic law, 111

Teleology, 12, 42, 121, 122
Tennessee v. Garner, 210n.3
Territorial law, 111
Terror, 234, 271n.197
Terrorism, 269
Texts, 46, 54, 211
Third World, 90
Third Reich, 71–72
Thom, René, 95
Thrasymachus, 12
Tort cases, 27
Totalitarianism, 43, 45
Trade usage, 168, 169, 170
Traditionalism, 3, 26, 31, 32
Transaction costs, 30–31
Traynor, Roger, 171
Trident Center v. Connecticut General Life Insurance Company, 162–66, 172n.36, 180, 239n.101
Trubek, David, 259
Truth, 17, 20, 26, 155; moral, 8, 121, 122–23, 140; nature of, Minow on, 32; foundation of, 40–45, 67; dis-

Truth (*continued*)
pute about, and law school curricu-
lums, 48; and the rule of law, 48;
foundation of, 49; and the integration of mind and body, 53; a priori,
54; claims of, and marginal people,
57–58; and partiality, 62–63, 72;
claims, and paradigmatic transitions, 97; concept, of foundationalist epistemologies, 98; neutral, of
justice, 121; and knowledge, 135;
and law's official story, 262
Tushnet, Mark, 244n.113

Unconscious, 51, 53
Unemployment benefits, 69
Unger, Roberto, 32n.14, 39n.26, 222–
23, 260n.165
Uniform Commercial Code, 166–67
Unionization, 117
United States Court of Appeals for
the Ninth Circuit, 162
United States v. Holmes, 224n.58
United States v. United Mine Workers,
224n.57
Universalism, 47, 60
Universality, 210; and the rule of
law, 36, 37, 39, 48, 67; and the rela-
tionship between knowledge and
power, 50
Utilitarianism, 20, 30, 130–57 passim;
ideal, 132–35, 136, 137, 140, 147
Utopianism, 2, 19, 85, 110, 114

Varela, F. J., 95
Violence, 11, 39, 209–73
Virilio, Paul, 100

Walker v. City of Birmingham, 224n.56
Wardens, 267, 273

*Warren's Kiddie Shoppe, Inc. v. Casual
Slacks, Inc.*, 168n.24, 172
Webb v. McGowin, 188–92
Weber, Max, 12, 81, 85, 94, 102,
218n.38
Welfare state, 56, 87, 97, 107
West, Robin, 8–9, 119–57
White, James Boyd, 139, 142–44,
198–202, 207, 246n.121
Will, 224, 237, 240; Hobbes on, 222,
223, 248–49; private, and judicial
misconduct, 243; law as, in
Dworkin, 245; and interpretation,
246n.121; Hamilton on, 249; and
law as the child of violence resistance, 250; absence of, in the law,
252; and legal judgment, 256; and
the space of law, 257; and interpre-
tation, 266; and law's violence,
271n.197
Williston, Samuel, 176
Wilson v. Block, 69n.83
Wittgenstein, Ludwig, 38, 52, 101
Wolford v. Powers, 181n.54
Women, 6, 15, 56; rights of, 22–26,
27, 33, 35, 59–68 passim; and the
rule of law, 36, 37; exclusion of,
54–59; subordination of, 54; as inferior, 55
Workers, 45, 66. *See also* Labor
groups; Working class
Working class, 86, 87, 91, 105
Workplace, 106, 108
World views, 49, 259–60
Worldplace, 106, 108

Yntema, Hessel, 258

Zell v. American Seating Co., 239n.101,
264n.177